D1453612

PROFESSIONS IN THEORY AND HISTORY

SCASSS

THE SWEDISH COLLEGIUM FOR ADVANCED STUDY IN THE SOCIAL SCIENCES

The Swedish Collegium for Advanced Study in the Social Sciences is a national scientific institution established in 1985. Its main objective is to promote theoretically innovative research with a comparative and long-range orientation.

PROFESSIONS IN THEORY AND HISTORY

Rethinking the Study of the Professions

edited by Michael Burrage and
Rolf Torstendahl

SAGE Publications
London · Newbury Park · New Delhi

© Swedish Collegium for Advanced Study
in the Social Sciences 1990

First published 1990

SAGE Publications Ltd
28 Banner Street
London EC1Y 8QE

SAGE Publications Inc
2111 West Hillcrest Drive
Newbury Park, California 91320

SAGE Publications India Pvt Ltd
32, M-Block Market
Greater Kailash – I
New Delhi 110 048

British Library Cataloguing in Publication data

Professions in theory and history: rethinking the study of
    the professions. – (SCASSS Series).
    1. Professions – Social perspectives
    I. Burrage, Michael   II. Torstendahl, Rolf   III. Series
    305.553

ISBN 0–8039–8252–6

Library of Congress catalog card number 90–60584

Typeset by Input Typesetting, London
Printed in Great Britain by Billing and Sons Ltd, Worcester

TP

Contents

Foreword

This book emerges in a new series of scholarly anthologies which are the outcomes of work within SCASSS, The Swedish Collegium for Advanced Study in the Social Sciences and published by Sage.

The book is a product of a three-year-long discussion among the authors and some other scholars. The initiative was taken in 1985 by Rolf Torstendahl as one of the directors of SCASSS. Three major conferences on the theme of theory of professionalism and several minor workshops and meetings have taken place since then. Some of the authors have also had the opportunity to work together as fellows at SCASSS.

The present volume is accompanied by another one, simultaneously published in the same series under the title *The Formation of Professions: Knowledge, State and Strategy.*

The editors would like to express their gratitude to all the contributors for their willingness to adapt their various drafts to the outlines for the two volumes presented by the editors. Thanks are also due to the publishers for their unfailing cooperation.

Michael Burrage and Rolf Torstendahl

Notes on the contributors

Klas Åmark is Associate Professor of History at the University of Stockholm. His works (in Swedish) include books on political opinions in the Swedish press, on the Swedish trade unions in general and on the trade-union policy in one branch, the building industry, specifically.

Svante Beckman is Associate Professor for the theme Technology and Social Change of the Department for Thematic Research at the University of Linköping. He has done research on Swedish social laws and their effects and is currently investigating technology as a power system.

Thomas Brante is Associate Professor of Sociology at the University of Gothenburg. His research has concentrated on questions relating the philosophy of science with social development. He has published several books (in Swedish) on sociological thought and theory.

Michael Burrage is Lecturer in Sociology at the London School of Economics and Political Science and a Fellow of the Institute of United States Studies at the University of London. His work on the professions has appeared in a number of American and European journals and he has recently completed a monograph on the Soviet *advokatura* under *perestroika*.

Randall Collins is Professor of Sociology at the University of California, Riverside. His books include *The Credential Society: An Historical Sociology of Education and Stratification* (1979) and *Theoretical Sociology* (1988).

Konrad Jarausch is Lurcy Professor of History at the University of North Carolina. He has written on German politics, student careers and quantitative methods. Among other works he has edited *The Transformation of Higher Learning 1860–1930* (1983) and has written *The Unfree Professions: German Lawyers, Teachers and Engineers between Democracy and National Socialism, 1900–1950* (1990).

Jürgen Kocka is Professor of the History of the Industrial World at the Free University of Berlin. He has written extensively on German social history and historiography including works on the management and white-collar strata in the Siemens firm and German white-collar groups. He has led research groups on comparative studies about *Bürger* in Europe and about *Bildungsbürgertum* at Bielefeld University which have resulted in publications in German. He is also the author of *White-Collar Workers in America 1980–1940: A Social-Political History in International Perspective* (1980).

Staffan Selander is Associate Professor of Education at Uppsala University. He has published and edited several volumes in Swedish on text content transformation through transfer and on professionalism.

Hannes Siegrist is Researcher attached to the University of Bielefeld. His publications include works on Swiss and German firms and their development, including personnel, on technicians in Swiss society, and on lawyers in a comparative perspective.

Rolf Torstendahl is Professor of History at Uppsala University and Director of SCASSS. He has published several works on Swedish historical problems, including technical education. He has written *The Dispersion of Engineers in a Transitional Society: Swedish Technicians 1860–1940* (1975) and *Bureaucratisation in Northwestern Europe 1880–1985* (in press).

1

Introduction: the professions in sociology and history

Michael Burrage

A marginal status in sociology

The study of the professions has been marginal to the mainstream of sociological theory and research and we can capture something of its present character and introduce the essays presented in this volume by explaining why.

There are two main reasons. The first is that two of sociology's founding fathers said virtually nothing about the professions. For Marx they were not significant participants in the class conflicts of capitalist societies. Some of his remarks suggest that he thought they would be aligned with the bourgeoisie, at other times he seemed to think they should be placed among the proletariat and at still others that they were *dritte Personen*, third parties or bystanders who might side either way. Weber ignored them altogether. They were, as Parsons correctly observed, his 'conspicuous blind spot', so the only guidance to be obtained from Weber's work are his analysis of status and his asides on occupational group closure in which the professions are not distinguished from other kinds of work groups.

Of course, the third founding father, Durkheim, said quite a lot about the professions but he provided no historical analysis of the professions in France, other than a few misleading remarks about their fate during the Revolution, and paid no attention to what French advocates, doctors, engineers and the rest were actually doing in his day. He was also unaware of the contemporaneous developments of the professions in Britain, the United States, Imperial Russia or any other country. One cannot therefore turn to Durkheim for any insight about the peculiarities of the professions in France, or for any guidance about how the professions in modern societies might be analysed, or about their institutions and behaviour. His discussion is solely concerned with the functions they might, could or should perform, both for their own members and for the rest of society, and pivots on the antithesis between professional solidarity and anomie.

This is not a lot but it is much more than one can say for either Marx or Weber. In any case, Marx and Weber did something far worse than merely overlook the professions. They provided two powerful and compelling concepts, class and bureaucracy, to ana- lyse adjacent, or even the same, social phenomena, which have overshadowed and diverted attention away from the study of the professions ever since. Marx's concept of class has acted like an irresistible magnetic force on the discussion of inequality and con- flict in capitalist societies and prefigured the emergence of a social formation that was going to be far more powerful, far more histori- cally significant, and far more worthy of attention than the docile, polite, numerically insignificant professions. Weber's ideal type of bureaucracy has similarly dominated all discussions of work relationships in modern societies and offered a powerful tool for analysing the way in which public and private corporations affect the actions of those who work in them. In a sense, therefore, Marx and Weber pre-empted ground that the professions might have occupied and directed attention away from the study of the distinc- tive impact of the professions on patterns of conflict and inequality or on the distribution of power and authority.

Sociologists of the professions have therefore always had to con- front the two super-concepts of class and bureaucracy and, some- how or other, to make their peace with them. Against that of class, they have made little headway; indeed, few sociologists have even tried. Instead they have preferred simply to place the professions in the class system. Given Marx's own uncertainty on this question, and given also that, in one or other respect, professionals may be said to resemble the members of every other class, it is no great surprise to find that some sociologists have placed them in the ruling class, or a 'service class' attached to it, some have placed them in the proletariat and some have thought they should remain in the middle, where they might perform a sort of mediating or bridging role. Sociologists have, in short, been engaged on a filing exercise for which empirical research on the class allegiances, class- related actions or supposed mediating role of the professions was apparently deemed unnecessary.[1] And once filed in what the researcher considered the appropriate place, the exercise was at an end. The professions were heard from no more because they could now play their part, along with dozens of other occupations, as constituent units of the class to which they were alleged to belong.

As the professions steadily increased in number in the second half of the twentieth century, sociologists dutifully continued this filing enterprise, and rather that seeking any new conceptual or theoretical apparatus, or trying to identify the independent contribution of professions to the stratification of modern societies, they just tried to make their filing more accurate and precise. In strikingly different ways, Daniel Bell in 1973 and Magali Larson in 1977 made a decisive break with this taxonomic routine. Bell, however, tended to see them as an emergent new class,[2] but Larson showed that the professions' distinctive forms of organization, distinctive resources and distinctive strategies enabled them to make an independent contribution to the construction of the class systems of contemporary capitalism and therefore merited analysis in their own right.[3] She has, thus far, had few followers in this respect. The filing continued.[4]

Perhaps one should not be surprised by this. The study of class formation and class conflict has long appealed to sociologists, and to their students, because it allows them to express their sympathy for the underprivileged and exploited and gives a vicarious thrill of participating in the class struggle, even while remaining in the comfort of the classroom and the library. The 'struggles' of well-placed and self-satisfied professionals can hardly be expected to generate comparable sympathy and passion. In any case, the conflicts professionals engaged in not only lacked violence and bloodshed but were often barely perceptible, and, despite Durkheim, they never offered a popular vision of a new kind of society. Their usual aim, after all, was not to disturb or overthrow the existing social or political order but to find a more comfortable place within it. The recent eclipse of class analysis is unlikely to alter the prospects of the professions in these respects, since ethnic or feminist or underclass movements are the natural heirs of this passion and commitment, rather than the professions.

Against bureaucracy, they have had rather more success. Beginning in the fifties in the United States, Kornhauser[5] and Marcson[6] among others showed that professionals within large bureaucracies constructed rival forms of social relationship, of authority and of control which challenged the imperative coordination by bureaucratic superiors and substituted collegial, normative forms of coordination. Mosher demonstrated that the rules of the US Civil Service Commission could be circumvented or undermined by the determination of professionals to control both admission to their work territory and behaviour within it.[7] Professional resistance to the inevitable, remorseless advance of bureaucracy has, however, usually been portrayed as guerrilla skirmishing, as an exceptional event leading to isolated professional enclaves, rather than as a major historical confrontation between two well-matched adversaries.[8]

The first reason for the marginal position of the subject therefore is because the founding fathers pushed it there, and sociologists ever since have shown a remarkable deference for their views.

The second reason is that the professions did not appear to be a universal, nor even a near-universal, social formation. In fact, until very recent times, they appeared to be peculiar to the English-speaking world and the subject of private Anglo-American exchanges. The British and the Americans seemed to prefer it that way. Most of them, including Parsons, were at their most insular or ethnocentric in these discussions, with never a glance to determine in what ways their own professions might be peculiar, never a hint that in order to explain the development or to construct generalizations about their own professions they might require comparative evidence from outside the English-speaking world.

There was a certain irony in these Anglo-American exchanges since the British and the Americans did not take much trouble to determine whether in fact the professions in their two countries were so similar. It was enough that both their countries clearly had professions while it was not at all certain that there were any professions in continental Europe or anywhere else. They knew for certain that continental societies had intellectuals, indeed a superfluity of them, since many landed on their shores. They could also reasonably presume that these societies had abundant legal, medical and engineering expertise, but professions were a different matter. In part, this was another example of 'Fog in channel: Continent isolated', and the fog obscured from British view all the associations and collective action of the lawyers, doctors and engineers of continental Europe. French and German scholars did not help the situation since few of them thought the professions worthy subjects to investigate. Indeed, they could hardly understand or translate the concept.

In these circumstances, it was difficult for English-speaking sociologists to treat the professions as a major social formation, or to make them the protagonists of any major social process. Parsons claimed that 'the professional complex . . . has already become the most important single component in the structure of modern societies', but only Daniel Bell and Ivan Illich seemed to believe him and they both tended to equate the modern world with the United States.[9] The British often tended to treat the professions as one more anomaly of which they were rather proud, rather like cricket: the king of sports, too bad nobody outside the Empire could learn the rules.

In the 1970s, the fog finally began to clear, as more and more evidence was collected about continental professions. The British themselves had little part in this. The OECD and EEC played a minor role, by discussing the practical issues of the free movement of professionals, but most of the work was done by American historians who discovered and investigated the professions of continental Europe, an enterprise in which continental historians and sociologists also participated. As a result, one could at last say, with some certainty, that professions did exist on the Continent and one could begin to explain why they had been neglected for so long and begin to identify their distinctive institutions and strategies. However, before considering the impact of this recent American historiography of the professions, it will be useful to look back at the earlier histories of the professions.

The professions in British history

Historians have, of course, always been aware of the professions. And occasionally they have presented full-length portraits of them, but more often the professions have been incidental to some other subject – the career of a politician, the development of some great institution, such as English law, or the background in narratives of great medical advances or significant engineering achievements. Professionals have also been found among the participants in protests or reform movements of various kinds or in revolutions. In recent times, however, there has been a shift of focus and the profession itself has become the subject of investigation as historians have investigated their recruitment and training, their systems of government, their relationship with the state and their clienteles.

The emergence of this new subject has probably to be explained by the decline of political history and the disenchantment with Marxism, especially the latter, since it had traditionally provided the ready-made concepts, scenario and rationale which allowed the historian to by-pass the great and the good and concentrate on the lives of ordinary people. Whatever the reason, the change is discernible in both British and American historiography, though if the destination is the same, historians in the two countries have come to it by different routes.

Until well after World War II, British historians focused on the creation, and the domestic affairs, of the corporate institutions of particular professions and therefore tended to concentrate on the elite of the profession and the issues that came to the attention of their governing bodies. They rarely sought to study the working practice of rank-and-file members of the profession, rarely referred to other professions, rarely sought to relate changes in the profession to changes in the wider society and rarely therefore found any reason to criticize the profession. Their main task was to recount the success story of responsible leaders coping with the problems that faced the profession. Indeed, these studies were frequently commissioned by the profession itself, as for instance (to give one of the later and more outstanding examples of the genre), Clark's history of the Royal College of Physicians,[10] or they were written as a labour of love by a senior member of the profession, like Cope's history of the Royal College of Surgeons.[11]

In 1933 Carr-Saunders and Wilson published what was in effect a compendium of much of this earlier kind of work, though it was distinctive because it included the histories of twenty-two professions and would-be professions in a single work.[12] Of necessity therefore, it invited the reader to consider the professions collectively, as a distinct set of occupations, a perspective the authors developed in their concluding reflections on the current and future role of the professions in British society. Given their sources, it is hardly surprising that little of the material they presented was other than complimentary to the professions and that little of it could help to locate them in the social structure. Their interpretation seemed to be much influenced by Tawney's 1921 essay, which saw the professions as the basis of an ideal socialist society, and they stressed the contributions of the professions to orderly social progress, as a bridge between knowledge and power.[13] A similar interpretation of the professions' place in British society subsequently appeared in the work of Mannheim and of Marshall, though Marshall placed more emphasis on the professions' role in mediating class conflict.[14]

In the inter-war period, the London School of Economics seems to have cornered the market in the studies of the professions since all these authors mentioned were connected with it. In 1967, another member of the school's staff, Brian Abel-Smith, in collaboration with an American, Robert Stevens, broke with this earlier tradition in a work that traced the history of the legal profession from the late eighteenth century and was sub-titled 'a sociological study of the legal profession'. This sub-title I take to be a statement of intent, since the book concentrates on the policies of the leaders of the two branches of the profession, their relationships with each other and with the state. The main sources for the study are statutes, reported cases and government reports, so it might more accurately have been described as the political sociology of the legal profession. Nevertheless, using these sources, it managed to say far more than any previous study about professional practice of ordinary members of the profession and it had one further outstanding characteristic in that it was far more critical of its subject profession than any previous British study.

It proved to be something of a turning-point. In 1972 Prest provided a detailed account of the Inns of Court in the early seventeenth century, including the background of their members, their training, their rules and system of government and their involvement in events leading to the revolution.[15] In so doing he inaugurated what has become a remarkable sequence of studies of English lawyers which has sought both to document professional institutions and relationships and to relate them to the rest of English society. They have frequently utilized sociological concepts and methods, and occasionally addressed sociological propositions, if only to dismiss them. A few examples will have to illustrate this new sociological perspective and give some idea of the vast distance that separates them from earlier histories of legal institutions.[16]

In 1983, Daniel Duman, an Israeli educated in Britain, documented the recruitment to incomes and careers of the nineteenth-century bar, the socialization and rules of etiquette of members, their working practices and their access to political office. He scotched the idea that the Industrial Revolution was a watershed in the history of the professions, by showing that by 1835 all the institutions which characterize the bar in the modern world were already in existence.[17] Three years later Prest also took up this theme in the second half of his portrait of barristers, which traced the careers, marriages, property-ownership of more than 100 barristers in the half-century before the Puritan revolution and enabled him to place the profession in English social, political and intellectual life at this time. In a provocative passage, he observes that 'Private law and litigation now play such a relatively insignificant part in the life of most modern western societies that a major effort of historical imagination is required to grasp their central prominence in early modern England'.[18]

In 1986, in his study of attorneys and solicitors, Brooks documented the astonishing increase in litigation first in the early fifteenth century, which was followed by a slight fall before the very rapid increase at the end of the sixteenth. Under the reign of the first Elizabeth and the early Stuarts, he discovered, the English were much more litigious than in the rein of Victoria, and in all probability more litigious than they were in the 1970s.[19] Moreover, he showed that at that time the courts were open to a wide cross-section of the population, so that only 20–25 per cent of litigants could be classified as 'gentlemen and above' and that the 'non-gentlemen' were apparently more ready to use the courts, and more likely to sue their social superiors, than to be sued by them. He further argued that lawyers were unlikely to have created the demand for their services since litigation began to increase rapidly before the number of lawyers started to catch up, and finally, that attempts to restrict the amount of litigation and attacks on the multiplicity of suits came not from below but from the legal and social establishment itself. The inescapable corollary of Brooks's work, though his study does not extend so far, is that, as the Law Society extended its authority across England and Wales, as it developed a code of ethics and enforced its rules of practice, as in other words the attorneys and solicitors professionalized, the market for legal services steadily declined.

There has been a similar interest in the history of everyday medical practice, though not on quite the same scale, and more in journal articles than in full-length studies which, for reasons of space, I will not cite. Marland, however, has provided a remarkably detailed account of medical practice and of the education, careers, and incomes of practitioners in two Northern cities right through the period of early industrialization. One of her 'vital themes' was that 'laymen both created a demand for medical treatment and went much of the way towards fulfilling that demand, with respect to both "orthodox" and "institutional" medicine and self-help forms of relief'. In other words, medicalization, a term she conspicuously declines to use, was not initiated by the professionals practising in these two cities. The role of doctors, she shows, was 'in many senses secondary and "inferior" to that of lay managers of the charities who provided the spur for the establishment of these facilities, the funding and organizational energy, and who made the key policy decisions'. Laymen also controlled admission decisions and 'retained absolute responsibility for authorising medical relief under the Poor Law'. Her other 'vital theme' was 'the value of examining medical options at the level of the known community against a social and economic backdrop', and her investigations on it lead her once again to stress 'institutional medicine's failure to create viable systems of medical care'.[20]

There has been no comparable surge of historical interest in any other profession, and sociologists have therefore been obliged to investigate for themselves the history of the professions they are studying.[21] For all the debate about the performance and status of British engineers since the late nineteenth century, there is little if any work which would illuminate their careers, attitudes and working life. Their history has been dominated by biographies of great engineers, engineering institutions and occasionally of educational institutions. Other professions – academics, architects, clergymen, social workers, teachers, midwives and nurses have occasionally found their own historian or historically oriented sociologist, but this work still has a pronounced emphasis on the activities of professional institutions rather than ordinary practitioners. Such a comment might once have been made about accountants too, but since the foundation in 1979 of *Accounting, Organizations and Society*, under the editorship of Anthony Hopwood, it is no longer altogether true, since this journal is encouraging a new kind of research on the behavioural, organizational and social aspects of this profession, some of which has subsequently appeared as full-length studies.[22]

The inclination of historians is to study a particular profession, over a specified time period, and few have also considered them collectively as a distinct social formation and tried to assess their significance for British society. In the 1960s, Reader and Perkin had both sought, *en passant*, to locate them into the class structure. In 1982 Holmes circumvented this issue and treated them merely as a distinct social strata, which emerged in Augustan England and provided new kinds of advancement and career, a new form of corporate loyalty and corporate action, and as a result constituted, what he termed a new 'civic influence', which he unfortunately failed to analyse.[23] Perkin has recently returned to the question and, dealing with a later period, from 1880 to the present day, no longer feels he has to fit them into the class structure or attach them to some other class, since in his view they all but displaced classes in mid-twentieth century Britain as a focus of collective loyalty, interest and action.[24]

The professions in American history

The United States naturally offers rather less scope to the historian of the corporate professional activities, since formally organized Bar associations did not spread beyond Massachusetts and these were disbanded after the repeal of bar admission requirements in 1835. Organized collective action of lawyers therefore only begins with the establishment of the Association of the Bar of the City of New York in 1876. Medical societies survived beyond the repeal of all the admission requirements on the practice of medicine, but they abandoned professional or regulatory pretensions and were little more than discussion circles. An organized medical profession therefore begins with the transformation of the American Medical Association (AMA) into a mass representative organization of doctors after its fundamental constitutional reform in 1901. The associations of engineers formed in the closing decades of the nineteenth century similarly became collectively significant only in the early decades of the twentieth.

Of necessity, this more limited time span means there are fewer historical investigations, but one can none the less identify certain trends and characteristics in the historical treatment of the American professions. There are, to begin with, a number of the polite and celebratory histories of the kind found in Britain. Charles Warren's history of the American Bar[25] and Shafer's history of the medical profession[26] fall into this category. Martin's account of the Association of the Bar of the City of New York is a recent example of a commissioned, institutional history.[27] In Britain, these kinds of work long had the field to themselves but in the United States they were accompanied by a politically inspired literature on both the legal and medical professions.

First, there were works which were closely related to the mass, popular anti-professional literature that had been part of the campaign to repeal the licensing privileges of lawyers and doctors. Indeed, what is probably the very first American study of the organization of medical politics straddles the line between political tract and academic history since it was written by an irregular physician who had himself taken part in the campaigns against the medical profession.[28] And the first analysis of the organization and politics of the AMA was similarly written by a doctor who opposed the AMA campaign to raise the standards of medical education.[29] These works are, of course, bitterly hostile to all the collective institutions and aspirations of the professions and anticipate several of the themes that are later developed in contemporary American sociological analyses of the professions, such as Freidson,[30] Gilb,[31] Illich,[32] Abel[33] among others.

The half-century or more during which there was no professional regulation of lawyers and doctors in the United States also generated a reform-oriented literature of reconstruction, most notably three comprehensive studies of the medical, legal and engineering professions by Flexner,[34] Reed,[35] and Wickenden[36] respectively. All three were funded by foundations, all three were explicitly policy-oriented, and all three, by virtue of the reforms or debates that flowed from them, are historical documents in their own right. They all also included valuable historical and cross-cultural material on the development of the educational or corporate institutions of their respective professions. Flexner's work developed into a penetrating cross-cultural comparison of medical education[37] and later of universities in general,[38] while Reed remains an outstanding history of the early bar and of the relationship between law schools and the reconstructed bar associations.

Finally, in the late seventies American historians began to illuminate what Boorstin had once described as 'a dark continent', the history of the legal profession. Bloomfield's account of the legal profession in the mid-nineteenth century, published in 1976,[39] was followed three years later by Gawalt's portrait of the Massachusetts bar from its beginnings in the 1760s up to 1840.[40] Both were sociologically informed studies of the profession but carried the burden of being explicitly 'revisionist'. Specifically, they both attempted to contest the conventional view that there had been an interregnum in American professional history. Bloomfield argued that, though there were no bar associations through most of the nineteenth century, a professional consciousness nevertheless survived among American lawyers through journals, schools and informal working relationships. Gawalt argued that the collapse of the bar associations formed part of the emergence of the profession, a sort of functional equivalent to the contemporaneous formation of the Law Society in England.

Neither of these revisionist arguments is persuasive because a profession that fails to unite cannot have a sense of identity or pursue the same goals as an organized one and must therefore be clearly distinguished from the latter. Both studies are, nevertheless, valuable for the information they contain about the recruitment, careers and working practices of American lawyers. Among many other things, Gawalt described the way in which barristers and judges of Massachusetts colluded to undermine the attempt of the state legislature to abolish the bar in 1784 and discovered that, before their disbandment, the Massachusetts bar had what appears to be one of the highest rates of self-recruitment ever recorded, 60 per cent. A number of other historians, without any such revisionist distractions, have investigated aspects of the careers, practices or organization of the early bars of Virginia, Maryland and frontier Michigan.[41] McKurdy, for instance, examined the backgrounds of the Massachusetts bar during the struggle for independence to test the proposition that those who supported the rebel cause were drawn disproportionately from the less successful, while the office-holding elite remained loyal to the Crown. The evidence was generally negative. The profession split down the middle.

The histories of the medical profession say rather less about the background and practice of ordinary members of the professions; perhaps this is simply because doctors generated less paper than lawyers and it is therefore more difficult to reconstruct the details of their professional practice. Or it may be that since medical knowledge changed more rapidly and dramatically than legal knowledge, the demands of narrative are that much more insistent. In any event, the histories focus more on the development of medical knowledge and on the institutions and elite of the profession.[42] Starr promised something different in the stimulating introductory essay in his 1982 work, but the work itself is rather conventional in its concepts, methods and judgements, although exceptional in covering the entire history of the profession.[43] Ten years earlier, Rothstein, a sociologist turned historian, had sought to re-analyse the history of American medicine in the nineteenth century with explicit use of sociological concepts and explicit reference to sociological propositions about the professions.[44] One of the incidental merits of this innovative work is that it includes an account of the internal organization of one group of irregular practitioners, the Thomsonians, who at one time were numerous enough to be a profession but had, of ideological necessity, to avoid professional institutions. As a result, they created a curious form of organization that combined elements of a revivalist sect and mail-order selling.

The histories of American engineers seems to have lapsed somewhat since Calvert's pioneering 'historical social analysis' of mechanical engineers appeared in 1967. This traced the professionalization of mechanical engineers between 1830 and 1910 and centred on the conflict between 'shop' and 'school' cultures. This conflict offered powerful insights into the disagreements and disorganization within the profession, though since his data on the social background, careers and working life of engineers were scanty, the study ended up with a decided elite and associational bias. Unless some as yet unsuspected source of data emerges, the history of American engineers will remain largely that of their professional institutions.[45] As in England, there is a pronounced disparity between the sociological and historical evidence about the working lives of engineers.[46] Noble's study of 'science, technology and the rise of corporate capitalism' focused on the struggle between engineering associations, schools and large corporations for the hearts and minds of practising engineers. However, working engineers, or engineers as a professional collectivity hardly put in an appearance.[47]

American trans-national historical enterprise

If the scope for histories of American professions is necessarily somewhat limited, American historians have more than compensated by studying professions in a variety of foreign countries, over many different periods of time. To begin with, they contributed enormously to the study of the English professions in studies such as Rothblatt's account of academic life in nineteenth-century Cambridge[48] and Abel's analysis of the development of the English legal professions.[49] For some reason, probably the creation of the NHS, the medical profession has attracted particular attention: Stevens's parallel studies of specialization in the English and American professions,[50] Berlant's comparison of their codes of ethics,[51] and Peterson's account of medical practice in mid-Victorian London.[52] Gottfried's investigation of a much earlier period included an unusual attempt to assess the intellectual quality of English medicine and to explain its 'failure' by reference to the corporate power of the College of Physicians.[53] However, American historians subsequently began to extend their interest beyond the English-speaking world and, by so doing, finally brought the private Anglo-American discussion of the professions to an end.

The impact of their work is especially notable in the study of the French professions, first under the *ancien régime*, whose professions are probably the most accessible and comprehensible of all the continental professions, simply because French professions under the *ancien régime* looked rather like a profession in the English-speaking sense of the term. In the sixties Dawson shed some light on the early history of the French bar, though this was incidental to a history of French law.[54] In 1975 Berlanstein documented the recruitment and training of Toulouse advocates, and then used a variety of measures, such as patterns of residence, inter-marriage and membership of freemasons' lodges, to establish their place both in the world of the *parlement* and in Toulouse society as a whole.[55] His analysis of their incomes suggested that economic motives played little part in the development of their corporate institutions. In 1981 Fitzsimmons traced the history of Parisian advocates from their dissolution of their order during the Revolution to their reconstitution in 1810,[56] a crucial period because it gives some insight into the effects of a breakdown and reconstitution of the state on the professions as well as the kind of legal practice that emerges when there is no corporate or state regulation of lawyers. Suleiman, an historically inclined political scientist, has recently investigated the *notaires* and provided a further example of the peculiarities of professional organization in France. To Anglo-American eyes the *notaires* are hardly a profession at all, since they are, in part, state functionaries, but Suleiman shows how they have nevertheless prospered and defended their collective interests within the state.

Studies of the medical profession by Gelfand and Vess[57] roughly parallel those of Berlanstein and Fitzsimmons on lawyers. Gelfand focused on the social and intellectual ascent of the surgeons through the last decades of the *ancien régime*, prompted by war but due largely to royal support for their academy, which was a distinctively French alternative to the corporate institutions of professional practitioners. More conventionally, Vess traced the medical profession's corporate institutions through the turbulent revolutionary years while Ramsey has investigated ordinary French medical practice from the *ancien régime* to the end of the restored monarchy.[58] Weisz examined medical politics surrounding the exceptional congress of 1845, and then the emergence of freely organized medical politics under the Third Republic which led to the annual closure of the Paris medical faculty in the years before World War I.[59]

All these works have, needless to say, drawn extensively on French historiography. American histories of advocates have, for instance, drawn on French histories of the law, of the *parlements* and other legal institutions; those about doctors on the histories of academies, schools, hospitals and medical care, especially *Annaliste* histories of medical care under the *ancien régime*. However, the American work has remained distinctive, because of its focus on advocates, *notaires* or doctors as professional collectivities. Until very recent times, there have been few French histories of the orders of advocates as a profession, as distinct from memoirs, biographies of leading advocates, treatises on their ethical codes and legal histories. In 1977 Mousnier included the orders of advocates in his study of the corporate bodies of the *ancien régime*[60] but French historical and/or sociological investigation of the advocates as a profession really begins with the work of Karpik[61] with Boigeoul's contribution to an Anglo-American comparative project on the legal profession and Dezelay's study of the division of labour between advocates, accountants and receivers.[62] There were no French histories of the medical profession until Leonard's remarkable *doctorat d'état* of 1978.[63] American scholars have therefore brought a new category to the study of French social history. French scholars more commonly frame their histories of professionals around an academy, a school, a faculty, a corps, a class and in the future will perhaps find 'a discourse' a more appealing category of analysis.[64]

One early French response to the importation of the term 'profession', by Jamous and Peloille, was decidedly hostile. They saw the term as 'an expression of the professional ideology of the dominant members' and decided they could not use the terms 'profession' and 'professionalization' to analyse the 1958 reforms of French medical education because it did not allow them to deal adequately with the 'duality and contradiction' or with the 'confrontation and conflict' this reform entailed. They then proposed what they evidently considered to be superior alternatives, though these turned out to be merely categories which were more familiar to French ears, such as 'corps', 'elite', 'caste', 'group' and so forth.

This reluctance and hostility reflects the differences in the way professions are organized in France and, as a result, differences also in the source materials available. In the case of medicine, there are also the rival attractions of the *Annales* perspective, focusing on patterns of disease and death or the *mentalité* of medical care rather than the doctor's professional concerns. By virtue of its multi-disciplinary perspective, the *Annales* perspective has probably provided better opportunities to relate medical care to the rest of society than the sociology or history of the professions.[65] In any event, it not surprising that the concept of profession has proved most attractive to students of French advocates, since advocates have always had a higher degree of corporate self-government than any other French profession, and therefore come closest to American or English forms of professional organization. American historians of French engineers have followed normal French usage and analyse the profession by focusing on a school or schools.[66]

While American historians have paid particular attention to French professions, a number have also discovered the professions of other countries. McClelland, for instance, has traced their rise in Imperial Germany[67] while Jarausch has unearthed an enormous amount of data about the fateful encounter of three professions with the Nazis.[68] Kagan's study of lawyers in late medieval Castile documented 'a legal revolution' during the sixteenth century in which litigation became 'a habit for peasants, nobles and merchants alike . . . a truly popular phenomenon embracing participants from all walks of life'. In the second quarter of the seventeenth century, the revolution began to 'run out of steam' just as the advocates belatedly began to develop some corporate solidarity and to subject the earlier 'laissez faire judicial culture to professional constraints'.[69] Kagan's work obviously invites comparison with Brooks's investigation of a roughly contemporaneous period in England. Cleaves's study of the professions in twentieth-century Mexico, by contrast, challenges all comparisons with the Anglo-Saxon world. Although the preponderant role of the state initially prompts comparison with continental Europe, the Mexican professionals have utterly failed to organize as professions. Instead, they rely on lesser, sectional forms of solidarity, such as the lawyers' *camarillas* or 'little mafias'. Doctors and engineers have organized as trade unions and agronomists only as university alumni associations. None of these have been able to exercise any control on entry to their professions or to protect their collective, professional interests. The closest similarity to a national professional association in contemporary Mexico is, in fact, the National College of Economists.[70]

The history of the legal, medical and engineering professions of Imperial and Soviet Russia has been virtually monopolized by American scholars. Imperial Russia provides a sort of experimental laboratory of the early development of the professions because of its distinctive relationship between the state, the universities and practitioner associations found there. Wortman has traced the emergence of a professional consciousness among Russian jurists within the imperial bureaucracy prior to the creation of professional institutions in 1864,[71] while Kucherov documented the short, wondrous history of the self-governing *advokatura* under the last tsars,[72] and in doing so provided one of the fullest accounts of the ethical concerns and disciplinary proceedings of any bar. One of the interesting themes in Frieden's history of the imperial medical professions is the physicians' attempts to secure a degree of self-government comparable to that of the advocates despite the gulf that separated the publicly employed *zemstvo* physicians from the private fee-for-service practitioners.[73] Bailes showed how the engineering profession survived the revolutionary trauma and was finally 'sovietized', or destroyed, by terror.[74] Although much remains to be discovered about the medical profession in the early Soviet years, Field has described its subsequent bureaucratization,[75] while Huskey has traced the anomaly of the *advokatura* and how it survived the early attempts to laicize the law, as well as the terror and collectivization.[76]

One further piece of trans-national American research deserves mention since it refers to a profession which precedes all the rest – indeed, which might be said to be the founding profession of Christian Europe, and was itself trans-national, namely that of canon law. In a provocative essay, Brundage has shown that the professionalization of canon lawyers began in the late twelfth century, at which time the canonists did yet not see their occupation as a full-time calling, but merely as a means of advancing within the state or church administration or the Roman curia itself. By the end of the fourteenth century, however, canonists had formed legal guilds or confraternities, which controlled admission to their ranks and curtailed the right of audience of non-professionals. At this time the canonists subscribed to a body of professional rules, usually considered the law a life-long career and had acquired high prestige.[77]

Two aspects of this early professionalization are of particular relevance to the analysis of the professions in the contemporary world. First, it was the bishops and other ecclesiastical functionaries of the late twelfth century in need of expert advice 'who first sought to circumscribe practitioners' freedom of action' by setting standards for the training and behaviour of canonists. And it was only *after* church authorities had begun to do this that the canonists themselves began to form associations to control admission and training and enforce professional ethics. In other words, it was the church and state bureaucracies which first prompted collective professional action.

Second, the profession first emerged within these bureaucracies. The early canonists were frequently employed or retained as consultants which they combined with private practice. One outstanding example is Pope Innocent IV (1243–1254) who 'continued to write academic legal commentaries and actually completed his great *Apparatus to the Liber Extra* while he was pope'. Canon lawyers faced a mid-career transition, comparable in some respects to that of engineers in the modern world, from fee for service to 'managerial' church appointments which gave a regular income and often meant that they moved away from technical legal matters into positions where law was applied or even where it was made. However, towards the end of the period they tended to avoid ecclesiastical appointments and to remain laymen and practise law independently as practitioners, advisers, academics or as some kind of judge, examiner or registrar, though they might engage part-time employments 'as keepers of student lodgings, as money lenders, and as real estate speculators'.[78] In sum, the relationship between professionals and bureaucracies begins not, as sociologists have tended to assume, with the large-scale employment of research scientists in American industry, but in the very earliest days of the very first profession.

The recent growth of American historical interest in European professions constitutes a decisive disciplinary shift, but to appreciate fully its significance we must note some other related changes. The first is the rise of trans-national studies in Europe. These have accompanied the American investigations and may even have been provoked by them, though they are distinct because these European studies invariably compare two or more societies. American studies seldom do. Thus, there are German studies of engineers in France, the United States, Russia and England,[79] Swedish studies of German, French and English engineers,[80] while a Swiss historian has compared the legal professions of Germany, and France and Switzerland.[81]

Simultaneously, sociologists of the professions seem to have become more interested in historical investigation. It is probably fair to say that they were always historically inclined anyway, since professional institutions are often unintelligible without reference to their historical development. Only field studies of the working life of professionals can afford to ignore history. None the less, in recent times more sociologists of the professions seem to be embarking on more historical enquiries. Some like Larson and Rothstein – have already been mentioned, but there are many more, such as Noel and Jose Parry who traced the collective social mobility of English general practitioners,[82] Larkin's study of the division of medical labour[83] or Abbott's analysis of the jurisdictional rivalries of lawyers and other professions.[84] The recent International Sociological Association survey of the legal professions of seven common law and eleven civil law jurisdictions edited by Abel and Lewis illustrates this sociological interest in history.[85] While this work was intended to provide sociological data on the contemporary professions, almost every country case study finds it necessary to begin with some sort of historical account either of the state or the profession or both.

If one puts these various trends together, the rise of a sociologically informed history, the growth of comparative studies and of historically inclined sectors of sociology, the study of the professions would seem to be on the brink of a truly historical and comparative social science. However, it seems unlikely that the historians and sociologists will simply join hands and advance towards this promised land, since they still have different motives for studying the professions, and different expectations therefore, about how the subject can and should develop.

The gains and losses of inter-disciplinary convergence

For the study of the professions itself, the arrival of the historians is no doubt an unalloyed good. And the historians have nothing much to lose. They can enjoy the exploration of new territory, borrow selectively and need not be very respectful towards what has already been done. They have, in fact, all but ignored social theory, taken almost nothing from Marx, the notion of status from Weber and most perhaps, though only in a loose sense, from Durkheim, that is to say, they make use of the concepts of role, of socialization, of institution, of function, formal and informal social control. Since they owe no fealty to Marx, Weber, or Durkheim, they seldom see any reason, as sociologists almost invariably do, to try to relate their conclusions to the work of these founding fathers. If they address sociological theory directly, they often find it difficult to contain their impatience. One exasperated historian described sociological theories as 'an unsatisfactory amalgam of a priori reasoning, casual anecdote and impressionistic comment'.[86]

For sociologists, the sitting tenants of the subject area, the arrival of these *Gastarbeiter* is not an entirely congenial experience. True, they obviously benefit from the extension of the historical data base that they may use to explain, analyse and comprehend professional actions and institutions. And these newcomers bring considerable enthusiasm and a belief that the professions are important. Prest echoed Parsons when he observed that the professions are 'one of the key distinguishing characteristics of Western civilization and society from the middle ages to the present'.[87] And if they continue at the present work rate, they may well persuade other historians and sociologists of the truth of this claim.

However, from a sociologist's point of view, the historians often seem rather promiscuous and irresponsible, starting and ending their investigations at what appear to be entirely random points in time, refusing to accept any responsibility towards the development of any kind of theory and being not too concerned about how their endeavours may contribute to the understanding of the professions or society in general. Indeed, they simply do not wish to *use* their history for any analytical or theoretical purpose and therefore seldom bother even to make inter-professional or cross-cultural comparisons. They are therefore reluctant to join sociologists' comparative and theoretical ventures or their attempts to use the professions as a means of understanding capitalist or industrial society. Their general rule is to analyse one profession, in one society, at a specific time.

Their arrival has also led to some sociological casualties, especially among the typologies, generalizations and 'theories' that sociologists had previously entertained. Some, such as the supposed 'natural history of professionalization', or the distinction between 'status' professions of the pre-modern and the 'occupational' professions of the modern world, were not great losses since they had never persuaded many sociologists. However, it was somewhat more unnerving when historians began to question assumptions which virtually all sociologists had accepted – namely that there was a marked difference between a rather static pre-modern dark age and a modern dynamic one, or that there was some intimate, and therefore causal, relationship between the rise of the professions and the rise of capitalism.

The professions is not the first field within sociology to take a drubbing of this kind. The sociology of the family provides an earlier, and even more embarrassing, example. Plausible-sounding theories sociologists had proposed about the transition from the extended to the nuclear family, or about the adoption of birth control, simply disintegrated with the first blast of historical evidence. This showed that the nuclear family was not the product of industrialization, that family limitation was not first adopted in the most industrially advanced country, and that whatever may be the cause of this momentous change in family relationships, it operated roughly simultaneously in Britain and Bulgaria. That self-same prop on which sociologists of the family, no less than sociologists of the professions had relied – industrialization as the prime cause of social change – was simply knocked away. Indeed, it may be that we are simply registering in one or two fields a fundamental realignment within the social sciences as the rise of social history threatens the foundations of sociological propositions.

A few years ago there was a little debate about the death of the sociology of the professions. Richard Hall conducted a content analysis of sociological journals over the preceding five years and concluded that it was almost moribund. Two sociologists subsequently contested this gloomy verdict and claimed that, in Britain at least, the study of the professions was alive and well, indeed thriving.[88] Wildly dissimilar assessments of the state of health of a marginal field are probably to be expected: one or two straws in the wind make a difference.[89] What is quite certain, however, is that the arrival of historians in some numbers presents sociologists of the professions with some entirely new challenges. The special relationship, the Anglo-American condominium, is all over. For them 1992 has already arrived and sociologists of the professions face new demands and requirements.

First, they must take account of an ever-growing body of historical evidence. They must also abandon one of the more seductive delusions that sociology inherited from two of its founding fathers – namely, that one can write about the institutions of one modern, capitalist society, about Britain, or France or the United States, as though it was typical, more or less, of all the rest. And since much of their earlier work has been neither historically or cross-culturally informed, they must also re-assess their concepts, categories and strategies of investigation, as well as their theories and generalizations, to discover those which enable them to move freely over the much larger terrain that is now open to them.

The contributors to this volume agree at least on the need to respond to the growth of historical and cross-cultural evidence and consequently on the need for some kind of conceptual and/or strategic re-assessment in the study of the professions. Thereafter they go their separate ways. In the first, and perhaps the boldest,

Collins suggests that the professions be treated as part of a general study of market exchange and their closure and monopoly strategies of markets compared with the rise and fall of similar strategies operated by other estates, castes, guilds and cartels. Torstendahl argues that the challenge of the subject is to combine essentialist and strategic studies of the same occupations while at the same time identifying the historical contingencies which determine the specific combination of properties and strategies at a particular point in time. Kocka compares the German uses of the concept of *Bürgertum* with the way English-speaking scholars have used the concept of profession, in the belief that this can produce new perspectives and hypotheses to the benefit of both.

The three next chapters, though utilizing Swedish empirical evidence to illustrate their arguments, propose concepts and classifications for general historical and cross-cultural application. Brante argues that to understand professional behaviour, formal membership of a particular profession is less important than place of employment. Åmark thinks that the concept of an 'open cartel' describes the way in which professionals seek to defend their status and remuneration more accurately than the commonly used term of 'monopolization'. Beckman suggests that in order to relate the analysis of the professions to that of other social institutions, it is necessary to locate the distinctive kind of authority they exercise with reference to the other, often conflicting, forms found in bureaucracies, families and political institutions.

The next three chapters propose varying strategies of investigation. Selander draws attention to the associative strategies that new occupations may use either independently, or in combination with the closure strategy of the older professions. Siegrist argues that future historical investigations should recognize that different images of time and different types of profession have informed previous studies of the professionalization. In chapter 9, I suggest that we might learn something about the professions by considering their history alongside that of manual occupations who have organized on a similar basis and for similar purposes.

The final chapter is, in a sense, the least ambitious in that it seeks merely to identify the actors and relationships which must be included in any satisfactory account or theory of the professions. In its original form it was intended to help identify some common ground and some common points of reference for the seminars for which these essays were first prepared. The participants tore it to shreds. In its revised form, it may help to locate the varying priorities and perspectives of the contributors and to show what kinds of professional action interested them – as well as those that did not.

Notes

1 For an exception, see Whalley, 1986.
2 Bell, 1973.
3 Larson, 1977/79.
4 Abercrombie and Urry, 1983.
5 Kornhauser, Jr., 1965.
6 Marcson, 1960.
7 Mosher, 1968.
8 Raelin, 1986.
9 Parsons, 1968:536–545.
10 Clark, 1964 and 1966.
11 Cope, 1959.
12 Carr-Saunders and Wilson, 1933.
13 Tawney, 1921.
14 Marshall, 1939:325–340.
15 Prest, 1972. Prest is an Australian educated in England.
16 Other notable examples are Ives, 1983, and Cocks, 1983.
17 Duman, 1983.
18 Prest, 1986.
19 Brooks, 1986.
20 Marland, 1987.
21 See Whalley, op. cit.; Glover and Kelly, 1987.
22 Loft, 1988.
23 Reader, 1966; Perkin, 1969; Holmes, 1982.
24 Perkin, 1989.
25 Warren, 1911.
26 Shafer, 1936.
27 Martin, 1970.
28 Wilder, 1901.
29 Strong, 1909.
30 Freidson, 1970.
31 Gilb, 1966.
32 Illich et al., 1977.
33 Abel, 1988a.
34 Flexner, 1910.
35 Reed, 1921.
36 Wickenden, 1930.
37 Flexner, 1910.
38 Flexner, 1930.
39 Bloomfield, 1976.
40 Gawalt, 1979.
41 Hall (ed.), 1987.
42 Kett, 1968; see also Haller, Jr., 1981.
43 Starr, 1982.
44 Rothstein, 1972.
45 Calvert, 1967; Calhoun, 1965; Perrucci and Gerstl (eds), 1969; Layton, 1971.
46 See, for instance, Zussman, 1985.
47 Noble, 1977.
48 Rothblatt, 1968.

49 Abel, 1988b.

50 Stevens, 1966; Stevens, 1971.

51 Berlant, 1985.

52 Peterson, 1978.

53 Gottfried, 1986.

54 Dawson, 1968.

55 Berlanstein, 1975.

56 In his Ph.D. thesis revised and published in Fitzsimmons, 1987.

57 Vess, 1975.

58 Ramsey, 1988.

59 Weisz, 1983:3–30. He is Canadian, not American.

60 Mousnier, 1979.

61 Karpik, 1985:571–600; Karpik, *Lawyers and Politics*; Karpik, 1988:707–736.

62 Dezelay, 1989.

63 Leonard, 1978. For an illuminating review of this and other works by Leonard derived from it, see Ramsey, 1983:319–338.

64 Jamous and Peloille, 1970:111–152.

65 Though as Gelfand notes virtually all the works published in the *Annales* itself have related to medical care under the *ancien régime*; see Gelfand, 1987:15–39.

66 Shinn, 1980; Weiss, 'Bridges and Barriers'; Weiss, 1982.

67 McClelland, 1985.

68 Jarausch, *The Unfree Professions*; Cocks and Jarausch, *The German Professions*.

69 Kagan, 1981.

70 Cleaves, 1987.

71 Wortman, 1976.

72 Kucherov, 1953.

73 Frieden, 1981.

74 Bailes, 1978.

75 Field, 1967.

76 Huskey, 1986.

77 Brundage, 1987.

78 Brundage, 1987:21.

79 Lundgreen, 1980:311–332; and Lundgreen, 1989.

80 Torstendahl, 1985b; Ahlstrom, 1982.

81 Siegrist, 1986:267–298.

82 Parry and Parry, 1976.

83 Waddington, 1984.

84 Abbott, 1988.

85 Abel and Lewis, 1988.

86 Prest, 1984:300–321.

87 Prest, 1986.

88 Hall, 1983:5–23.

89 However, the *Handbook of Sociology*, which surveys the discipline as a whole, provides some support for Hall's verdict, since it gives no separate treatment to the professions in its twenty-two chapters (Smelser, 1988).

2

Market closure and the conflict theory of the professions

Randall Collins

How are we to understand professionalization as part of a larger range of social phenomena, and as a process which varies across historical contexts? I would like to approach these questions from the point of view of sociological conflict theory.[1] Conflict theory follows from an interpretation of Max Weber. The basic premises are that we can explain social behaviour and social structure in terms of the interests of individual actors in maximizing their power, wealth and status. The key variables are the resources available for controlling or evading the control of others in organizations and social networks. Individuals are not necessarily or even usually conscious of their interests; that is because the most important interactions tend to be social rituals, which produce moral beliefs and ideals which permeate the thinking of local groups. Group members, in effect, believe in their own ideologies, even as they press for advantage against other groups.

In many ways the key is Weber's conception of status groups. These are communities of life-style and of cultural consciousness. One might say, incorporating the themes of Durkheim, Mauss and Goffman into the stratification perspectives of Marx and Weber, that status groups are those networks of people within the larger formal structures of stratification, who perform interaction rituals among themselves and thus arrive at a common conception of their identity, their purpose and their status honour. Weber contrasted status groups analytically with classes. Classes are categories of persons who have similar economic interests because they are in similar positions within economic markets. Classes can be transformed into status groups when they go beyond the cold material calculation of market interests; that is to say, when they become communities, sharing a felt identity, ideals and standards for the conduct of life. This has usually been thought of as something that classes do in their leisure time, as consumers rather than in the realm of work and finance. An important extension of Weber's idea, though, is that status groups can also appear within the division of labour itself; status groups appear not only as groups go off the market, but structure the market itself.

A broader name for this process is market closure.[2] Instead of seeing occupations as having fixed positions on a market, we see that occupations themselves can become status groups in the realm of work. Instead of merely responding to market dynamics, as in the model of class conflict stemming from Marx, occupations attempt to control market conditions. Some occupations are relatively success-ful at this, others less so. Those which are especially successful are the ones which we have come to call 'the professions'.

Moreover, market closure is a much broader phenomenon than what occurs among occupations; its more fundamental form is mon-opolization among capitalist enterprises. It is necessary, then, to examine markets and capitalism generally. We are now beginning to see that there are a variety of market economies, ranging much further than our conventional notion of modern capitalism – the capitalism of the last few hundred years. Seen in this light, the closure of occupations on the market is part of a larger structural pattern. There is a long-term dynamic consisting of endless conflict over market closure. Occupational structures, like capitalism and markets in general, do not stay put; they are constantly changing, as some occupations gain new resources in the struggle to gain closure over their markets, and other occupations lose some of the privileges they have gained. This happens for at least two reasons. One is that markets themselves are unstable. We do not yet have much agreement on the long-term dynamics of markets; Marxist crisis theory is somewhat discredited, but it may well be that certain kinds of periodic restructuring are deeply ingrained, perhaps con-nected to processes of over-reaching power in financial, geopoliti-cal, fiscal or other spheres.[3]

There is another reason why markets are unstable, even in the face of deliberate efforts to monopolize activities and take them off the market. The appropriation of opportunities upon one market tends to create another market on a higher level; for instance, as the appropriation of land as private property opened up a new market in land; or the appropriation of manufacturing capital opened up new markets for stock ownership. Within the specific realm of professions, as occupations which have organized to restrict their work from market competition, this creation of supra-markets takes place through a process of status emulation. The success of older occupations in acquiring privileges for them-selves sets up models towards which other occupations can strive. This happens especially because the ideal-typical professions do not merely monopolize but also transform their work into status honour. As I have suggested, professions are Weberian status groups, formed within the division of labour. But the nature of a status group is to play down its utilitarian aspects, to direct attention away from the work which is done, and on to the style, the honour, the moral standards displayed by its members. It is precisely these cultural and honourable aspects of professions which are more portable, easier for other occupations to emulate.

The strong professions are those which have surrounded their work by social rituals, and turned their mundane jobs into the production of 'sacred' symbols. The importance of education in forming the professions reflects the fact that education is the peculiarly modern and secular form of ritual. Thus occupations which wish to raise their social status, to become professionalized, have an ever-more commonly available resource with the expansion of mass higher education. The market monopolies which the classic professions had at one point in history come under pressure by the rise of a supra-market for cultural credentials. Once again, monopolization at one level is threatened by the emergence of a market for the instruments of monopolization. The shifting contours of modern professions must be seen in the context of this larger process. Thus our contemporary malaise about the professions is itself a product of what has happened to the production of 'sacred' symbols as the competition over market opportunities, and over the formation of occupational status groups, goes on into a new phase.

Market closure in Weberian theory

For Weber, the process of monopolization or market closure is a fundamental characteristic of capitalism. His analysis goes much further in this respect than Marx and Engels, for whom the growth of capitalist monopolies is merely a side-effect of cyclical crises. Weber describes monopolization and de-monopolization as a comprehensive force throughout the economy, affecting labour, capital, finance and land as well. It each case, it is human actors who band together, establish formal regulations, and acquire political enforcement as a 'legally privileged group'.[4] This sounds like a definition of a profession; but it could also be a medieval craft guild or a business cartel. Weber also points out that this is the source of property in land, and of the feudal estate (status group, *Stand*), the landowning aristocracy. The formation of status groups and of classes more generally are part of the same process of monopolization.

This process itself is dynamic, carried along by struggle. Moreover, it is undermined by its very success. Groups are constantly manoeuvring over control. But their victory creates a new line-up of resources, which themselves become items for exchange and targets for further struggles. In Weber's own example, a tribal society, such as the ancient Germanic tribes outside the borders of the Roman Empire, may have no private property in land. As powerful households appropriate land for themselves, land now becomes monopolized. A landowning class emerges. But appropriation not only cuts down some opportunities (only some persons have control of land), but also opens up new possibilities (land becomes potentially an item for sale upon a market).

This process has been repeated numerous times. The medieval European aristocracy was formed when a closed, hereditary status group monopolized not only ownership of land but also military service as armed knights. (Thus we might regard this military aristocracy as one of the first groups to establish a true professional monopoly over an occupation.) When kings attempted to establish their own patrimonial-bureaucratic hierarchies, the aristocracy sometimes attempted (but with only partial success) to monopolize higher administrative positions as well, just as they typically monopolized positions as officers when larger armies of foot-soldiers and artillery were formed. But even the success of these tendencies towards monopolization eventually contributed to undermining the position of monopoly-holders. The restriction of governmental offices in parts of late medieval Europe to an aristocracy of birth also opened the way to treating positions as property, and thus kings in search of cash could put the same positions on a market and sell them to the highest bidder. A similar process motivated aristocrats who had monopolized landownership to attempt to realize its value on a market which was open even to outsiders, provided they had sufficient money.[5]

Thus there are processes both creating monopolies, removing certain items into the realm of private ownership, and by the further extension of property rights, dissolving them again on a financial marketplace. Weber's picture seems congruent with Schumpeter's emphasis on both sides of the monopolization process. For the entrepreneur has a monopolistic position merely by the fact of being the first.[6] Without the protection of some degree of monopoly, businesses could not afford to innovate at all. Monopolies thus are part of the dynamism of the economy. The other side of the same coin is the principle that monopolies are temporary over the long haul. Ultimately, a business which is not moving ahead is falling behind. It cannot merely remain in place, because it will lose out in the competition with other organizations, even those in quite different sectors of the economy, because of the pervasive competiton for capital (credit) which ties together all economic sectors. Weber agrees both with ubiquity of monopoly (at Schumpeter's innovation stage) and its transitoriness (as the competition for money and its pressure upon prices throughout the economy forces monopolists who are no longer growing to sell their holdings).

Weber proposes that modern capitalism develops through a *series of monopolizations:* first, of money capital by entrepreneurs who make advances to labour; then, of market information and hence of sales opportunities; subsequently, of all material means of production, thereby expropriating workers from their tools as well as excluding seigneurial and other outsiders' control over the place of work.[7] Finally there is the expropriation of the manager and even the owner, who becomes in effect 'a trustee of the suppliers of credit, the banks'.[8] Weber subsumes Marx's concern with the expropriation of workers, into a larger process of monopolization which was directed against feudal lords as well as against workers, and which ultimately expropriates the owners themselves – only in Weber's 'dialectic', it is not socialism that triumphs, but the credit market.

Various stages of the up-and-down process of monopolization may go on simultaneously in different areas. The monopolistic medieval guilds and the hereditary land-holding estates were circumvented as their individual members succeeded in appropriating their own shares for sale on the market, at the same time that new occupational and trade monopolies were being created. Having monopolized the means of production in particular branches, capitalistic enterprises were transformed into entities to be sold and recombined according to the vicissitudes of stock markets and banks. This goes along with the growth of new monopolies, both by Schumpeterian innovation and by cartellization and other forms of monopolistic business politics.

It should be stressed that our term 'monopoly' or even 'monopolization' carries rather misleading connotations. Even disregarding the practice of Marxist commentators to speak of 'monopoly capitalism' (or the 'monopoly sector' in dual labour market theory), when what is actually referred to is 'oligopoly', the term 'monopoly' implies less dynamism and tension than is actually the case. More accurately, we are speaking of a process of appropriation of market opportunities, although the instruments of appropriation themselves can thus become available for transactions on a superordinate market. The sale of monastic ordination certificates in medieval China,[9] or the comparable sale of governmental offices in early modern Europe, was both a 'corruption' of the usual channels of open occupational recruitment, and at the same time it opened up a market in which financial speculation and investment could take place. A modern analogy would be the growth of the highly credentialized occupational world, which fragments occupational markets and appropriates ('monopolizes') opportunities for groups of specialized degree-holders; at the same time, it creates market-like phenomena in the realm of the credentials themselves, such as the 'credential inflation' which has diluted their value in recent decades.[10]

The market economy exists even in this situation, but its laws do not consist of the familiar processes of adjustment of supply and demand to produce equilibrium prices. Rather, the key dynamic may be the up-and-down fluctuation of monopolization in various sectors. Weber gives the outline of this process as it applies to labour of all degrees of skill and power, including managerial and 'professional' labour (the latter being only a modern phrase for a successful type of licensed monopoly legitimated by a technocratic ideology). Schumpeter concentrates on monopolies of productive organizations, which emerge and dissolve regularly within the economy. Together they add up to a general process of appropriation covering all aspects of the economy.

The world history of markets

We can see that Weber's view of monopolization spills over the edges of conventionally defined capitalism, by including medieval guilds, the venality of offices, and even the formation of the feudal aristocracy. This is only one reason to broaden 'markets', or even 'capitalism', beyond their usual modern reference. We are becoming used to the idea that socialist states nevertheless act as capitalist units in the capitalist world system, as do state-owned enterprises within a given economy.[11] Corporate or political ownership is no bar to participation in the dynamics of competitive market systems. We may also push the historical edge of capitalism backwards in history.

Medieval capitalism
I have proposed elsewhere that the capitalist take-off in Europe took place in the high Middle Ages (in the years 1050–1350), as the corporate capitalism of the Christian monasteries.[12] A similar 'Weberian revolution' in institutional forms, my argument continues, took place in medieval China (AD 400–1000), as the entrepreneurial capitalism of Buddhist monasteries. Even within the anti-market structure of patrimonial/feudal society, the religious

capitalism of corporate entrepreneurs created a market system, which went on (with various vicissitudes) to spread into other sectors, eventually destroying the religious economy itself.

It may seem surprising that what we have always regarded as pre-capitalist society can have its own market dynamic. Yet it has always been a problem, in evolutionary 'stage' theories, how the seeds of the new capitalist form emerged within a non-capitalist structure. Marxism classically assumes the growth of bourgeois classes as a kind of alien growth within feudalism, which eventually chokes and takes over its host. The most sophisticated Marxist analysis of feudalism goes beyond this rather *ad hoc* model to propose that feudalism has its own economic dynamic.[13] In this model, the rent struggle between feudal lords and peasants stimulated both of them to increase productivity as well as bring new land into cultivation. The medieval economy thus expanded, until it reached a general crisis from its own inner contradictions. Prices, profits, inflation and workers' standards of living, all move in this 'feudal' dynamic of expansion and contraction, raising the question: is it accurate to call this 'feudalism' rather than another type of 'capitalism'?

Exchange theory, cultural capital, and kinship
A more appropriate perspective is to recognize that market processes of various sorts are ubiquitous throughout history. What changes is the shape of the market and the contents of what is exchanged – and monopolized. Exchange theory, although used mainly as a social psychology for analysing contemporary small-scale interactions, proposes quite generally that all interaction is governed by the exchange of rewards and costs – in short, by inter-personal markets.[14] Various kinds of purely social markets have been theorized: assortive mating in marriage markets;[15] 'friendship markets' which sort people into status groups by matching personal and cultural traits.[16] Relatedly, we have the reproduction of social classes through the circulation of cultural capital;[17] and the inflation of educational credentials.[18] In very general form, moreover, exchange theory proposes that market phenomena will exist in any society whatever, including the most primitive.

This requires us to make some distinctions. The phenomena just mentioned – marriage and friendship markets, cultural capital, educational credentials – are specific to forms of society in which individuals bargain freely for marital and personal connections, and in which institutions exist to produce specialized cultural currencies and tokens. How can these apply to tribal societies, in which specialized currencies do not exist, and the inter-personal network is itself prescribed by kinship and other ritualized connections? Yet one of the earliest forms of exchange theory was formulated for precisely such societies: Mauss's theory of gift exchanges, as elaborated by Lévi-Strauss into a structural theory of tribal kinship.[19] Here we have exchanges that are *not* bargained for on the open market; the main focus in Lévi-Strauss's analysis are the sets of kinship rules which specify who must marry whom, thereby perpetuating the exchange of women which links families together repeatedly over the generations.

This teaches us two points. First, exchanges, and the advantages and disadvantages that follow from them, are the essential ingredients of an 'economic' dynamic. The range of people that an actor may exchange with – that is to say, the extent or openness of the market – is a variable, and a secondary factor. When markets are 'wide open', so that everyone can potentially bargain with everyone, we have one type of economic structure. At the opposite end, there are Lévi-Straussian structures which specify exactly who must exchange with whom. Both ends of the continuum are ideal types. In reality, the wide-open market closes down, in varying degrees, through monopolization (as well as other factors, such as local accessibility of exchange partners); and the Lévi-Straussian world of pure marriage rules is always leavened by individual preferences and violations or by local contingencies (such as when a family which is supposed to marry a son to a mother's-brother's-daughter has no son).

Second, all exchange structures have a dynamic. We have seen various processes by which open structures move towards monopolization, and again to de-monopolization and 'marketification' at a higher level. There are well-known processes of price changes by supply and demand, as well as less clearly understood processes of inflation, growth, crisis and decline. This might be thought to apply only near the 'open' end of the continuum (although the fact that monopolization itself is part of the market dynamic should give us pause). But Lévi-Strauss shows that different structural forms, at the ideal-type end of the continuum where all relationships are pre-structured and closed, have their own historical dynamics. Some of them ('short-cycle' kinship exchanges) tend to reproduce the same kinds of kinship structures repeatedly. Other marriage rules (which may also be called 'alliance strategies') are more like risky 'investments' for families ('long cycles'), which eventually result in some families becoming 'rich' in kinship connections, while others become 'kinship-poor'. The end result of this particular path, Lévi-Strauss theorizes, is that the dominant families set themselves up as an aristocracy, thereby creating the state and going off the rule-constrained tribal kinship market entirely.[20]

Lévi-Strauss does not hesitate to describe this as a kind of 'kinship capitalism', complete with its self-transforming crisis culminating in a 'kinship revolution'. Thus the static rules of a closed, anti-market exchange structure can result in long-term dynamics, and even overthrow itself. Similarly, Mauss suggested that the gift-exchange system has at least one variant which is dynamic and results in economic growth.[21] This was the potlatch, found among the tribes in resource-rich environments. Mauss points out that the feverish competition and destruction of goods is a strong stimulus to production, and likens the Kwakiutl and the other North-west Pacific tribes who practised the potlatch economy to competitive capitalists.

We have not yet arrived at a completely general theory about markets. It is clear that conventional economics, both in neo-classical and Marxist form, have picked out only a limited sector of the larger phenomena. It is apparent, too, that the shift between more open and more closed situations of exchange is not merely a definitional frame, within which to locate various systems of 'capitalism' – or whatever we should call it! We cannot simply rest with taxonomies, because the dynamic of exchange systems is itself intimately connected with processes which move along the continuum between 'open' and 'closed'. The forces that produce what we have called 'monopolization' and 'de-monopolization' are themselves the essence of a theory of markets or exchange.

Occupational closure

Closed occupational groups have occurred in various forms, and in societies ranging all the way from tribal to industrial capitalist (and even socialist). Perhaps this is not surprising, in view of the preceding overview, which finds that market structures of various sorts exist almost everywhere: *kinship markets* in tribal societies; *corporate religious capitalism* in feudal societies; as well as *modern market economies*. Presumably these have had spillover effects, fostering network connections which could be used for other forms of exchange. Even the most primitive societies traded goods, sometimes over very long distances. In addition, there are social exchange systems, of which *educational credentials* are just a part, along with *cultural capital* more generally. There have been many sorts of market structures, with their own forms of monopolization. Hence it is not surprising that virtually all societies have versions of occupational closure.

Tribal societies generally have closure of esoteric activities. Iron-working, for example, was usually carried out by secret societies. The earliest specialized occupation was probably shaman, which was both secret and highly ritualized, and generally was structured round an apprenticeship. From this later was to evolve the closed corporate practitioners of medicine and priestcraft. Aspects of this secret-society structure are found in much later epochs, surviving in the Shakespearean term 'mystery' in the sense of a craft. For instance, stone-masons were organized as a religious lodge, a structural form which was taken over for social and political purposes with the emergence of the Masonic orders in the 1700s.[22] It may be noted that tribes had secret societies that were not occupational specialties: tribes with a men's house structure usually maintained ritual secrecy, even if closure was only against women and children; while religious ceremonies were often carried out by a closed group. The structure of closure, in other words, is broader than occupational closure, and its forms were available to be adapted for the latter purpose when specialized occupations appeared. Conversely, occupational closure is structurally related to status-group organization of the larger community, which it often reinforces or even creates.

Some agrarian state societies, with their more elaborate division of labour, had crafts guilds. Since production was small-scale, these doubled as monopolies of business as well as of labour – for example, in the European Middle Ages. Not all agrarian societies had closed guilds, however. They were notably lacking in ancient Greece and Rome, largely because crafts were typically occupations of slaves. India, on the other hand, developed an extreme version of occupational closure in castes and sub-castes. Structurally, a caste is the same as a guild (which also existed at periods in early medieval India) with the addition of endogamous marriage rules in the larger society.[23] That is to say, India as a whole was organized as a set of hereditary occupations. The guilds of medieval Christendom, too, were largely hereditary, in that occupation could be passed like property from father to son. But there was no rule against marrying into the occupation, whereas the presence of such a rule in India is what transformed them into castes. This most extreme form of occupational closure occurs when a monopolizing occupational group is reinforced by endogamous family structures. The whole was legitimated and enforced by becoming part of the dominant religious practices, and thus of the status system of society.

What conditions foster the various degrees of occupational closure? One factor is revealed if we consider the conditions that limit or break down closure. Metal workers in tribal societies were generally esoteric enclaves protected by the rituals of secret societies; but in late medieval European mining, this type of structure had largely disappeared. The difference, I would suggest, is that small-scale or individual craft work was displaced by larger organization – enterprises with a hierarchical structure, a property-holding boss supervising hired labourers. De-monopolization is fostered when the individual producer is separated from the market by a collective organization of production.

This process has interesting theoretical ramifications, in view of Williamson's doctrine that production can be organized either by markets or hierarchies.[24] Williamson proposes that activities are taken off the market and brought into permanent hierarchies when transaction costs are high because of uncertainties, while the input itself is repeatedly needed. Hence this activity is brought under a permanent authority instead of being bargained for in each instance. However, the ideal-type professions (law, medicine) are those in which uncertainty is high, yet they are organized primarily in the market and resist being brought into hierarchies. Professions may thus violate Williamson's principles. It is true that demand for their services may be intermittent, which should reduce the tendency to bring them into hierarchies. But in fact intermediate patterns are very common, in which some professional activities are brought into hierarchies (such as the employment of lawyers by government or business bureaucracies), but the occupation still retains its community structure and its distinctive status honour.

The question then arises: when are hierarchies de-monopolizing, and when are they compatible with professional monopolization of particular activities? The answer requires us to see that there is a struggle among occupational groups to control one another. The more powerful group is that which is able to maintain a monopolistic structure for its own members, while controlling the labour services of other occupations through keeping them unmonopolized and subject to market pressures. Both processes can go forward at the same time. De-monopolization at some levels of the organization (usually the lower) can go along with the renewed importance of group closure at other (usually middle to upper) levels. As crafts workers lost their privileges in bureaucratic employment, there took place a parallel growth of 'staff' specialists in the administrative sector, which often have been able to monopolize positions for possessors of licences and educational credentials.

A particularly clear case is the military profession. Its history reminds us that there is no simple evolution either towards or away from professionalization/closure; particular complexes of conditions have shifted the pattern in either direction at various times. The military was most sharply closed as a profession at the time of feudal knights; their monopoly on the profession of arms went along with their legally enforced, hereditary position as the aristocratic estate. (This was a move in the direction of a caste system, but did not reach it for lack of strict marriage endogamy.) But ancient Mediterranean armies, fighting in mass phalanxes, fostered no closed professional group; and again, modern mass armies have broken down the exclusivity (and the status honour) of the military profession. Some vestiges of it survive, however, in the modern officer corps: the caste-like division of order-givers (commissioned officers) and order-takers (enlisted men), with the upper group maintaining some of the ritual and themes of closure carried over from the knightly tradition. But here we have a 'profession' only within the privileged part of the hierarchy, above all in the activities of dramatizing their rank above the mass of de-professionalized subordinates.

The degree of technical skill, and how widely available such skills are in the population, seem not to have affected how much closure there has been in the profession of arms. In the modern army, the technical experts are most likely to be on the lower side of the ritual divide, in the ranks of the enlisted men. In the Greek phalanxes, technical military skill seems to have been very widely diffused. Instead, the difference in professionalization seems to have hinged on the extent to which there were relatively few important military positions in a given society, and on whether resources were available for creating a special elite ethos around the persons in these activities. It may be intrinsic to high professional status, then, that there be relatively few such people in a society; they must be out of the ordinary, quite apart from how valuable their services may happen to be. The ordinary Greek citizen-soldiers or Roman legionaries were too large a group to be a high-status profession. Stratification thus seems to be a cause of professionalization.

Occupational status honour

Relatively small size, and pre-existing privileges thus seem to be some of the conditions which make possible an elite, monopolistic occupational group. What makes such a group a 'profession' is the addition of one more ingredient. The professions are not merely occupations which have achieved closure against market competition; they also have occupational status honour. That is to say, they surround their work with an ideological covering. It is a 'calling', not merely a job. It is carried out from high motives of altruism, of glory, or of moral, spiritual or aesthetic commitment, rather than for mundane gain.

The fact that the high-status professions are also ones with high pay and power, moreover, suggests that the idealization of work is something additional to other rewards, and not a substitute or compensation for them. High occupational status honour is a major factor in producing the high pay of the most idealized, and presumably altruistic, occupations. Their status honour demands a 'status-appropriate' wage, so that they can maintain the appropriate life-style (as Weber commented generally about status groups).[25] Conversely, occupations which have low status honour are believed to merit low wages. This is one factor which determines the low wages paid to women workers, especially in occupations, such as secretaries, which are generally all-female enclaves.

It is the conditions which determine status honour which make trade unions (and especially industry-wide rather than crafts unions) structurally different from the professions, even though they share a similar form of market closure. Status honour, too, can be positive or negative. The Hindu castes are occupations, ranked from those of high and positive status (priestcraft, military) down to those of a very low standing (untouchables who carry out the 'dirty work'). (The latter exemplify what Durkheim and Mauss referred to as negative mana.) What we mean by the 'professions' is *a combination of market closure with high occupational status honour.* Presumably the closure and the status honour are each resources for attaining the other, although we have seen enough examples of each existing separately to know that their interaction cannot be the only determining factors. There are many instances (bureaucratically controlled priests or military officers) where high status honour is maintained even in a setting where horizontally controlled closure is limited by hierarchy.

It is here that education has played its crucial role in professionalization. Most treatments of education (from the conflict side, if not the technocratic theory) have seen it as producing primarily the closure of occupations. Bourdieu and Passeron's cultural capital theory, and other analyses which indicate the advantage of higher social classes in surviving a lengthy educational sequence for admission to occupations, all stress that education is merely a convenient device for monopolization.[26] (Some have noted, too, that education conveniently obfuscates its monopolizing tendencies, by operating under the legitimating ideology of openness of opportunities, of meritocratic or technocratic beliefs.) Here I would like to stress the other factor, the role of education as producer of status honour.

I have suggested that the ideal-type professions are those possessing high occupational status honour. (The quasi-professions or would-be professions usually are ones that fall short, not so much in closure, but in matching these high levels of status honour.) How are they able to generate this honour? Part of it comes from occupations which wield power (lawyers, military officers), since order-giving tends to produce self-idealization.[27] But this cannot be the whole answer, since order-givers in bureaucratic hierarchies do not usually acquire the same degree of corporate status identity. Another factor is that these are specialists in ritual. This is most obviously the case with the priesthood, the descendant of the earliest profession (shaman). Other high-status professions – medicine, law, science – also have a ritual cast, from operating in conditions of high uncertainty, and sometimes high dependence and potential distrust by clients, which foster ritualized procedures and the ceremonial impressiveness of practitioners before the uninitiated.

The modern 'high professions' tend to stake their status honour on their educational qualifications. Interestingly enough, would-be professions try to follow this route too, but with less success; the escalation of credential requirements for employment as a business manager in a large US corporation (now at the MBA level, but conceivably pushing via market oversupply towards Ph.D.s in Business Administration) has not resulted in managers sharing the same symbolic glory as religious ministers, medical doctors or scientists (or even of military officers who have attended the traditional military academies). What, then, is the nature of education in these high-status enclaves?

We can dismiss, I think, the proposal that this elite education is peculiarly laden with technical expertise. Education in medicine, for example, for all the technical skills which the modern profession exercises (although it did not possess much such skill before the twentieth century), nevertheless is not basically technical. We know this because the actual technical skills are learned in practice; the content of medical schooling is largely background materials in the sciences that have little bearing on actual performance; scores in medical school bear no relation to professional success.[28] Similarly, the status derived from studies in divinity (in societies where this has been high status) was not the result of the technical skills imparted by theology. The proper interpretation must be that it is education for ritual specialists; the nature of elite education itself must be a particular kind of ritual.

Education as ritual

All education is a ritual in a certain formal sense. A ritual involves the assembly of a group; their common focus of attention; the enhancement of a collective mood; and as a result, the symbolic significance of the content of the ceremony, which now becomes an emblem loaded with moral overtones and representing membership in the group.[29] Participation in rituals not only forms group identities, but gives the members symbolic tokens they can carry around with them, to use in guiding and idealizing their own activities, and in recognizing other members of the group. If we distinguish between explicit formal rituals, and 'natural rituals' which have the same structure but occur without explicit ceremonial intention, then it is clear that education is a 'natural ritual'. There are, of course, various methods of education that have been used historically: the group of students chanting together under a master, the lecture, the oral debate, the written examination and others. The point I would like to focus on does not deal with these differences (although a comparative examination of the varieties of educational ritual would be quite interesting), but with the most general structure. There is almost always the group of students, the focus of common attention, the common mood which sets the classroom occasion apart from ordinary 'profane' reality (in the Durkheimian sense), and the sacred objects which are exalted by this ritual process – usually the content of the curriculum, but also sometimes the teacher and even the student.

The status honour of elite education comes particularly from the last point: not only is education here especially 'sacred', especially successful in building an intense bond among those who participate in the schooling ritual, but it makes the completed student into an emblem of this sacred realm. This is very explicit in the case of training in divinity, which ends with the ordination of the priest; similar rituals exist for military officers, and for medical doctors. An explicit ritual induction into the profession upon completion of education is less apparent for scientists, since the formal granting of a degree is much less important here, but the identification of the individual with the 'sacred' realm is nevertheless very strong; this suggests that it is not the ritual induction at the end that is crucial, so much as the overall process of elite educational ritual.

Why does education sometimes have this effect, but sometimes not? For it is clear that much of education is an 'empty ritual', generating few shared moods except boredom and alienation, or at most passive acquiescence, as found in the classrooms of public schools, especially in compulsory secondary grades. One difference is that the students are merely physically present, but lack the motivation to focus their attention intently on the curriculum, or on the teachers, and thus keep ritual intensity from building up. This happens because differences in cultural capital, and recognition of objective probabilities of success in the system, de-motivates many students with low resources, at the same time that it super-motivates the select few who anticipate moving through education into prominent careers. The aspiring professionals, and above all those who have built up a stock of cultural capital that makes them comfortable with ritual occasions, are best able to throw themselves into the educational procedure. It is most ritualistic, in the Durkheimian sense, for these particular students. In fact, their participation in it is so intense that they end up identifying *themselves* with the subject matter. At the same time that this intense focus makes the curriculum contents 'sacred', it also makes the students, by participation, members of the 'sacred' realm in their own right.

The contemporary status problems of the professions

If education has provided the ritual resources by which occupations have professionalized, it has also produced, in the late twentieth century, an ambivalence around the professions in advanced industrial societies. This is the modern guise in which has appeared an old structural process: the tendency for forms of monopolization to undermine themselves through the appearance of a supra-market for the resources of monopolization.

On the one hand, there is still a widespread tendency in contemporary societies to adulate the professions. Partly this is due to their attractiveness as careers, prompting many career applicants. Also the non-professional classes in general, especially at the working-class and lower-middle-class levels, have a ritualized respect for such professions as medicine and science. Their claims of technical skill are taken as wonder-working, and they are invested with far more of a heroic aura than the bureaucratic commanders who actually hold power in modern society.

The adulation by the lower classes of the professions may be understood as the product of the ritual circumstances of the different social classes. Whereas the professionals epitomize the 'natural rituals' of the cosmopolitan sector, oriented towards the production and communication of symbols, the lower classes inhabit far more localistic social worlds. The 'natural rituals' of their daily lives have a particularistic focus, a repeated and largely enclosed set of interactions with a personal circle of family and acquaintances, resulting in conformity to a reified set of person-oriented symbols.[30] The world of the lower classes is a world seen in terms of personalities, not structures and processes, and is judged by conformity to traditions, not by abstract reflection. One might suppose that the cosmopolitanism of the mass media would break down this localism, but this is not so: the world of television and mass entertainment is just a larger world of personalities, not abstractions; actors and rock stars become just so many more personal figures of local gossip, but raised to a level of eminence that makes them 'sacred objects' of this personalistic world-view.

When individuals from this localistic ritual milieu view members of the professions, they have no way of understanding them except by assimilating them to their own cognitive categories. The power of the professions is precisely that they work in the realm of abstractions, and that they take part in cosmopolitan networks of non-personal connections with associates and strangers across long distances. But this is what the localistic world-view cannot comprehend. For them, the professions are merely heroic personalities, when they can see who they are: famous scientists, doctors who perform heart transplants, and the like; otherwise, the more technical and esoteric parts of the professions are invisible to the public. The skills and resources of the professions are misinterpreted. Since abstractions and network connections do not enter into the popular world-view, the success of the professions is taken as a kind of magic, 'science' as an object of uncomprehending adulation. This is entirely parallel to the way that people living in the milieu of localistic rituals of isolated tribal or peasant communities (Durkheim's 'mechanical solidarity') are superstitious about those larger, impersonal processes which impinge on their world from outside.

Ironically, then, the respect which the popular classes have for the professions is based on an entirely unprofessional way of seeing the world. It is the worship offered by the localistic ritual milieu to an entirely different realm of ritual structures. This 'magical' faith in the professions is potentially volatile, however, because it takes them on false premises, expecting miracles and capable of becoming scandalized, perhaps, when the miracles do not always happen. Popular distrust of the professions remains as yet largely a potential for the future. The public still trusts its magicians (more than, at least in the United States, it trusts other institutions, such as business, government, or labour) and has not yet turned against them.[31] But there is another source of distrust, which is already in full bloom. This is the distrust of the professions against themselves.

We may note, first of all, the auto-critique of the professions. It has been professionals themselves who have raised the issue of closure, of bias in their own ranks, of failure of their own standards of altruism. Current intellectual sophistication, moreover, has turned self-reflective and relativistic, denying the universal validity of its own cognitive claims. This crisis of conscience is structurally produced. The professional mentality, as we have seen, is produced by prolonged and self-willed immersion in educational rituals. The result is identification with the realm of symbols. At one time, this was a naïve identification: professionals had science, they had truth and right method, as well as dedication to doing good. But over time this naïvety has eroded. To be more exact, it has gone beyond itself. The educational rituals have intensified: because more candidates press for qualifications, credential requirements have escalated, individuals spend more time in education and go through further levels of symbolic abstraction. The intellectual content of professional training has become specialized, relativistic and reflexive. The magicians, in the privacy of their classrooms, are becoming self-conscious of their own tricks.

At the same time, the educational world has evolved. Teachers at these high levels (that is, 'professors') make their own professional careers by innovating or at least adding new layers of commentary on to the sacred symbols, the texts which make up the focus of attention in the curriculum. This reflection of symbols results in consciousness at higher levels of abstraction. It includes the discovery, which has been the prime intellectual theme of the twentieth century, of the recursive and constructed nature of symbols themselves. The current critical sociology and social history of the professions, like parallel developments in the sociology, history and philosophy of science, comes out of a larger process of academic self-reflection that has been building up with the expansion of mass higher education in this century.

The result is that the professions are beginning to be undercut at their ritual core. This does not mean that the professions are prepared to abolish themselves (although some sociological radicals, including myself, have sometimes made suggestions in this direction). After all, it is on the basis of the academic enclave, the core of professional self-generation (and of protected material resources for carrying out these intellectual activities) that these critiques have been mounted. Sophisticated professionals nowadays may talk self-critically, but they do so as part of their professional activities. They undercut themselves only in terms of confidence and subjective legitimacy, not in their salaries and autonomous conditions of work. And since this professional auto-critique is among the most esoteric topics in the culture of the professions, it is, as yet, well shielded from outsiders' awareness.

Nevertheless, the potential seems to be building up for a serious crisis of the professions. If the internal self-critique of professionals' legitimacy is ever combined with a popular upheaval of elite distrust, a repudiation of the 'magicians', we could see a future wave of massive de-professionalization. Such developments are not without precedent. We have seen above that the general process of monopolization, found in many spheres of exchange, is met by an equally general process of de-monopolization. Specifically in the sphere of professions, too, there have been waves in particular historical periods rolling back the professional closure of the time: there was a democratizing reaction against credential and licensing requirements for law, medicine and divinity in the United States in the early 1800s;[32] and entire credentialling systems fell into delegitimation and institutional crisis at the end of the European Middle Ages, as well as again in many European societies in the 1700s.[33]

It is a peculiar historical pattern that the developments regarded in one period as liberating become later to be regarded as oppressive. The reified traditional symbols of the *ancien régime* were attacked by revolutionary upheavals which glorified science and reason, later embodying them in professions which achieved some structural closure around their possession. Now, for the pre-revolutionary *'philosophes'* of the late twentieth century, it is science, reason and the professions themselves who are the oppressors to be overthrown. Ironically, it is only the reified traditional consciousness of the unsophisticated popular classes who uphold respect for these ageing idols, precisely because they themselves have not acquired the cosmopolitan consciousness. When and if this happens, it will be a revolution by 'combined and uneven development' within the class cultures themselves. What will happen after such an anti-professional revolution remains to be seen. That we are still in an early stage is implied by the fact that de-monopolization thus far remains at the level of critique, and has not yet created its own mythical saviour for the future.

Notes

1 Collins, 1975, 1988.
2 A concept elaborated by Parkin, 1979, and Murphy, 1988.
3 Wallerstein, 1974, 1980, 1988; Collins, 1988:96–101, 135–137; Goldstone, 1989.
4 Weber, 1922/1968:341–342.
5 Weber, 1922/1968:343, 638.
6 Schumpeter, 1911/1961; 1942.
7 Weber, 1922/1968:144–150.
8 Weber, 1922/1968:148.

9 Collins, 1986:72–73.

10 Collins, 1979.

11 Wallerstein, 1974.

12 Collins, 1986:45–76.

13 Anderson, 1974.

14 Blau, 1964; Lindenberg, 1985.

15 Waller, 1937; Walster and Walster, 1978.

16 Collins, 1975:80–81, 111–152.

17 Bourdieu and Passeron, 1970/1977; Bourdieu, 1979/1984.

18 R. Collins, 1979, 1981.

19 Mauss, 1925/1967; Lévi-Strauss, 1949/1969.

20 Lévi-Strauss, 1949/1969; 1984.

21 Mauss, 1925/1967.

22 Roberts, 1972.

23 Thapar, 1966:109–113.

24 Williamson, 1975.

25 Weber, 1922/1968: 932.

26 Bourdieu and Passeron, 1970/1977.

27 Collins, 1975:67–79.

28 Collins, 1979:201–202.

29 Durkheim, 1912/1954; Collins, 1975:153–155.

30 Bernstein's 'restricted code' in working-class speech is one instance of this; Bernstein, 1971/1973.

31 Lipset and Schneider, 1983.

32 Collins, 1979:139–142, 148–151.

33 R. Collins, 1981.

3

Essential properties, strategic aims and historical development: three approaches to theories of professionalism

Rolf Torstendahl

Identification of the problem

Researchers approaching professionalism tend to do so from one of two sides. Either they start out from the properties which are thought to characterize professionalism and professionals or from the types of collective action on which the groups of professionals rely. The two approaches are not directly related to fundamental schools in meta-theory, even if an indirect relation may be found. It is hardly accidental that structural functionalists were much more occupied with the characteristics than with collective action[1] and that neo-Weberians, conversely, devote their interest rather to the forms of collective action which they tend to say are constitutive for the standing of professionals.[2] It is noteworthy, however, that Marxists often are more interested in the classification of professionals in a class schema than in the specific activities which may characterize the part of a class or middle layer where the professionals are thought to be at home.[3] It will be shown here that a third approach is also at hand, and has become clearer during the last decade, and this is the historical or developmental perspective. It has become more and more clear that professions have not always been what they are today. It has even been questioned if they are not receding under the strain of something called 'de-professionalization' (a line of thought especially used by Marxist authors), which is most often thought of as a new tendency in social development in the West. If there is a new tendency, a time perspective is required in the analysis, and time horizons have thus become vital in new ways.

The three main approaches to the study of professions and professionalism may then be stylized in the following way:

1 The characterization of professions, professionalism and professionalization in order to get an adequate ground for classification of occupations and people. It is then taken for granted

that professions have their specific place in society and that professionalization is taking place in a specific way. A proper way to study professional groups is then, often, to examine their history and prehistory.

2 The identification of relations/conflicts between a (professional) occupational group and other groups and the overall intentions guiding the actions of the first group against another or several others.

3 The examination of the relations of one occupational group, taken to be professional, to other groups during a long time sequence, not in order to follow a 'professionalization process' but in order to see changes within a 'profession' or in the conditions for professions in society at large.

This difference is not primarily intended to be one between 'static' and 'dynamic' points of view, even though traits of this kind may appear. More important than this is, however, that the first approach is to be applied to those occupations which are clearly identifiable as professions, while the second approach will make it possible to identify groups which have applied strategies of professionalization but have been unsuccessful in their attempts to attain recognition as of a professional standing or groups which have used strategies of professionalization as well as other strategies. The third approach will help to discover both internal changes in professions and their adaptations to a changing society. This means that the three approaches differ in their way of tackling questions of professionalization. The first approach aims at identifying which are the professions, while the second approach aims at finding out which groups *act* professionally and the third approach wants to show how professional groups *change* (though remaining professional). From all sides it is possible to claim that the other approaches beg the question. It is impossible to find out empirically which are the characteristics of professions without having a stipulation or enumeration of which are the professions. And it is equally impossible to identify which groups act in a professional manner without deciding first which kind of action is to be considered professional. Likewise, it is impossible to analyse the changes in professional groups without first being able to pick out the professional groups which may be subject to change.

It ought to be mentioned, even if it is rather self-evident, that the three approaches do not exclude one another, even if researchers often treat them as exclusive.

The essential property approach

The first approach is essentialistic, something in line with an old tradition in Western thinking. It has long been considered vital to direct all kinds of scientific analysis towards the most essential properties or traits of what is the object of analysis. These are sometimes described as the only analytical approximation of the 'thing in itself' (*Ding an sich*), sometimes they are made the 'prime mover' in a theoretical body of sentences regarding the analysed object. Logically these two alternatives are quite distinct from each other. In fact the difference in research is not always that clear. Both the predicative (seeking essential logical predicates) and the causal analysis may be examples of the aim to find the essential properties, but the difference is – or ought to be – that only the causal analysis is apt for use at the starting-point in a social theory. However, in actual social science, it is not always possible to make the difference between a predicative analysis (that is, showing the adequate logical predicate) and a causal analysis when we come to essentialism: it is not easy to say if education is the basis of professionalism in some analyses because it is the inner core of what can be said of (that is, the logical predicate of) something which is called professionalism, or because it is the causal origin of a social chain of dependencies which are known as professionalism.

This statement is not an empty play on words. On the contrary, it is important that we cannot easily identify why we find education with diplomas and licences 'essential' for the standing of professionals. Three possibilities open up. First, it may be that the concept of professional is really unthinkable without the property of educational qualification and licensing. This is the sense of the essential logical predicate and a standpoint which is in line with a Platonic tradition taken up in (for example) Thomism. The second possibility is that only with education as a driving force, according to an established theory of 'social forces', could a profession be established. The third possibility refers it all to language and implies that the way in which people actually talk about professionals refers explicitly or implicitly to education and licence.

The intention is not to go into philosophical depths here but just to show that it is by no means evident what is really essential to professionalism. Whichever is the analytical platform, it has to start out with presuppositions. Only if we already know what it is to be professional, may we claim also to be able to identify what is essential to professionalism. It never works the other way round. Essential properties may be identified (if it is accepted as possible to identify essentials) after the stipulation of a definition of the concept. Other types of definitions are possible as well, but the analysis of essential properties must follow, not precede, definition.

We may ask if the essentialist analysis really leads towards the intended goal. A sound (irrefutable but also unavoidable) question is why we know that an analysis of professionalism should start out from the social relations of lawyers and doctors. This has been taken for granted in research on professionalism since it started. Why isn't it equally proper to start from nurses or engineers or journalists or primary school teachers? Their social relations and experiences might give a basis for an essentialistic study which might make lawyers and doctors part of the periphery. The reason is that doctors and lawyers 'are' professionals. The logical extension of the concept – that is, which persons may be classified properly by the concept – is already known. This is a definition by use. We know from empirical semantics of everyday life that English-speaking people call lawyers and doctors by this name.

This means that the ultimate rationale for the essentialistic approach lies in the linguistic habits of the English-speaking world. It is, then, most intriguing to imagine another linguistic world where engineers and primary school teachers were called 'infessionals', and a theory of 'infessionalism' was formed from an essentialistic analysis of the things engineers and primary school teachers have in common. Especially intriguing would be to note the explanations that might arise for an (imagined) fact that more and more groups were affected by 'infessionalism' and were applying the concept to themselves. Would this be nonsensical? Would it be worthwhile to study this phenomenon or not? Would it give a deeper insight into the social reality where engineers and primary school teachers were to be found?

Such questions are not immediately answerable. If we really take for granted that a language pattern was formed, where 'infessional-ism' played a role, it is pretty certain that an analysis would give interesting results. Language – especially then the concepts for social relations and social structure used in everyday life – reflects 'social reality' (whatever it is) or, in a still more demanding interpretation, makes out this 'reality'.[4] It may be rewarding to find the common traits that have made engineers and primary school teachers what they are and also (the causal approach) what may be the causes for their special positions in society.

This means, of course, that language plays an important role in social habits. We conceive as common traits in social groups what we give the same name and we tend to think that, once the common name is established, there must be 'something' at bottom to be discovered and also, perhaps, 'something at bottom' which is the driving force for a common development. On the one hand such convictions may be discarded as 'illusionary' effects of language. On the other hand, it is hardly advisable to give up essentialistic analysis altogether. It is the way to discover social 'reality'. We would know nothing about what constitutes credentials, education and knowledge if analysis had not been devised to make these things clear. And only if these concepts are analysed in their empirical application can we know something of the 'real' basis of professionalism.

Most theorists of professionalism and of professionalization have tried this essentialistic approach. They have identified necessary traits of professionalism in groups or they have identified stages of professionalization or they have defined degrees of professionalism and/or professionalization (or even de-professionalization or re-professionalization). A gradualism and a development perspective is not at all excluded from this first approach. But if one stops there, one ought to note the limitation of the perspective. The foundation is the English language and its use in the nineteenth and twentieth centuries. Other societies and their differences from the social habits and their reflection in the language of the English-speaking world are not considered. What is essential to professionalism thus tends to be analysed only from the perspective of what has been essential for the groups identified in English as professionals. If the same properties are not essential to the corresponding groups in other societies we must realize that the essentialistic analysis is no good basis for a general theory of professionalism.

The strategic approach

What Frank Parkin has developed out of the closure concept in Weber's *Economy and Society* is one main example of the second approach. Parkin's closure theory contains two action lines, the strategies of exclusion and usurpation, and one 'dual' strategy which is a mixture of the two action lines.[5] Even if other researchers have not to the same extent hung their theories on strategies, it seems clear that strategic action has been in the centre of interest in many specific analyses of professional behaviour.

The analysis of closure is not exclusively, not even in the first place, an analysis of professionalization. One of the closure strategies, the strategy of exclusion, is applicable on professionalization and that is all. It is all that can be said about the general relation between professionalism and exclusion. Closure is a more general phenomenon, the keeping of other people away from the advantages someone has got in society: capital assets as well as all other marketable valuables. Usurpation is conceived by Parkin to be the opposite of exclusion: the usurpation of the advantages that exclusion lines try to keep for the privileged group. Usurpation is thought of as the (or a) typical trade-union strategy.[6]

Even in Parkin's analysis of closure there seem to be some points that ought to be cleared. First, it seem to be empirically debatable to what extent usurpation is really a trade-union strategy. It may be argued that it is not the only trade-union strategy: to ask for a rise in wages seems not to be a usurpation in any clear sense of excluded values or valuables. Further, someone may want to dispute that it is ever a trade-union strategy to usurp those values that were denied and to form new closure lines from this. It may be argued that trade unionism is rather to find relations which are non-closure solutions; that is, to form an 'open cartel' which anyone may join who is in principle a subject in the cartel's field of relevance (and not only an object for the activities regulated through the cartel).[7] It is important to note that cartelization as a strategy is quite different from exclusion, but that they are possible to combine by applying first one (exclusion) and then the other (cartel among accepted practitioners).

I don't want to go into this interesting field here but rather discuss two other questions, namely: is exclusion always the same, and how do we recognize professional strategies? The latter question is relevant only if my considerations regarding the former question are valid. It seems not to be self-evident that closure strategies of exclusion are always the same.[8] Exclusion, as a name for the whole genre of closure strategies that deny to those who are not inside a privileged group access to some assets which give the group a monopolistic position on the market or at least some sort of control over the market, seems to cover at least two situations that are different in a significant way. One is the situation where the asset is marketable in itself. All normal capital assets are of this kind, real estate as well as stock and securities and goods. They are not bound to the abilities, qualities or disposition of a specific person. This means that they can easily be re-distributed through any social upheaval either peaceful or violent. New groups may become the asset-holders and they may – or must, in order to keep their new possessions – apply the exclusionary strategies against the former possessors as well as the less lucky people who were without these possessions both before and after the upheaval.

Another situation is the one where the assets are not *per se* transferable on the market. Only as part of the individual bearer – if he or she accepts – are these assets marketable on the labour market. It may be argued that individuals are not always in a position to refuse a job. This is true, but all the same there is a difference between that situation and the situation where someone is robbed of their assets, because then they have not got them any more. The doctor, the engineer and the school teacher will never be robbed of their abilities whatever hard conditions may be thought out for them in their society. Only they themselves can then apply exclusionary strategies on the basis of their professionalism.

Professionals thus seem to be in a special position in applying their strategies of exclusion. They share this position with some categories which are normally not counted among the professionals, such as successful athletes or performers of different sports, or even players, artists or gamblers, honest or fraudulent. What these people have in common is that they have access to personally acquired skill and/or knowledge which is marketable through themselves and which they can make a basis for an exclusionary strategy. This, however, applies very widely in society. Many groups of people have personal skill and/or knowledge which is marketable through them and in demand in the labour market. The nursery school teacher, the electrician, the glazier and many others have such assets. They are not normally considered professionals. So, the conclusion seems to be, that not all exclusion strategies are the same and that, yet, the strategy which is based on skills and/or knowledge and so on is not used only by the groups which are normally known as professional.

It would be rather easy to decide that one strategy was 'the professional strategy' by using one of two methods: one may look at the strategies of groups defined as professional groups and empirically determine which is their strategy or strategies, or one may decide that one of the alternative strategies which can be discerned by analytical work is called professional because it is applicable to professionals (among others or exclusively).

It seems that Parkin's usage is of the latter kind. He examines the application of closure strategies in general and puts forward the use of exclusionary closure as professional. As a stipulation this is quite acceptable. We must know, however, that the application of exclusionary closure may not coincide with any definition of 'professionalism' in terms of essential properties.

Another complication has to be considered as well. Only if closure strategies are conceived of as the sole strategies applied in society or incompatible with all other strategies can we leave other strategies out of consideration. In fact this seems not to be the case. At least three strategies which are used by collectivities and are not varieties of closure seem to be discernible: politicization, cartelization and status quo. Politicization as a strategy means that someone tries to reform the 'rule regime', to use Tom Burns's phrase. It means that the normative system is to be changed either by legal reform or by social acceptance.[9] The creation of open cartels means that all people working within a social field are invited to form a price regulation of the work in the field and nobody is excluded who accepts the price list. Status quo as a strategy means accepting the existing normative system in all respects as it is and trying to apply it to oneself and others. Politicization is then another strategy for change other than exclusionary closure or any closure strategy, and politicization and cartelization compete with closure strategies regarding which changes should be given priority by a collectivity, while status quo as a strategy opposes change.

One further comment has to be made on Parkin's use of the strategy conceptions before we turn back to the question of how to choose between the essentialist and the strategic aspect of professionalism. This comment is about dual closure and semi-professions. Dual closure – that is the application of both exclusion and usurpation at the same time – is said to be characteristic of the semi-professions.[10] As has already been stated, some objections may be raised against usurpation as a trade-union strategy. Another point which deserves mentioning is that if usurpation is taken to describe trade-union strategies which are not exclusionary, it is necessary to observe that exclusionary strategies are combined with trade-union strategies by many groups which are not commonly regarded as semi-professional: doctors and surgeons in many cases ask for (*sic!*) a rise in their salary from their counterparts on the labour market instead of using exclusionary strategies in order to enforce a rise in the social evaluation of themselves that might result in pecuniary gains. In fact, the combination of a professional strategy of exclusion and a trade-union strategy of cartelization (and the use of bargaining to make cartels effective) seems to have become quite common after World War II in groups that did not use this combination earlier. A change has taken place.

Still one important observation regarding the 'dual closure' concept has to be made. Dual closure means that two strategies are applied simultaneously. As already mentioned, it is of fundamental importance if, on the one hand, strategies are recognized as being possibly of different natures and if, on the other hand, the actors are considered capable of applying more than one strategy at a time. It seems that the surrounding world asks for the applicability of simultaneous strategies of different content or nature.

The conclusion of the deliberations on strategy as an instrument for the delimitation of professions is, thus, that professions as collectivities must be able to apply several strategies at a time. If the strategy of exclusion is found – through empirical research – to be the most commonly used strategy by professional groups, and most empirical investigations made seem to point to this result, this is important. Exclusion seems to be an important action line for professionals. Obviously they are not, and have not been, insensitive to other means of increasing their influence or payment. And it is also important that exclusion is not a strategy confined to the groups which are generally recognized as professional groups in the English language. A definition based on strategy thus has considerable limitations.

Weighing essential properties against strategy

The preceding analysis leads us to two related questions for the starting-points of analyses of professionalism:

1 Can advantages of the essentialistic approach to the strategic approach – or the reverse – be identified in order to make it possible to select one of them as preferable?
2 Is it possible to combine the two approaches in one theoretical body which is not only circumstantial and sophisticated in an elaborate way but has also advantages compared to any of the two approaches in its pure form?

The advantages of essential properties as starting-points are first of all the 'firm ground' one might find in everyday language. This firm ground is, however, confined to the English-speaking societies. It is not sure, and it is even contested and doubtful, whether the concept in its everyday English usage is applicable to other languages. The French *professions libérales* (and still more *cadres*) are something different, and so are the *Akademiker* in Germany and Sweden. Thus there is 'firm ground' only if one is willing to confine the study to one social unit defined by language.

In the strategic approach it is not taken for granted that linguistic usages are the appropriate starting-points for social theory. The theory is hinged on the group's own (linguistic or non-linguistic) behavioural patterns and it is up to the researcher to label them as professional or non-professional.

Stated in this way it is obvious both that each approach has its advantages for certain purposes and that they do not denote the same things. It must be possible, however, to do research according to one of the approaches and then check if the results would be very much different as regards the groups concerned, if an approach of the other kind had been used.

One difficulty remains. Both approaches are vague in the general sense that several definitions and specifications are possible within each of them. Manipulation of cross-checked results is easy ('Having concluded that professionals X behaved 'a'-like in relation to the state during the whole period between 1920 and 1986, I have also found that theory 'a'-strategy was an exclusion-based closure strategy').

It is necessary to emphasize that cross-checking of results from investigations with the 'essential properties approach' and the 'strategy approach' cannot be used for purposes of verification. They do not confirm each other. The cross-checking has to be a heuristic device in order to limit the range of possible outcomes.

Of course, the most important of all such measures that can be taken is to specify more precisely what is the 'essential property' which is regarded as indispensable for the standing as professional, for the practice of professionalism and for the process of professionalization. Only groups which have acquired a considerable amount of 'abstract knowledge' (not necessarily in the form of theories but rather, in some instances as, for example, lawyers, in the form of normative systems) are accepted as professionals.[11]

There seems hardly to be any doubt that knowledge belongs to the 'essential properties' that have to be sought in the groups that are to be regarded as professionals. The groups admitted into the circle of professionals in the British and American literature on the subject rely on university training, and Randall Collins seeks the roots for professionalism far back in history but only in the educated layers of society.[12] Jürgen Kocka and Werner Conze, in their introduction to a volume on *Bildungsbürgertum* (which in its turn is a German concept without a close equivalent in English) emphasize higher education as well as modernization as essential parts of the meaning of the concept.[13] Recently, in another introduction to an anthology, Hannes Siegrist has questioned the relation between 'free and academic occupations' (*freie und akademische Berufe*) and professions, but the 'ideal type' of professions with which he wants to contrast specific historical investigations contains as a fundamental element occupationally relevant knowledge which may be generalized and has a theoretical element.[14]

It is important that investigations which start out from other linguistic premises than those of English tend to emphasize education and knowledge rather than a specific set of 'professions' as the basis around which a theory has to be formed. Several of the Anglo-American authors who have dealt with the subject tend to make the same thing central in their analysis, but they, notably Collins,[15] place the emphasis on credentials rather than on knowledge and tend to make such credentials the basis of a strategy rather than the essential property of the professions. The same is true of Murphy, who wants to connect professions with guilds rather than to make a clear distinction between them.[16]

As several of the British model professions – lawyers, physicians (at least to an extent) and engineers – have been without a specific university training for their standing (always or for a long time) it seems that a condition of education cannot be 'institutional education'. Other forms of education are difficult to specify. It seems advisable, then, to withdraw the condition of education. The only remaining part of the essential property condition, which is not definable only in terms of the English language usage, is knowledge.

Thus, we may define knowledge-based groups as the groups which may develop professionalism. They can do so through applying certain strategies, which presupposes that the two approaches – essential properties and strategies – are regarded and used as compatible with each other. If compatibility is to mean something beyond sheer simultaneous existence of 'professional properties' and 'professional strategies' (an ontological compatibility which can hardly be denied to theoretical constructs of any kind) it has to bear upon the denotations of the two conceptual approaches if the preceding discussion of the conceptual differences between the two approaches is correct.

Denotation again points to the important empirical foundations of statements on professionals and professionalization. There must, in short, be important coinciding classes of phenomena, which are pointed out as well by analysis of essential properties as being professional as by strategic analysis as acting professionally. If the two approaches 'cover' some phenomena in the same manner (but in different conceptual schemas) and these phenomena are regarded as central in both conceptual approaches, then they are empirically compatible in the sense alluded to here.

I want to argue that there is a compatibility of this kind between the two approaches as far as we know their competing qualities. Having reconsidered some analyses of professional groups, I have found that they seem compatible with the strategic approach as well. And it is also evident that many analysts have used strategic analysis as an additional argument for their vindication of a thesis on professionalism in groups which they consider important but questionable from an essentialistic point of view.

Of course, it has not been possible for me to make any real, thoroughgoing analysis of vast empirical material for the investigation of the compatibility of the two approaches. It seems that engineers – the group with which I am personally best acquainted – are interesting as an example of a group with some essential properties, some professional strategies, some non-professional properties and some non-professional strategies.[17] Civil servants, another group about which I happen to know something are also a group where one can find some (indeed many) professional properties, some professional strategies but rather more strategies for status quo or politicization.[18]

In both cases, engineers as well as civil servants, it is worth noting that what is important for the classification from essentialist points of view is not so for the strategic classification and vice versa. What coincides is results or classifications, not the bases for them.

This brief summary of results in the research concerning the two groups of engineers and civil servants may serve as an indication that it may be worthwhile to analyse more closely the empirical connections between the two approaches. Above all, such investigations may be rewarding since many analyses based on essential properties (especially as taken for granted in English by English-speaking authors) have been mixed with occasional pieces of evidence from strategic points of view. This combination of approaches has seldom been regarded as a combination because the starting-point in the English language has been taken for granted.

If the observations related so far have a significance they must mean that acting professionally (in the strategic sense) is characteristic of professional groups (in the essentialist sense). It must be important to check if that is true, and to make sure that strategic analysis means a substantial addition to an essential analysis of professionalism.

However, such an analysis of professional strategy in relation to professional properties must not be supposed to show a complete empirical agreement. It would be mistaken to expect all cases of essentialistic professionalism to show strategic professionalism and the reverse. Strategic action of a professional kind may *often* be taken by groups that are essentially professional, but the absence of professional action cannot be used as evidence for any misuse of the essential properties. Likewise, as I have already made clear, a professional strategy may be used by groups or individuals who cannot be classified as professional from an essentialistic point of view. The two concepts overlap, but they do not coincide.

This means also that groups, where some professional properties are at hand, may or may not act professionally, and it is an empirical question if they act professionally less often than groups which are more solidly professional from the essentialist point of view. The activities of Swedish elementary school teachers (with few essentialist criteria) were clearly strategically professional in the late nineteenth century (as shown by Christina Florin),[19] perhaps even more so than the activities of engineers (with more essentialistic criteria). Once again, it is important to point out that investigation of the empirical relations between the two approaches to specific groups are important in order to show the wealth of possibilities in social reality. The statistical relations that ought to be found are not implicitly self-evident and not the main thing. Most important is that the conceptions of being professional and acting professionally are connected empirically but not by definition.

Another subject for empirical analysis is the relation between unsuccessful professional strategies and professional properties. As groups applying professional strategy may vary in their 'degree of professionalism' according to essentialist criteria, it is natural that they should vary also in applying unsuccessful strategies of this kind. But it cannot be shown analytically to what statistical extent this should be true, and if the two should correlate or not. Maybe some properties regarded as essential criteria were more often coupled with unsuccessful strategies than other essential properties.

I have frequently alluded, in this chapter, to the need for empirical investigations of the relations between theoretical alternatives from different approaches. Such investigations have not only an esoteric theoretical interest; their main objective is to pin two theoretical maps over a social terrain one over the other in order to compare them with each other and with the terrain at the same time. The basic idea is that they both have contributions to offer, but that we do not yet know exactly which are their respective advantages and disadvantages and that it would give a better orientation to be able to read them together than to use only one of them at a time.

Is there a temporal approach?

It is necessary to emphasize that the professional complex can be viewed from more aspects than from those of the professionals as individuals and as groups. Both properties and actions have the professionals as subjects. They are, as professionals, the centre of interest both in the essentialistic and the strategic approach. It is, however, possible to regard professionals as participating in or as the objects of a social process, where the individual professional is not acting – or is not interesting – from his or her professional point of view but as forming a social group with a pattern which is interesting for its own sake. Here we may distinguish between two varieties of viewpoints. One is the tradition of professionalization theory which tries to define comparable phases in the development of each professional group. The stages of professionalization, discussed by Wilensky and others,[20] are the points of reference here. Another is the effort to compare different kinds of development in different times. This is a macro-sociological (or, rather, macro-social-scientific) way of looking at social developments, as it takes for granted that social phenomena look different in different types of societies but that a correspondence between phenomena and processes may exist all the same.

There is a premise for the second type of argument, and a premise that is often misunderstood. This premise is that concrete social formations form a mass that can be divided into types and that the formations of one type show more similarities to each other than they do to those of any other type. But it means, also, that the social formations of different types are similar in some respects, for otherwise it would not be fruitful to compare them.

However, the supposition is mistaken that the premise of the argument is that all societies 'function' in the same way, or that all societies can be defined in a set of essential 'functions' which have to be filled (and thus can be identified) in all social formations and all types of societies. I do not want to deny the existence of valid arguments on functions in all cases but only that 'functions' (if meaningfully defined) must not be taken to be constants.[21] It is impossible to show that new 'functions' of this kind do not arise and develop.

The argument I want to point out as important for professionalization theory is the contention that in social formations of types A and B there may exist occupational groups which are related to occupationally relevant knowledge as well as demand for special services and market control in ways that make it interesting to say that the A type societies represent an A-form of professionalization and B type societies a B-form. If we find that the A-form arose earlier than the B-form, and that many societies have – through a period of time – changed their appearance from A to B and that during a certain period there is a coexistence of the two forms while the A-form becomes extinct in some societies but not in all which have the B-form, then we have grounds for a temporal dimension of professionalism theory.

It is important to point out that a temporal dimension of the theory of professionalism should not consist of stages that are regarded as a compulsory path for the development of professionalism in any given society. The temporal dimension must be much more closely related to the actual development of world history, and it is clear that some societies (or groups of societies) have gone through developments which have no real counterparts in other societies (for example, industrialization in Europe and the United

States during the nineteenth century, which was based on the development of railways and consequently of the iron industry and engineering).

A temporal dimension of the theory of professionalism (as distinct from stages of professionalization) is thus important in so far as we want to relate professionalism to other societies than to the societies of industrial capitalism in its European and North American forms. Further, it is probable that the phases of capitalism in the West[22] have not passed without leaving their marks on the development of professionalism. We should not be astonished, then, to find that professionalism has not always been the same in the capitalist world. The forms of professional market relations (knowledge output control through the state in continental Europe and through associations in Britain and the United States) of the early nineteenth century obviously were no longer dominant in the early twentieth century. Professional relations to industrial, mercantile and state bureaucracies became a new dominant factor which made politicization and professionalization sometimes compatible and sometimes competing strategies for realization of professionalist goals. There have been long-term changes in the realization of professionalism in Europe.[23] There are also several indications that professions have found a new form in these capitalist societies since World War II through their intimate cooperation or symbiosis with trade unions and the adoption of trade-union strategies.

Regarding a temporal approach to professionalism, the following points ought thus to be observed:

1 Temporality is a dimension of the study and a temporal approach is no alternative to the approaches based on analysis of essential properties or strategies.
2 A temporal approach dealing with professionalization in a limited sense must fall into the sterile discussion of stages in an evolutionary path: which stages have to precede which, and so on.
3 A temporal approach to the theory of professionalism will be fruitful when the temporal dimension is used to compare types of societies and how occupational knowledge, certain service functions and the market are related to one another in order to detect types of patterns which succeed each other, overlap or come back in cyclical revolutions.
4 Within the capitalist societies of Europe and North America from the beginning of the nineteenth century – only one type (or two types) of societies – there seems to be a developmental

sequence of phases in the socio-economic and political development which have close relations to phases in the development of the standing of professionals and their activities. From a limited knowledge control strategy by the professionals (Britain and the United States) or by the state (Germany, France, Sweden and so on) to a strategy for bureaucratic control in private businesses or the state through exclusionary strategy or politicization, and, further, to a strategy alternating between knowledge control in the classical manner and trade-union strategy in another well-known manner, professionalism has changed its appearance when the social environment has changed.

Conclusion

This chapter implies that current research of professionalism and professionalization has been fundamentally chained to the English language and, through the language, to the society where this language has its current usage, where social reality and conceptual subtlety were formed together. Many social phenomena are not confined to one specific country with its social setting. For example, 'state' is used and understood in many different social contexts, even if it is almost certain that it does not mean the same 'thing' in all these contexts. Professionalism and professionalization are, however, bound to the English language. It is argued here that this is not by chance. There is no immediate counterpart to these concepts in other countries.

Nevertheless, in this chapter an attempt has been made to form an argument for the elaboration of the theory of professionalism and of professionalization. One first condition, in order to make such a theory valid and interesting in spite of the linguistic and social barriers, is to break the basic connection with the English language. The 'essential properties' of professionals must not be decided by how the concept is used in English. It is argued that essential properties must, instead, be connected with knowledge (abstract knowledge), and both education and certificates have been discarded as the basis for the groups which ought to be considered. These groups may be called 'knowledge-based' groups.

If knowledge-based groups are recognized as the basis around which a theory of professionalism has to be formed (irrespective of whether these groups are called professionals or not in Britain or the United States), this solves only part of the problem for the theory formation. The next problem is what it means to act professionally. Here it has been argued that professional activity has to be connected with exclusionary closure as a strategy for collective action. It is further argued that there is no logical link between the knowledge-based group as such and the exclusionary closure strategy. This means that it ought to be fertile – and there are good indications from current research that it has shown to be so – to cross-check being professional with acting professionally. Knowledge-based groups have not acted and will not act only from the exclusionary closure strategy. To what extent do they rely on this strategy, and which other groups use this strategy? These are important questions.

With a mind open to different answers to these questions it is possible to relate the activities of knowledge-based groups in different societies and in different historical social settings to their surroundings. It is obvious that there have existed knowledge-based groups far back in history and also that the exclusionary closure strategy has been used.

The enormous leap forward that was taken in the development of the theory of professionalism in the late 1970s through the efforts especially of some American and English social scientists[24] focused attention on the activities of the professionals. Taxonomy, which had dominated the previous discussion, became obsolete. In order to make another step forward possible and widen the scope of the theory, it is necessary to cut the conceptual links to one specific social context. Through empirical research on a historical basis it is then possible to examine the changes in the use that has been made of professionalism. As a basis for group formation, knowledge is but one alternative, as a strategy exclusionary closure is but one alternative. It has been used, sometimes frequently, sometimes seldom. Sometimes states have been promoters, sometimes private interests.

In showing this and in analysing historical developments in different social settings,[25] researchers have in fact let the theory of knowledge-based groups win ground. It is time now to accept its conceptual premises.

Notes

1 Parsons, 1963; Wilensky, 1964; Hall, 1968.

2 Parkin, 1979; Collins, 1979; Larson 1977/1979 ought to be regarded primarily as neo-Weberian rather than Marxist.

3 E.g. Johnson and O'Donnell, 1982; for the Marxist approach, see further Murphy, 1985.

4 Linguistic philosophers of different schools have put forward such interpretations. Influences from Wittgenstein's *Philosophical Investigations* in Winch, 1958, as well as from Austin, 1961, in Harré, 1979, may be mentioned.

5 Parkin, 1974; Parkin, 1979.

6 The ingredients in Parkin's analysis are well analysed by Raymond Murphy in Murphy, 1983, 1984, 1986 and (partly summarizing his earlier works) Murphy, 1988. Murphy presents a thorough discussion of the consequences of Parkin's and Collins's premises for their respective use of closure theories.

7 On the concept of 'open cartel', see Åmark, 1986:27–33, esp. 28, and Åmark's essay in this volume.

8 A penetrating discussion of closure strategies is found in Murphy, 1988, especially chs 4 and 8. Its results have inspired parts of this essay, even if the conceptions do not completely coincide.

9 Burns and Flam, 1987:13.

10 Parkin, 1979:101–102. This is the second case, where Parkin applies the dual closure concept. The first case is within the working class; for example, relating to the position of the labour aristocracy.

11 See Burrage, Jarausch and Siegrist, ch. 11 in this volume.

12 R. Collins, 1979, 1981. See also his contribution in this volume.

13 Conze and Kocka, 1985:9–26.

14 Siegrist, 1988c: 13f.

15 Collins, 1979, especially chs 5 and 6.

16 Murphy, 1988:185–188.

17 The literature on engineers is very rich and constantly growing. The types of research questions have been partly dissimilar in the American and the European investigations of engineers. See Torstendahl, 1975, 1982 and 1985b and literature referred to there.

18 See, for example, Mayntz, 1982, and Burrage, 1988b and literature cited there.

19 Florin, 1987.

20 Wilensky, 1964. For a pertinent critique on the stage theory of professionalization, see, for example Hellberg, 1978:12–14.

21 This is not the place to go into the recently mentioned discussion on 'neofunctionalism' advanced by J. Alexander.

22 I have tried to show that there is a common sequence of phases in the societies of industrial capitalism in Western Europe from the middle of the nineteenth century. See Torstendahl, 1984a.

23 See, for example, Siegrist's contribution in this volume.

24 Larson, 1977/1979; Collins, 1979; and Parkin, 1979, are main examples, but there were others working in the same direction at the same time.

25 See, for example, *The Formation of Professions: Knowledge, State and Strategy*, edited by Rolf Torstendahl and Michael Burrage, London: Sage, 1990, and also Siegrist (1988a).

4

'Bürgertum' and professions in the nineteenth century: two alternative approaches

Jürgen Kocka

I

It is difficult to translate the concept 'professions' into German. While *'freie Berufe'* (liberal occupations) refers to self-employed professionals only (not to those in salaried positions), the concept *'akademische Berufe'* (academic occupations) excludes those nineteenth-century professionals who were not trained in universities or similar institutions (like the English barristers), and it does not carry with it the notion of autonomy and self-controlled closure which usually define the 'professions'.[1] It is true, the concepts 'professions' and 'professionalization' have been used by social historians and sociologists writing in German.[2] But they are not 'home-grown'; they maintain the flavour of imports, and they are not easily applied to a social reality which has been conceived by and structured around other key concepts. Notions of class and the manual–non-manual distinction have structured the German social language much more than structural-functional categorizations.[3]

It is, vice versa, equally difficult to translate the German *'Bürger'* and related concepts into English. *'Bürger'* carries at least *three* different levels of meaning which overlap and intermix both in the common and in the scholarly use of the word. First: with respect to the late medieval and early modern period the word refers to urban burghers, a corporate group defined by specific legal privileges, life-styles and status in contrast to other townsmen and the rural populations; since the evaporation of the corporate distinctions between town and countryside, between burghers and other townsmen took a relatively long time in nineteenth-century Central Europe, this traditional meaning of *'Bürger'* has survived though in a continually weakened form.[4] Second: particularly with respect to the late eighteenth, nineteenth and twentieth centuries, *'Bürger'* refers to those who belong to the social formation *Bürgertum*, which included (1) the bourgeoisie in the strict sense of the word (namely, businessmen, entrepreneurs, capitalists, managers, *renti-*

ers and so on) and (2) what is often called '*Bildungsbürgertum*' (educated middle classes); that is, lawyers, judges, academically trained civil servants, ministers, many journalists, later on engineers and so on. Usually the nobility, the petty bourgeoisie, the lower and working classes, the peasants, artists, the military, and the Catholic clergy were not included in the concept of '*Bürgertum*'. Perhaps 'middle class' is the best translation for '*Bürgertum*' in this second meaning (which will be the focus of this article). Third: '*Bürger*' has the meaning of 'citizen', and the adjective *bürgerlich* can be translated by 'civil' or even 'civic', '*bürgerliche Gesellschaft*' by 'civil society'. While the German language seems to differ from most other European languages in that it does not clearly differentiate between '*bourgeois*' and '*citoyen*', this ambivalence cannot be regarded as a mere semantic incidence. It rather points to the interconnection between the rise of the middle classes and the rise of civil society in late eighteenth- and nineteenth-century Central Europe, a connection which may not exist any more today, but which survives on the semantic level.[5]

In contrast to 'profession', the concepts '*Bürger*', '*Bürgertum*' and '*bürgerlich*' are frequently used in German historical literature. In recent years research on this topic has expanded. The bourgeoisie and the *Bildungsbürgertum* (educated middle classes), their social composition and economic situation, their cultures and politics have drawn much interest, and continue to do so.[6]

Obviously, the social history of the professions and the social history of the *Bürgertum* partly deal with the same kind of people, although they categorize them in different ways. How do these two approaches compare? Can they learn from each other? Before discussing these questions, the German *Bürgertum* approach should be introduced in some more detail.

II

Which were the defining attributes of that social formation *Bürgertum* (middle class) in the late eighteenth, nineteenth and twentieth centuries? Which were the characteristics shared by businessmen, *rentiers*, doctors, lawyers, experts, clergy and others, in the socially relevant way – characteristics which at the same time distinguished them from other social categories not belonging to the *Bürgertum*? What was the common denominator and the *differentia specifica* of the *Bürgertum*, and how did they change over time? Certainly, the *Bürgertum* cannot be seen as a 'class' in a Marxist or Weberian sense, since it included self-employed and salaried persons, and, more generally, persons with very different market positions. Certainly, in contrast to the burghers of the late medieval and early modern times, the nineteenth-century middle class cannot be seen as a corporate group (*Stand*) either, since it was not characterized by specific legal privileges. Rather, there are two plausible and compatible arguments with respect to the unifying and defining characteristics of the *Bürgertum*.[7]

It is generally more likely that social categories are transformed into social groups with some cohesion, common understanding and a potential of collective action if there is tension and conflict with other social groups. By setting oneself apart from others, one gains identity. This is well known from the history of classes. The same holds true with respect to the Central European *Bürgertum*. When the modern *Bürgertum* emerged as a post-corporate supra-local social formation in the second half of the eighteenth and the first part of the nineteenth century, merchants, entrepreneurs and capitalists, professors, judges, journalists, ministers and high-ranking civil servants differed in most respects, but they shared a critical distance from the privileged aristocracy and absolute monarchy. By stressing the principles of achievement and education, work and personality, the concept of a modern, secularized, post-corporate, self-regulating, enlightened 'civil society' emerged, which was supported by many *Bürger* and held against the privileges and the despotism of the *ancien régime*. It was a complicated and multi-faceted process with many exceptions. Still, the different sub-groups of the emerging *Bürgertum* were to some degree united by their common opponents: the nobility, unrestricted absolutism and religious orthodoxy. On this basis, they developed common interests and common experiences; a certain degree of shared self-understanding and common ideologies emerged; the *Bürgertum* constituted itself as a social group or formation, which encompasses different occupational groups, sectors and class positions.

In the course of the nineteenth century this line of distinction and tension lost much of its structuring power, without fading away altogether – due to the gradual destruction of the legal privileges of the nobility, the rise of constitutional government and increasing *rapprochements* between the upper grades of the middle classes and parts of the nobility. Simultaneously, another line of distinction and tension came into play, which had not been altogether absent around 1800, but which became more manifest, more clearly perceived by the contemporaries and even dramatized in the second third of the nineteenth century: a line of demarcation setting the *Bürgertum* apart 'from below', from the lower classes, the emerging working class and the 'small people' in general (frequently including many master artisans, small merchants, inn-keepers and clerks, now frequently lumped together as petty bourgeois and distinguished from the *Bürgertum* proper). Whatever the many and great differences between late nineteenth-century industrialists, merchants and *rentiers*, lawyers and higher civil servants, professors, high school teachers, scientists and others, they usually shared a defensive-critical distance from 'the people', the 'working class' and the labour movement, and this meant much with respect to self-understanding and life-style, social alliances and political commitments at that time. Consequently, where and when a strong tradition of aristocratic dominance was absent (as in the USA); where and when the gap between nobility and (the higher echelons of the) middle classes was bridged and integrated early (as in eighteenth-century England); where and when the integration of the upper strata of the middle class and the nobility into a new composite elite was also followed by a marked weakening of the tension so that both 'social fronts' faded away (as in most of Europe today) – a distinctive *Bürgertum* was less likely. The existence of a distinctive *Bürgertum* depends on constellations, which vary over time and place, and the national differences of sociological conceptualization reflect these variations.

The second attempt to define the *Bürgertum* refers to its culture. According to this view the bourgeoisie and the *Bildungsbürgertum* (educated middle class) shared a specific respect for individual achievement on which they based their claims for rewards, recognition and influence. They shared basically positive attitudes towards regular work, a propensity towards rational life-styles, and a fundamental striving for independence: individually or on the basis of associations and self-governed initiatives. Emphasis on education (rather than on religion) characterized middle-class views of themselves and the world. Simultaneously, education (*Bildung*) served as a basis on which they communicated with one another, and which distinguished them from others who did not share this type of (classical) education. There was much respect for scholarly pursuits (*Wissenschaft*) and a particular aesthetic relationship towards music, literature and art. For middle-class culture a specific ideal of family life was essential: the family as a purpose in itself, a community held together by emotional ties and basic loyalties – also by the dominance of the husband and father – an inner sphere protected from the world of competition and materialism, from politics and the public, a sphere of privacy (although not without servants, whose work made it possible for the middle-class mother to give sufficient time to the cultural dimensions of family life, including the transmission of the 'cultural capital' to the next generation). Middle-class culture could flourish only in towns and cities.

For there had to be peers with whom one could meet in clubs and associations, at feasts and at cultural events, something that a rural environment could not really offer. If one sees the cohesion and the specificity of the *Bürgertum* as defined by its culture, one appreciates the importance of symbolic forms in the daily life of the *Bürger*: table manners and conventions, the quotations from the classical literature, titles, customs and dress.[8]

Middle-class culture claimed universal recognition. In contrast to aristocratic or peasant cultures, it had an in-built tendency to expand beyond the social boundaries of the *Bürgertum* and to imprint the whole of society. The *embourgeoisement* of non-middle-class groups was an essential element of middle-class culture. The school system, the workplace, public life, and, finally, the sphere of organized leisure were the most important arenas in which middle-class culture could express its hegemonic force and its attractiveness. In the long run, it spread widely and dispersed. To the extent that this happened, middle-class culture ceased to define the *Bürgertum*. The more clearly a whole society was imprinted with middle-class culture, the more difficult it became to identify a specific *Bürgertum*. This is the situation in most Western countries today.[9]

On the other hand, there were (and there are) obstacles preventing an easy spread of middle-class culture beyond the *Bürgertum* proper. For, in order to participate fully in the values and practices of middle-class culture, certain economic and social conditions have to be fulfilled. One needs a stable income clearly above the minimum. Life must be relatively secure, in the long run; otherwise, long-term planning is impossible which, in turn, is needed to build up a systematic, rational, disciplined conduct of life. Within the family, the wife and mother as well as the children must be, to some degree, set free from the necessities of work and from the compulsion to contribute to the family's income – impossible in all lower-class and many lower-middle-class milieus. Again, the availability of servants appears to be central.[10] Middle-class culture cannot flourish without plenty of space (functionally specialized rooms in the house or the flat) and time for 'purposeless' cultural activities and leisure. In order to take part in the game of middle-class culture and to obey its rules, such conditions had (and have) to be fulfilled, which were (and are) beyond the reach of the majority. This explains why the middle-class status of most of the petty bourgeoisie (master artisans, small retailers, small businessmen, inn-keepers and others) was highly precarious and questionable, and why peasants, workers and lower-class persons in general did not qualify as *Bürger* at all. A tension between universalist claims and limited accessibility was typical for middle-class culture.

But the degree to which it spread beyond the social boundaries of the *Bürgertum* has varied in the course of history.

On the basis of such considerations, one can ask interesting questions and pursue fruitful research. One can study processes of middle-class formation and devolution, by looking at the relation between sub-groups of the *Bürgertum*, at its outer boundaries and its relations to other parts of society. One can ask how *bürgerlich* different social phenomena were – the literature, the educational system, entrepreneurial behaviour, a society's dealing with its minorities, the political system, and so on – that is, to what degree they were influenced by the middle classes and imprinted with their principles. One can compare whole societies as to the degree of their *Bürgerlichkeit* (middle-classness). In fact, a powerful though controversial line of comparative interpretation holds that a specific weakness of *Bürgertum* and *Bürgerlichkeit* characterized German history during the nineteenth and part of the twentieth centuries, due to the strength of surviving pre-bourgeois elites and traditions, and particularly due to the strength of bureaucratic structures and static traditions.[11]

III

There are similarities and congruences between the historical study of the professions and the historical study of the *Bürgertum*. Doctors, lawyers, university professors, perhaps high school teachers, scientists, university-trained engineers and other groups of experts and well-educated persons are subject to both approaches. Both approaches deal with long-term processes of group formation and group development. This is why both approaches are interested in social distances and affiliations between persons and groups. Both approaches try to find out to what degree, with which consequences, due to which factors social formations emerge and dissolve. Both try to relate economic, social, cultural and political factors to one another.

The *Bürgertum* approach is broader, more synthetic and less specific than the profession approach. Within the *Bürgertum* approach it seems to be easier, in fact unavoidable, to place the historical analysis of single groups in the context of the whole society; the profession approach narrows the topic more specifically down and allows a more concise operationalization. It is easier to make controlled cross-cultural and inter-national comparisons of single professions than of whole middle classes. Sociological theory seems to be more fruitful with respect to the problems of professions than to the rise and fall of the *Bürgertum*.[12] Different types of theories play a role: the concepts of 'profession' and 'professionalization' are closely related to the notion of modernization, and they continue to be so, even if professionalization is seen as a process of competition, conflict and power re-distribution in which certain groups gain at the cost of others.[13] On the other hand, the *Bürgertum* approach is closely related to notions of class and class formation even though the *Bürgertum* cannot adequately be described as a class. Professionalization theory developed out of English and American discourses and experiences; the *Bürgertum* approach is continental in origin.

IV

Relating both approaches to one another may produce new perspectives, hypotheses and results. The historical study of the *Bürgertum* can make good use of some insights derived from the historical study of the professions. On the other hand, in the light of the *Bürgertum* research, some findings in the literature on the history of professions and professionalization may look different. Cross-fertilization produces new questions on both sides. The following remarks concentrate on what this may mean for the debate about professions and professionalization.

First, professionalization can be seen as a strategy to get into the *Bürgertum*. According to this viewpoint, Hannes Siegrist has analysed the gradual professionalization of Swiss attorneys during the nineteenth century.[14] For him, professionalization appears less as a process of monopolization of market opportunities and increasing professional autonomy, and more as a process of collective upward social mobility and cultural adjustment.

Siegrist has also shown how important social integration into the middle class can be as a factor of professional success, at least in the case of client-oriented professions. Social connections and shared cultural experiences tend to increase confidence, which may be more important for an attorney's (or a doctor's) success than expert knowledge. Siegrist warns against over-emphasizing the role of formalized knowledge, which is often stressed within studies of professionalization.

Following this line of questioning, one has to investigate professionals' membership in clubs and civic associations, marriage and mobility patterns. With respect to Germany, these indicators show that in the first half of the nineteenth century the members of different academic professions had close relations with one another but only limited contact with the bourgeoisie (business community). In the course of the nineteenth century, the gap between some professions and the bourgeoisie was bridged by increasing intermarriage, intergenerational mobility, and other contacts. At the same time, the distances between single professions became more pronounced, setting – for example – ministers and lawyers further apart, and increasing the life-style and economic differences within single professions, such as among lawyers in one large city.[15] The members of fully professionalized occupations belonged to the *Bürgertum*. On the other hand, as Mario König has shown with respect to Swiss white-collar employees (bank clerks, for instance), those who try to professionalize in vain or behave as would-be professionals, do not fully belong to the *Bürgertum*.[16]

The failures of professionalization projects have different causes. Certain types of activities (such as in the arts or journalism) seem to be less suitable to professionalization than others (for example, law, medicine or engineering), because the knowledge they require is not easily expressed and transmitted in theoretical form. But as the *Bürgertum* research suggests, there are social and cultural factors explaining the failure of professionalization, as well. Without regular and foreseeable income on a satisfactory level (such as nineteenth-century elementary teachers), without a family of the middle-class type (most white-collar employees), without a certain distance to manual work (nurses) professionalization is doomed to fail.

Dealing with the professions in the context of *Bürgertum* research draws attention to the social and cultural prerequisites of professionalization projects. After recognizing the outstanding importance of culture and life-style for the constitution of the *Bürgertum*, one wonders whether one could identify a culture of professionalism as well. Until very recently, it was a male culture, which may have helped to make the entrance of women more difficult.[17] It certainly had achievement-oriented, meritocratic elements, which stood against democratization of all kinds. It stressed specialized knowledge over general education, and it probably lacked the universalistic claims of middle-class culture in general.

Second, in German literature the *Bildungsbürgertum* (educated middle class) plays a major role. The *Bildungsbürgertum* (persons who have at least higher education, usually on the university level, and who make their living from it) is usually seen as one of the two fractions of nineteenth-century *Bürgertum*. (The other one is the bourgeoisie: entrepreneurs, merchants, bankers, capitalists, managers among others.)[18] There is, it is true, some debate on the problem to what degree the nineteenth-century *Bildungsbürgertum* is just an *ex-post facto* construct of retrospective research and/or to what degree it was a social reality – that is, not just a category but a real sub-group of the *Bürgertum* with clearly marked outer boundaries, internal cohesion, common self-understanding and collective identity. But at the present stage of research it seems that in nineteenth-century Germany this supra-professional entity *Bildungsbürgertum* has been a reality to a larger degree than in France and England. The social language[19], marriage circles[20] and voting patterns[21] provide evidence which points in this direction. In order to understand this German feature, one has to take into account the relative weakness, status inferiority and late development of the German bourgeoisie (compared with Western Europe). One also needs to consider the important role of the *Gymnasium* (secondary school) and the university – results of the neo-humanistic educational reforms of early nineteenth century. In contrast to Britain (with its strong stress on a guild-type apprenticeship-based training of attorneys, barristers, doctors and others, in the early part of the nineteenth century) and France (with its specialized Grands Écoles, at least until the 1870s, when much of the German university system was imitated), the different German professions received their education in common institutions, increasingly specialized, but still 'under the same roof' and with many common experiences.[22] Consequently, cognitive, normative and aesthetic elements of general education were shared across the lines separating specialized professions; and something like a broadly defined *Bildungsbürgertum* could emerge.

There is a certain tension between general education (*Allgemeinbildung*) and specialized education (*Fachbildung*). Max Weber, among others, feared that the rise of the expert (*Fachmann*) would, in the long run, help to destroy 'das alte Kulturmenschentum', the broadly educated and cultivated personality.[23] Following this line of thought, one can see the *Bildungsbürgertum* (based on the recognition of the high value of general education) and the professions (based on the high value of specialized, functional knowledge), to a certain extent, as competing identifications. Given the emphasis on general education and the existence of a comprehensive *Bildungsbürgertum* (at least to some degree, and more than in other European countries) in Germany, the emergence of clear-cut professional groups and identifications must have been slowed down – another explanation for the absence of an endogenous German discourse on 'professions' and 'professionalization'. On the other hand, there can be no doubt that, also in Germany, professionalization advanced in the course of the nineteenth and twentieth centuries. In the last decades of the nineteenth and in the twentieth century, the rise of more specific professional identities on the basis of expert knowledge helped to fragment the *Bildungsbürgertum*. There are several reasons why the *Bildungs-bürgertum* is more a phenomenon of the first two-thirds of the nineteenth century, and why it has slowly lost its cohesion and profile in the following decades. But one of the reasons can be found in the process of professionalization and in the concomitant rise of the *Fachmenschentum* (expert).[24]

Third, within the German *Bildungsbürgertum* civil servants played a major role: administrators with a university degree (usually in law), judges, university and *Gymnasium* professors, in addition some government-employed doctors, architects and engineers. At the beginning of the nineteenth century, the majority of the *Bildungsbürger*, at the end a sizeable minority of them, were civil servants (*Beamte*) with specific loyalties, obligations and claims to the government. In terms of recruitment (on the basis of general-ized qualifications to be acquired in a standardized and hierarchical system of public schools), seniority rights, tenure, and bureaucratic work situations (hierarchical, functionally specific, on the basis of written records and generalized rules), the status of this higher echelon of academically trained *Beamte* became increasingly similar to the ideal-type developed by Max Weber after 1900.[25] In Prussia and Bavaria and in other German states the modern civil service had originated in the absolutist period of the late eighteenth cen-tury. It underwent basic reforms at the beginning of the nineteenth, but it was never challenged by a successful revolution from below. The Prussian civil service became the model of the national bureaucracy, which very slowly developed after 1870. The early and continuous rise of relatively autonomous, powerful, well-educated and highly prestigious civil servants distinguished Ger-many from Britain and the United States, where a modern civil service did not emerge before the last decades of the nineteenth century, and even then it differed strikingly from the Central Euro-pean type of bureaucracy, which was indeed the empirical basis for Weber's ideal-type.

While the French development resembled the German as to the absolutist origins, the early rise, the basic continuity and the relative strength of the public bureaucracy, its structure was very different. The French administrators came from different schools (not from an integrated university system); corporatist and clientelist types of patronage survived; the whole set-up was more centralized but less systematic; parliaments and the public helped to reduce the bureaucracy's autonomy. In general, the bureaucratic impact on the fabric of society was much less pronounced in France than in Germany.[26]

This strong and peculiar German bureaucratic tradition deeply influenced the development of the German *Bürgertum* and helps to explain its state orientation as well as other features. It also influenced the German pattern of professionalization in at least three respects.

In the first place, an important part of professionalization occurred *within* the public administration. After all, these civil servants increasingly became academically trained professional bureaucrats, who largely determined the rules of recruitment – that is, access to their sphere of work, the kind of university training needed, the type of examination to be passed, the preparatory service required in addition. Partly, their authority rested on their knowledge (*Sachwissen*). And they gained a certain amount of collective autonomy *vis-à-vis* the clients (or 'subjects') and *vis-à-vis* the political rulers, either the monarchs or the parliaments. But, of course, it was a bureaucratically crippled professionalization: autonomy on the basis of self-governed associations did not really develop; the authority of civil servants rested not only on knowledge and competence, but also on the delegation of formal authority by the superiors; and they served in a strictly hierarchical structure, which required their obedience and limited their responsibility – quite in contrast to pure professionalism.

The rise of this bureaucratic professionalism partly hindered, partly facilitated professionalization outside the civil service. Prussian attorneys, for instance, had to have indirect civil service status until 1878; this made the development of a self-regulated, professional bar difficult. On the other hand, bureaucratic models seem to have cleared the way for an early adaptation of professional management techniques in the railway companies, large manufacturing enterprises and banks.[27]

In the second place, as recent comparative research has shown, professionalization inside and outside the civil service was based in Germany, from the beginning, on government-regulated academic training and examinations. The university education of government officials served as a model. Guild-type apprenticeship systems played hardly any role, in contrast to England. But, in contrast to France, the central bureaucracies did not suppress the associations of the emerging medical, legal, engineering and other professions. Rather, a close cooperation between relatively autonomous professional associations and government bureaucracies emerged – a symbiosis which did not prevent but facilitated the professionalization of doctors, pharmacists, lawyers, engineers, architects and others, although it provided for a particular bureaucratic flavour of German professionalism.[28]

In the third place, for the emerging professions the civil servants seem to have frequently played the role of a normative reference group. To reach the high status, the clearly defined credentials and the secure position of an academically trained civil servant was an attractive aim for the members of emerging professions, like the engineers. To give just one example: in the 1870s the chairman of the Association of German Engineers (*Verein Deutscher Ingenieure*) demanded a civil service-type state examination for professional engineers, as a basis for their social upgrading and their professional consolidation.[29] It was not the successful entrepreneur whom the striving German professional wanted to imitate, as seems to have been the case in the United States.[30] Rather, the professional *Beamte* served as a model, in the case of the engineers without complete success. The civil service status with its formalized qualifications, seniority rights, salary classifications and tenure guarantees was not fully applicable in capitalist firms which became the main field of employment for engineers, managers and other experts, nor was it fully applicable in the world of the 'liberal' professions of self-employed lawyers, doctors, pharmacists and others. Still, the widespread acceptance of the civil service status as a model within the professions was significant. It influenced the way in which they formulated their demands and expected the state to support them. It indicated the close affinity between professionalization and bureaucratization in Germany.[31] And it said something about the place of the emerging professions within the *Bürgertum* at large: about their relative proximity to the higher civil servants, and their relative distance from the bourgeoisie.

Notes

1 Cf. Conze and Kocka, 1985:9–26; Larson, 1977/1979; Murphy, 1988; Feuchtwanger, 1922; McClelland, 1985:233–247; Jarausch, 1987:280–299; Jarausch, 1986a:107–137; Cocks and Jarausch, 1989 (forthcoming).
2 Cf. note 1; Huerkamp, 1985b; Burchardt, 1980:326–348; Siegrist 1985:301–331; also see several other contributions to the same volume, and Dilcher, 1986:295–305; Siegrist, 1988b:11–48.
3 Desroisières, 1988; Desroisières, 1977; Kocka, 1989b.
4 Cf. Walker, 1971.
5 Kocka, 1988a:11–78; Hobsbawm, 1988:79–106.
6 Cf. Kocka, 1987b:21–63 (review of the literature); Siegrist, 1988b; Frevert, 1988.
7 Evidence and literature in support of the following paragraphs: Kocka, 1988b:20–33.
8 Cf. the contributions by H. Bausinger and T. Nipperdey in Kocka, 1987b:121–148; Nipperdey, 1983, ch. 4; Bourdieu, 1979.
9 Consequently, the concept of '*Bürgertum*' has developed as a major tool for

analysing social developments from the late eighteenth to the early twentieth century, but it is less helpful and indeed marginal for the analysis of present-day societies.

10 Cf. the observation in Sombart, 1986:11.

11 At least in comparison with Western Europe. Cf. Kocka, 1988c:3–16.

12 But cf. in the tradition of Max Weber: Lepsius, 1987:79–100. Also see the synthesis in Wehler, 1987, vol. I, pp. 177–193 and vol. II, pp. 147–241.

13 Cf. Parsons, 1939:457–467; Parsons, 1968:536–547. Also see Johnson, 1972; Larson, 1977–1979.

14 Siegrist, 1988c, vol. II, pp. 92–123. Also see note 2 above.

15 Cf. Henning, 1972; Henning, 1978:1–30; Zunkel, unpublished paper, 1986. I also draw from unpublished work by B. Dornseifer (Bielefeld) on the professions in Hamburg.

16 König, 1988, vol. II, pp. 220–251.

17 Cf. Huerkamp, 1988:200–220.

18 Cf. Engelhardt, 1986; Turner, 1980:105–135; Vierhaus, 1980:395–419; Vondung, 1976. The concepts of '*Intelligenz*' and '*Intellektuelle*' are slightly different. Cf. Geiger, 1949; Pascal and Sirinelli, 1986.

19 Contemporaries spoke of '*gebildete Stände*', later of '*akademische Berufe*' and '*Bildungsbürgertum*'. Cf. Engelhardt's history of the concept (note 18). Apparently contemporaries found it necessary to identify a group larger than single professions but smaller than the *Bürgertum* as a whole. Such conceptualizations reflected and influenced perceptions, which in turn were related to experiences and structures.

20 R. Zunkel has summarized the evidence which shows – for the first part of the nineteenth century – a strong tendency of daughters and sons of families with academic backgrounds to inter-marry while marriage connections with the bourgeoisie proper and with the lower-middle-class groups were much less frequent. Towards the end of the nineteenth century inter-marriage between the offspring of academic families and the offspring of bourgeois families became more frequent. Cf. note 15 above.

21 H. Best has shown a distinctive voting pattern of *Bildungsbürger* in the 1848–1849 National Assembly of Frankfurt, while he did not find corresponding patterns in the French National Assembly of the same time; cf. Best, 1989:75.

22 Cf. Lundgreen, 1988: 106–124.

23 Weber, 1964:737.

24 This interpretation is doubted by Siegrist, 1988a:19. But see Huerkamp, 1985a:358–387, 384.

25 *Wirtschaft und Gesellschaft*, pp. 162ff, 775ff. Cf. Wunder, 1986; Hattenhauer, 1980; Süle, 1988.

26 Burrage, 1988b:51–83; Kocka, 1981:453–468; Thuillier, 1980; van Riper, 1958; Karady, 1985:458–468.

27 Cf. Kocka, 1980a:77–116; Kocka 1987a:259–277.

28 Cf. Huerkamp, 1987; Heidenheimer, 1989; Späth, 1988:84–105; Lundgreen, 1988:106–124; McClelland, 1985:233–247; Osborne, 1983; Rueschemeyer, 1973.

29 Lundgreen, 1988:117; Kocka, 1969:171–190.

30 Burrage, 1988b:70–79.

31 It was very difficult in the United States. Here, professionalization came late but clearly preceded bureaucratization. I have discussed the effects of this German-American difference on the formation of white-collar groups: Kocka, 1980b:44–45, 89–92, 144–150, 189–191, 263–264.

5

Professional types as a strategy of analysis

Thomas Brante

By and large, modern studies of the professions have followed two lines, two avenues of research. In the first, attempts have been made to identify the essence or true nature of professions as such. This approach has mainly been taxonomic: empirical findings and historical facts have chiefly been employed merely in order to illustrate and exemplify theoretically motivated definitions of professions, and delineations between professions and other occupational groups. The second avenue has been historical and empirical; the histories of single professions have been carefully scrutinized and mapped out. Here, theoretical definitions and explanatory concepts have played a minor role.

In the academic division of labour the first line of research may be called philosophical, conceptual or semantic, the second historical or historiographic. The question I want to address in this chapter concerns the role of sociology in studies of the professions. What specific perspective, what kind of research, and consequently what type of results, can sociology contribute?

Before I begin to discuss this question, let me point out that there are reasons to be somewhat dissatisfied with the contributions sociologists so far have offered in the field. Crudely put, sociologists have tended to follow one of the two avenues of research mentioned; that is, an autonomous sociological approach to the professions can scarcely be said to have been pursued. Further, among sociological-taxonomic studies, too often obvious value-biases have permeated both initial assumptions and conclusions. In a previous article, which surveyed different approaches to the professions, I have tried to show how and why sociological-taxonomic studies tend to fall into one of two broadly defined categories with ideological underpinnings. In order to emphasize the ideological premises behind the approaches, I labelled them the naïve and the cynical perspective.[1]

In short, the naïve perspective, which dominated the scene up to around 1965, defined professions à la Parsons; namely by constantly underscoring their (positive) functions for society at large. Professions are conceived as the prime bearers and distributors of rational norms (for example, teachers at schools and universities), and the foremost in developing society in economic, technical and general welfare respects (such as engineers or physicians). Professions are distinguished from other occupations by prestigious attributes such as strict ethics and integrity, a universalistic and functionally specific relation to their clients, and, above all, by employing skills based on scientific knowledge. They are society's most important spearhead groups, working towards a better future.

During the 1970s and 1980s, the cynical perspective forms an alternative to the naïve perspective; in fact, it may be seen as the inversion of the former. Professions are still understood as occupational groups with long and high education. But the resulting credentials and alleged theoretical competence is employed strategically to seek monopoly of sectors of the labour market; a speciality (knowledge monopoly) is used to obtain occupational monopoly; that is, to eliminate competition. Professions are seen as instruments, as resources by which their members can gain higher income, power and prestige – a kind of collective egoism. Society is not conceived as a harmonious whole, but as a market permeated by competition between rival groups. Thus, professional strategies are analysed from the notion of social closure, namely, a general theory of the dynamics of society.

Ordinarily, these two perspectives are separated by being labelled 'essentialist' and 'strategic', respectively; but basically, both are essentialistic in proposing all-embracing, universally valid definitions. They employ trans-historical concepts while they should, according to Eliot Freidson, use 'generic' concepts.[2]

This leads to the suspicion that both the naïve and the cynical perspective should be understood from the point of view of sociology of knowledge. Naïvism was chiefly developed in post-war USA; that is, during a period when a harmonic, idealist and conservative social ideology was predominant. Cynicism emerged during the 1970s and 1980s, during a period of labour market conflicts and legitimacy crisis, and – *nota bene* – during a period of economic cutbacks of the universities and a general questioning of the utility of social science, forming a good ground for cynical reflections on the part of students of the professions. Both perspectives generalize 'the obviousnesses' of their times to the whole of history, and all societies.

So what should a more 'genuine' sociological approach involve? First, sociology is an empirical discipline, and sociological research on the professions should therefore start with elaborations of empirical research programmes. Second, sociology has explanatory ambitions, hence sociological research on the professions must make use of and apply general sociological knowledge and explanatory theory that – after all – already does exist. Third, and to refer back to the foregoing, it should be neither too general nor too specific; that is, it must try to avoid both the taxonomic and the historical approaches to find a middle way between definition and narrative.

What is the general task of sociology? Peter Blau has given a useful definition. He claims that the task of sociology is to find the structural parameters that cause differentiation between individuals and social groups, in turn affecting social interaction, role relations and so on.[3] Hence the task of sociological research on the professions would be to find structural parameters which differentiate professions from other occupations, and professions from other professions, that in turn can explain differences in interaction, behaviour, ideology and so on.

During the 1980s several overviews and historical summaries of modern studies of the professions have been published. In these we most often find, on the one hand, critical appraisals of studies undertaken so far, and, on the other, general suggestions concerning what routes research should embark upon in the future. Before I start sketching how I think sociology can fruitfully contribute to professional research, I want to connect to some of these suggestions. As point of departure I use an anthology in which several of the most distinguished contemporary scholars of the professions offer their views of the problems and future options of the subject.[4]

Professions and social context

The history of modern studies of the professions from the pioneering works of Talcott Parsons and Everett Hughes in the 1930s is nowadays quite well known, and I will not recapitulate it here. Suffice it to say that most overviews identify a series of turning-points in professional research (around 1940, 1965, 1970, and 1980), and also a set of problems and anomalies in contemporary research. The situation of the 1980s is depicted by Dietrich Rueschemeyer as in 'turmoil',[5] and by Robert Dingwall as on the road to an inevitable 'turning point', since established traditions have reached some kind of limit.[6] Eliot Freidson is also very critical, arguing that 'there has not been any significant advance in developing a theory of professions over the past decade or so', since theoretical discussions have 'either addressed false issues or issues which are essentially insoluble because of the very nature of the concept of profession itself'.[7]

What solutions are proposed to this unsatisfactory state? Of course, different writers emphasize different possibilities, but they have some preferences in common.

First, professions must be studied in a much broader context. Celia Davies holds that the conventional perspectives 'play down and sometimes totally obscure the material and ideological conditions for different kinds of work organization, and that the phenomenon of study [professions] therefore must be located . . . in the wider social structure'.[8] Dingwall claims that 'Professional work must be studied not just in the context of a division of labour but as part of a network of social and economic relations'.[9] Discussing the proposal that professions must be analysed by being related to their political power, Rueschemeyer argues that such an extension is still not sufficient: we must go even further, exploring 'the conditions of this power'.[10]

To me this recommendation implies that we must relate studies of professions to extant sociological theory. (The alternative would be to create a completely new social theory, which might be a bit too ambitious.) Only if professions 'lived their own lives', so to speak; that is, if they were entirely autonomous, following their own laws of development, would it be justified to study them *per se*, without connecting them to the general social development. This proposal forms the most important point of departure for the thesis I will propose presently.

Second, the importance of the comparative approach is emphasized; professions must be related to one another and to other occupations, and professions in different countries must be compared. We cannot assume that 'profession' is a natural category but must carefully explore similarities between professions and differences from other occupations. Comparative studies may provide us with important clues in this respect.

Third, we have the related problem as to how 'profession' should be delineated and defined. Taking 'profession' as a given, Talcott Parsons did not discuss the issue. Everett Hughes regarded it as a matter of degree, which is also common today (cf. expressions such as 'semi-profession', 'proto-profession', and the like). A related line of thought is to understand 'profession' as an ideal type. Others, such as Terence Johnson, reject all attempts to formulate a 'structural' definition. Instead, Johnson employs the concept of 'professionalization' to denote historical processes.

Universal definitions of professions

On the one hand, we cannot avoid delineating the object of study; that is, the phenomenon of profession. Talking about 'professionalization' as a process is of course no solution; indeed, a process must be distinguished from other processes, thus be defined. (What is the starting-point and direction of the process? What does it consist of? Why at all call it 'professionalization'?) On the other hand, as the endless attempts to define 'profession' indicate, it is very easy to reach an impasse right here. No matter how the problem is twisted and turned, we always seem to be faced with a so-called Scylla–Charybdis dilemma. It seems to be possible to raise objections to each definition that seeks to be precise; it is either too narrow (for example, by certain definitions, engineers are excluded, which appears intuitively wrong), or too wide (plumbers become professionals, which opposes the intuitions of many scholars of the professions).

On the one hand we need a delineation; on the other hand we cannot find a definition that is both all-embracing and sufficiently precise. To my mind, this problem is primarily epistemological. It is related to the standard demand of rationalist philosophy; namely, that scientific concepts must be carefully defined *prior to* the instigation of empirical research. However, there are a number of very useful concepts in contemporary social science possessing the same status as the concept of profession, such as 'paradigm', 'discourse', 'incommensurability' – and (why not?) 'class'. In the vocabulary of Paul Feyerabend, they refer to 'complex historical-anthropological phenomena which are only imperfectly understood',[11] and in need of closer examination, but it would be detrimental to use the ordinary logical rules of exclusion, inclusion and overlap on them – that is, try to specify them too much in advance. Hence, if we disregard the postulates of rationalist philosophy, which is entirely legitimate nowadays, we may begin with a softer delineation providing us with certain characteristics of professions, and later let the empirical material react back upon the specification of the definition.

Therefore I now propose a tentative definition, inspired by Jürgen Kocka, which I will come back to later. Professions are 'non-manual full-time occupations which presuppose a long specialized and tendentiously also scholarly . . . training which imparts specific, generalizable and theoretical professional knowledge, often proven by examination'.[12]

Professions must be studied in a broad context, and explanations must be related to relevant sociological explanatory models. This is of course exactly what has been attempted by the sociological taxonomies described above; namely, Durkheimian functionalism and Weberian social closure. To my mind, both perspectives provide us with valuable knowledge, but to a great extent they reflect their own times, implying that we must be careful as regards their attempts to universalization, and their latent idealism. Bengt Gesser expresses it well in pointing out that it is 'necessary to study professions in the context of their institutionalization and class character in order to avoid the idealistic overtones resident in the description of professionals as executors of power, inferred from a monopoly of knowledge'.[13]

This leads us to Marxism, which can be understood as a third tradition, besides the Durkheimian and the Weberian. Marxists have also struggled with taxonomies for the classification of professional occupations. From a class perspective, many suggestions are put forward; Alvin Gouldner regards specific intellectuals as a new class, the Ehrenreichs puts them in 'the professional-managerial class', following Nicos Poulanzas. Michael Ornstein views them as a new petty bourgeoisie. John Urry and Scott Lash understand them as a part of the new 'service class', while Göran Therborn defines them as 'specific functionaries' of capital (and the state?).

My main objection to the Durkheimian, Weberian and Marxist approaches is that they exaggerate the unity of professionals, tending to regard them too much as a homogeneous group. Apart from this, the Marxist approach seems to be the most proper one, in accordance with the recommendations mentioned above; that is, a broad, comparative, historical materialist perspective must be the right route today. Moreover, I think the Marxist conceptualizations above are all partly correct; that certain professional groups do belong to the petty bourgeoisie, others to the higher middle strata, while yet others are 'specific functionaries of capital'. The problems arise when attempting to compress a heterogeneous group like professionals into *one* category.

To sum up: we should – at least for the present – suspend attempts to formulate an abstract, universal definition of 'profession', and instead try to break down the concept to more manageable and practical categories. Further, the resulting categories should be anchored in a broader social context. Let me now propose such a categorization.

Four professional types

The unit of analysis of conventional professional research has been particular *occupational groups*. Physicians constitute one unit, lawyers another, engineers a third, teachers a fourth. Individuals within a particular profession form natural units because of a number of prevalent, common denominators. By and large, they have a shared education and practice the same activity (for example, to cure the ill). Together with special associations, labour unions and so on, this background engenders loyalty, collegiality and shared interests. Of course, these are significant parameters for the explanations of the ideology and political behaviour of professionals.

On the other hand, from the point of view of sociology, it is also an important fact that different individuals within a particular profession frequently work in dissimilar social contexts. Being a private doctor is radically different from being employed by a big public hospital, in regards to income, prestige, retirement security and so forth, and thus also, presumably, in regards to political opinion and general world-view. In principle, the private doctor and the private lawyer may indeed have more in common than the private doctor with a private practice and his colleague in a big city hospital. The objective or material context – the basic conditions of private practitioners of various occupations – display great similarities. ('Objective' should here be understood in contrast to subjective; even though the basic objective conditions may be similar, they are not necessarily influential at the level of consciousness, nor in relation to the organization of the political scene.) The objective conditions for an occupational activity form the base for a particular *rationality* concerning attitudes to general political issues such as (for example) the question of private and public market, possibilities of small-scale enterprising versus the powers of big corporations, and so forth.

Therefore I think it might be fruitful to commence not from professional occupations as the basic unit of analysis, but rather from *types of professions*. Professions are categorized and analysed from their objective conditions, making the analysis amenable to and anchored in social theory.

Tentatively, I distinguish four main types of professions: 'free' professions, academic professions, professions of the (welfare) state and professions of capital. Thus the basic unit of professional research would be altered; the point of departure is not an occupation such as (for instance) physician, but, rather, types of professions. Physicians come under all four types.

Free professions is the classic professional type, described primarily in the Anglo-American literature. Crudely put, they are oriented towards the market in general, and are thereby governed by the rationality of the traditional petty bourgeoisie. Historically, they can be likened to specialized craftsmen, small-scale business, contractors or entrepreneurs.

Academic professions primarily turn inwards, towards the scientific community and its particular reward system. The material base for academicians is mainly employment as lecturer, while careers are determined by research contributions, evaluated by colleagues. Academic professions are 'reputational organizations'.[14] Historically, at least some academic disciplines can be likened to monastic orders. As Eliot Freidson notes, the relative freedom of academic professionals provides opportunities of acting as 'free intellectuals' in public debates – thereby they can have a cultural function and position outside the university (even though Sweden is not a very good illustration).

Professions of capital are subjected to the general terms of survival of capitalist firms; that is, ultimately, by rationalizations and innovations of the activity in question they are oriented towards increasing the profit of their corporation (technicians, engineers, company doctors, lawyers and so on).

Professions of the state are primarily service agencies subordinated to state bureaucracy and local authorities, similar to other civil servants. Primarily they carry out reproducing, distributing and uniting tasks (such as health personnel, civil servants, teachers). In Sweden, they are subject to the values expressed in the Law of Social Service (*Socialtjänstlagen*).

The most important difference between the two large professional types of today – capital and the state – is related to the development and consolidation of the modern welfare state during the twentieth century, and the resulting political economy. The expansion of the public sector implies a 'de-commodification' – that is, a decrease in traditional market forces to the benefit of new distributive principles. The public sector creates a new type of labour market, involving new employment opportunities and labour tasks. Employment conditions in the public sector differ markedly from those in the private economy; according to some scholars, the former adopt a quite new and different 'class character because they are no longer so closely tied to market principles'.[15]

The development of the welfare state in turn creates a new form of rationality, especially for professions that are dependent upon the public sector: 'Many of the professionals responsible for the welfare services, such as doctors and teachers, have developed also important interests in the defence of the welfare state.'[16] Different professional types involve different institutional logics, generating different ideologies.

The political profession

I further believe that in Sweden today it is possible to discern a fifth professional type, the *political profession* (government, the top people of the parliamentary parties, the labour unions and the state bureaucracy). The reason is that to an increasing extent, the political elite is sheltered by 'social closure' of the classical kind, and that this closure is based upon specific knowledge claims, obtained by a long 'education'. A contemporary Swedish politician most often has an academic degree. He or she has gone through a long process of socialization, starting with political school associations (and parents), thereafter political youth associations, student corporations, summer schools, local political work, courses and so forth – a series of refinements, preparations and contacts generating the group from which top politicians are later recruited. Increasingly, the political profession has obtained a relative autonomy, often carrying across party lines. The autonomy is based upon a specific discourse, specific kinds of knowledge, a specific political *habitus*, entrance barriers, career patterns, specific systems of reward and loyalty, together with an increasingly unique safety system such as special retirement advantages, ambassadorial posts, and so on, to those who, due to age or other pressing reasons, are forced to leave the political game.

But is it meaningful to talk about a political profession? Of course, this is a matter of definition. Traditionally, professions have been defined as non-manual jobs with a high academic education, legitimized by examinations (cf. Kocka's definition above).

I think it is reasonable to alter this definition somewhat. University education and academic credentials should not be over-emphasized. The crucial point is, rather, that it concerns knowledge that on the one hand is in demand on the market and at the same time is relatively esoteric and inaccessible to the common man, and on the other hand that this knowledge and the skills are linked to high status and relatively high material rewards. High values on *both* these variables distinguish the top professions. Semi-professions fail on one or both variables, together with older, obsolete professions such as (for example) priests in Sweden. Occupations that rank too low on one of the variables are not regarded as professions.

Formal education and examinations should not be emphasized too much, partly because many professionals obtain many of their occupational skills *after* formal education. Engineers are a good example; they receive further education by most employers. Nowadays, many companies offer 'trainee-programmes' for them. Furthermore, to a great extent professional knowledge is obtained by practice, by an apprenticeship process or 'enculturation process';[17] an unwritten know-how or 'tacit knowledge' that cannot be standardized and formalized to a university course is transmitted. This mode of knowledge constitutes the base for the delicate balance between technicality and uncertainty which is another important ingredient of the professional repertoire. As Randall Collins expresses it:

> Where the practitioner is able to provide a sense of security against the unknown that nevertheless continues to remain at least somewhat predictable, he will be in the strongest position. This requires that the practitioners depend upon each other; they are engaged in a form of ritual reality-creating of emotional manipulation the object of which is primarily to convince others that they are a pillar of strength in the storm (although at the same time, they must make sure that there still continues to be a storm). Such ritual self-assurance depends upon the closure of the group of practitioners in supporting each other's claims.[18]

Do politicians constitute a profession? If the formal aspect of 'professional' is too strongly emphasized, they fall outside the concept; there is as yet no university course for the political occupation. On the other hand, if 'profession' is not formally interpreted but understood as a special form of knowledge that is linked to high status and high material rewards, a political profession can be identified. First, most contemporary top politicians in Sweden do possess an academic degree. Second, they have undergone a long apprenticeship. Third, and most important in this context, they possess a particular form of 'tacit knowledge'. Let me give just one illustration.

It is a familiar fact that ministers of government can swap posts. It would not be unreasonable to believe that ministers are required to possess a competence correspondent with the department's subject matter; for example, that the foreign minister had at least some education as a political scientist, the minister of social affairs as a sociologist, the minister of law as a jurist, and so forth. However, a minister can change departments, sometimes several times during his career. In this respect, ministers are 'exchangeable' with one another, in the Durkheimian sense. From the point of view of knowledge, this leaves us with two possibilities; either no special knowledge is required for being a minister, or else there exists *another* kind of knowledge, a special political qualification. Competence is not primarily determined by the particular branch, but by expertise in 'political technology', a competence that transcends departments and party lines. This tacit knowledge, which incidentally is poorly examined by political scientists, constitutes the knowledge base of the political profession.

The foregoing may be summarized at three levels of abstraction, where the first level provides a conceptual delineation of 'profession', the second level outlines the professional types, and the third level comprises professional occupations (Table 5.1). The professional types at the left-hand side of the horizontal dimension are more dependent upon and oriented towards the market, whereas the types at the right-hand side are more dependent upon bureaucratic organization.

Table 5.1 *Professions and professional types*

General definition of professions				
Free professions	Capital professions	Political professions	State professions	Academic professions
Self-employed physicians, lawyers, accountants, engineers, psychologists, etc.	Privately employed engineers, accountants, physicians, lawyers, etc.	Government, political elites, higher civil servants, etc.	Publicly employed physicians, teachers, social workers, psychologists, etc.	Natural and social scientists, scholars of the arts

Professional types, interests and loyalties

But is the theory of professional types a suitable and fruitful instrument for the analysis of professions? Of course, this question cannot be answered simply, especially not without being empirically applied and tested. In the following I will offer a few arguments for the theory, simultaneously proposing some possible routes for more detailed empirical studies.

The first argument is historical. As mentioned above, professions are nowadays understood as unitary and natural occupational groups, not least in professional research. An important reason for this is their political organization into associations. Indeed, in contemporary research a profession often seems to be identified with its association, especially in studies of 'the profession's' (that is their respresentatives') union strategies – for example, in wage negotiations and various attempts at closure. In addition, the associations have a formally democratic structure, and an egalitarian ideology. It is in the interest of the association to portray the member organization as a unity. This tends to obscure differences in work conditions, differences in the rationality and particular interests of professional types, professional hierarchies and so on.

However, historically, professions have definitely not constituted homogeneous occupational groups in regards to organization or collegial loyalty. On the contrary, the position of professionals has been closely tied to the surrounding stratification system. From the Middle Ages to the middle and end of the nineteenth century – that is, during a period of 700 years – the positions and privileges of professionals were determined by their class background and possibilities of serving wealthy patrons; that is, to their 'employment conditions' in the modern sense. There was a stratum of lawyers, doctors and others who served the aristocracy and the state: they were linked to the social elite; while others survived by the guild system and by 'serving the public' (by trying to sell their services on the market). Crudely put, we can distinguish the professional types of the elite and of the public (although this distinction of course can be refined). These two types had nothing in common; according to Magali Sarfatti Larson we cannot even talk about internal hierarchies of the professions during this time, 'for "common" and "learned" practitioners inhabited different social worlds'.[19]

We cannot do so until the nineteenth century, during 'the wave of association', unification and, thereby, ideas of collegiality, arises within the professions. And this is not a result of a sudden realization that individual practitioners, after all, work within the same 'calling' and therefore should be associated, but as a result of external pressure. The centrality of the market and increasing competition is one factor enforcing familiar strategies of survival such as control and limitation of recruitment to the occupation, standardized education, credentials and so on – that is, attempts to obtain occupational monopoly in order to preserve and enhance material privileges and exclusive status. Another important factor accelerating and expanding organizational efforts during the twentieth century is the new allocation system with negotiations between representatives of interest groups, in which it is crucial to be organized into a strong group.

The argument here, then, is that organization – that of professional associations – is historically 'circumstantial', a result of surrounding social conditions. Organizing is reinforced by notions of collegiality, loyalty, internal equality and democracy and altruism – the modern professional ideology. This conjecturally conditioned unity has been universalized and turned into the 'essence' of professions by modern professional scholars. Hence even professional research of the 1980s must be understood from the perspective of the sociology of knowledge – as merely reflecting the labour market of our times. Beyond organization on the political scene we find the political and economic structures ultimately determining whether unity and associations are powerful instruments, or whether alternative loyalties are more rational from the point of view of the individual (see below).

The second argument concerns the international, comparative perspective on professions. A problem in modern professional research is the great difference between continental and Anglo-American professions; as often noted, the differences are so big that it is difficult to transfer Anglo-American definitions of professions to the European context, and vice versa. It is hardly meaningful to employ the same all-embracing concept for them. However, a categorization into professional types facilitates the comparison of the 'professional structure' of different countries. To mention just one obvious example: in nations that have carried on the *laissez-faire* politics of the nineteenth century, the position of free professions is still very strong (such as the USA), while the reverse holds for the Continent, and perhaps especially for Sweden, where the professions have always been intimately associated with the state. The state has been more active, organizing both training and employment, which provides one reason why the free professions are comparatively small and weak in our part of the world. In England and the USA, the professions had to organize their own training and credential institutions; dissimilar conditions generate different strategies.

Thirdly, since 'profession' is a historically and geographically relative concept, dissimilar conditions during various epochs and social systems can be grasped by breaking down the concept – for example, by the proposed theory of professional types. Consequently, the theory can contribute to the exploration of the ideology or identity patterns of professionals. Do professionals identify themselves with their association, the occupation, the company, the department, the state, or the small businessman, the profession or the employment?

Of course, this is also historically and geographically variant. Joseph Ben-David gives an example concerning nineteenth-century Germany and France: 'the technically competent . . . do not primarily identify themselves by their professional qualifications, but by their employment. If they are in private practice, they tend to consider themselves officials of a certain rank, rather than chemists or engineers.' Eliot Freidson comments: 'This is a far cry from Anglo-American professions, which gain their distinction and position in the marketplace less from the prestige of the institutions in which they were educated than from the substance of their particular training.'[20] Due to this variance, we cannot assume or infer anything concerning the attitudes of professionals from, for example, the statutes and political programmes of professional associations. Rather, we need the approach of the sociology of knowledge – for instance, empirical applications of Mary Douglas's grid-group model – in order more closely to explore the complex interplay between profession, employment and ideology.[21]

Fourthly, different professions display dissimilar forms of organization, various types of internal control mechanisms, and hence different degrees of closedness. Differences *between* professions are highly conditioned by what professional type is dominating each profession. For instance, private business is not particularly interested in *formal* competence, and thus engineers tend to be comparatively weakly organized – therefore, engineering is sometimes referred to as 'the profession that failed'. In the welfare sector and at the universities, formal competence is an imperative issue, an effect of these professions' own demands for closures of their occupations. Consequently, state professions are typically safeguarded by sets of requirements for credentials, rites and so on.

Fifthly, tensions *within* a single profession may be at least partly accounted for by observing that it includes several professional types, implying that it encompasses contradictory political and other interests. Recent empirical studies of professional development corroborate this suggestion. For instance, concerning US lawyers, Richard Abel writes that

> Until after World War II, a single role dominated the profession – the private practitioner . . . Since then, however, several changes have threatened this clear professional identity. First, the number of employed lawyers has increased to the point where it approaches the number of independent practitioners. Second, as law firms have expanded, many independent practitioners have become employers of numerous subordinates and members of large bureaucratic organizations. Third, several distinct subgroups have grown in both size and coherence: judges, government employees, lawyers employed in business enterprises, and law professors. These changes have profound implications for the profession. Increasing differentiation and stratification undermine the sense of professional community.[22]

Evidently, Abel's sub-groups correspond to the types depicted above. He also delineates a category of 'lawyers-politicians', parallel to my 'political professional' type, and his emphasis of the historical relativity of professional unity and solidarity is tantamount to my first point above. Likewise, the explanation for the postwar diversification of this formerly unified profession, as well as for the consequent emergence of alternative associations to the American Bar Association, is broader, underlying socio-economic trends such as the concentration of capital and the relative impoverishment of the public sector. For the case of Canada, Harry Arthurs et al. go one step further, discussing and criticizing what they call 'the myth of a single legal profession', a notion 'patently at odds with the facts'. They hold that the explanation for the emergence of the myth is that 'a unified profession can better protect its autonomy and influence public and governmental opinion than one that speaks with many voices'.[23]

The same differentiating tendencies are found among Swedish lawyers. In the internal jargon of Swedish lawyers, one nowadays distinguishes between the 'A-team' and the 'B-team'. The A-team includes private lawyers and company lawyers while judges and other state-employees constitute the B-team. Capable jurists choose or seek to go to the private sector where payments and job conditions are much better, while the less talented are compelled to remain in the public sector.[24]

Similar conditions are currently facing Swedish physicians, psychologists, therapists and engineers. Generally, Sweden of the 1980s is characterized by (attempts to) escape from the public professional type to professions of capital, and free professionals. The beginning of the 1970s was different; the state offered comparatively better job conditions. Generally, during an interventionist and expansive conjuncture with an expanding public sector, the influence and scope of the welfare professions can similarly be expected to increase, and vice versa. In other words, the development of the professions must be understood from the background of economic conjunctures, the relationship between private and public sector and the government's educational policy.

Sixthly, to employ the notion of professional types facilitates connecting the development of the professions to wider social trends, ultimately to the type of social formation. The content and historical evolution of professional types should be contrasted and understood against the background of general class context and power positions. One viable option in this respect is to relate the types to theories of society articulated by Marxists such as Etienne Balibar, Nicos Poulanzas and Erik Olin Wright, and by Swedish sociologists such as Göran Therborn. Göran Ahrne and Bengt Furåker. Society is conceived as combinations of different modes of production, to which different classes are related. The bourgeoisie and the working class are related to the capitalist mode of production, the petty bourgeoisie to the petty bourgeoisie mode of production, and a greater section of those publicly employed are

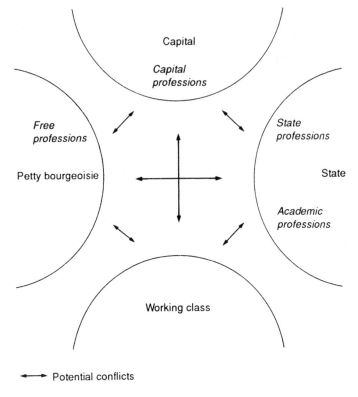

Figure 5.1   *Professions and class*

associated with the 'embryonic' (Hoff) or 'state bureaucratic' mode of production (Furåker).[25] The idea can be summarized in the model, shown in Figure 5.1.

During the twentieth century, the professions have increased in number and scope, globally as well as in Sweden. The causes of the increases are both common and country-specific; different countries have dissimilar 'professional structures'. As is well known, in Sweden the public sector has been strongly built out, as illustrated in table 5.2. In 1985, publicly employed had increased to 38.2 per cent. The decrease of self-employed is primarily caused by the transition from agriculture to the other sectors; namely, the decrease in farmers. At the turn of the century, there were approximately 110,000 publicly employed, in 1985 approximately 1,644,000. From 1963 to 1985 the publicly employed more than doubled: from 0.75 million in 1963 to 1.6 million in 1985, which means an increase from 20 per cent to 38 per cent of the total workforce. The increase primarily concerns health care, administration, education and social care.[26]

Table 5.2 *Self-employed, privately employed and publicly employed in Sweden 1930–1975 (percentages)*

	1930	1965	1975
Self-employed	31	14	8
Privately employed	59	64	56
Publicly employed	10	22	36

Comparison of the general development to the professional structure demonstrates on the one hand partly the same tendencies – that is, the self-employed do not increase, and professionals of the welfare state increase drastically. However, the increase is considerably larger as concerns professional groups. The public sector employs more than 70 per cent of the professionals (this figure is of course dependent upon how we delineate 'profession' – if so-called semi-professional groups such as nurses are included, the figure will be even higher), while the private sector employs only approximately 20 per cent.

Thus, while private industry still dominates the Swedish labour market – it employs over half of the working population – the reverse relation holds for the professions. This professional structure is unique to Sweden.

We find one example among physicians, a group that has almost tripled between 1965 and 1985. In 1985, there were 21,600 active physicians in Sweden. Of these, 18,600 were publicly employed, and 1,000 were private practitioners. Approximately the same dominance of the public professional type holds for nurses (around 70,000 in Sweden in 1985), teachers (140,000), university lecturers and researchers (14,000). The chief among the professions of capital, civil engineers, number around 26,000 privately employed, 9,000 publicly employed and 7,000 free practitioners.[27] Jurists (judges and lawyers) form a middle group, including around 9,000 publicly employed and 8,000 privately employed or free practitioners.

What are the causes of this development? It is inappropriate to go into this issue here, but let me sketch two general causes, in need of further elaboration. One cause is historical. Since at least the time of Gustav Vasa, Sweden has had a strong central power, and since at least 'The freedom era', it has fostered and employed an intellectual elite for state services; in other words, a comparatively large and university trained civil service has existed for a long-time.

During the twentieth century, in particular since the party of the working class took political power, 'the Swedish model' has developed. Essentially, it has involved a series of reforms, initiated from above. From the beginning the Social Democrats engaged the expertise – well-educated professionals (such as the Myrdals) – as designers of the Swedish 'folk home'. Postwar development of the welfare state provides great possibilities for professional occupations in several areas: in health care, education, administration and also politics. The public sector becomes the important labour market for professional occupations. Hence, the expansion of the public sector is one reason for the increase of (welfare state) professionals.

On the other hand, professionals themselves constitute a cause for the development and institutionalization of welfare. Professional groups have established themselves by their own power, by discovering problems, pointing out needs, presenting suggestions for reforms, and at the same time demanding occupational monopoly, various kinds of closures, formal credentials and so on, backed by the state. The welfare sector has been both an end and a means for professionals. In other words the activities of professionals result in effects which reproduce themselves. These dialectics between external demands and internal strategies form a crucial research task that must be analysed against the background of the general social development.

Conclusion

At present, I regard the presented theory of professional types as a supplement to conventional approaches to the professions, not as a substitute. They may very well be united. By employing the professional types, a set of structural parameters constituting the objective conditions and conditions of possibility surrounding the professions can be outlined. The focus will be on basic factors such as class position, the importance of economic conjunctures and governmental regulations for different types, primary 'consumers' of various types, latent conflicts between types and so forth. In a Marxist vocabulary, such a study belongs to the structural level, in contrast to the level of organization.

Ordinary professional research focuses upon the level of organization and 'the political scene'; for example, the development and political behaviour of professional associations. To my mind, such an analysis of manifest political conduct must be based on the objective conditions constraining and enabling action. The theory of professional types forms an intermediate link between political action and social structure, thereby satisfying the demand that professions must be analysed by being related to 'a wider social context'.

Notes

1 Brante, 1988.
2 Freidson, 1986, ch. 2.
3 Blau, 1974:615.
4 Dingwall and Lewis, 1983.
5 Dingwall and Lewis, 1983:11.
6 Dingwall and Lewis, 1983:38.
7 Dingwall and Lewis, 1983:20.
8 Dingwall and Lewis, 1983:184, 182.
9 Dingwall and Lewis, 1983:12.
10 Dingwall and Lewis, 1983:55.
11 Feyerabend, 1975:269.
12 An altered version of Jürgen Kocka's definition, in Jarausch, 1986.
13 Gesser, 1985:245.
14 Whitley, 1984.
15 Prandy, Stewart and Blackburn, 1983:103.
16 King, 1987:857.
17 R. Collins, 1981.
18 Collins, 1975:343.
19 Larson, 1977/1979:3; and ch. 1.
20 Freidson, 1986:34.
21 Douglas, 1982.
22 Abel, 1988a:188.
23 Arthurs, Weisman and Zemans, 1988:151, note 22.
24 Nowadays, this situation is a serious problem for jurists, and it has been carefully examined in an extensive survey, demonstrating that the 'escape' from the public to the private sector is increasing. (In 1984, 52 judges left their jobs; for 1985 the figure was 76; and for 1986, 109.) The reasons are primarily economic and secondarily other job conditions ('Rekryteringen till och avhoppen från domarbanan. Domstolsverket', Rapport no. 1987:1).
25 See, for instance, Furåker, 1987.
26 Furåker, 1987.
27 The number of free practitioners is estimated by the civil engineers' union in Sweden, Svenska Civilingenjörsförbundet.

6

Open cartels and social closures: professional strategies in Sweden, 1860–1950

Klas Åmark

In the many-faceted debate on the theory of professionalization, particular interest has always been devoted to the efforts by professional occupational groups to maintain a monopoly over their professional markets and their knowledge and skills.[1] It is this problem – the effort to form a monopoly within an occupation and to restrict competition – which is the main subject of this chapter, my aim being to complement the prevailing Weberian research tradition within this area with ideas from Karl Marx and Swedish history. As regards the latter, I draw not only on the history of professional and semi-professional occupational groups, but also on the history of other economic interest groups. Chronologically, I shall deal with the period 1860–1950, and in so doing identify two of the most important strategies for professional occupational groups, the first of which I call the 'open cartel', and the second, following Weber, that of social closure. I examine and compare the components of these two strategies and consider whether and how they can be used together.

I shall concentrate on the actions of professional occupational groups and, in particular, the actions of their organizations. There were of course other important actors in the context, especially the state, whose representatives often presumed that the type of abstract knowledge forming the basis of professional occupational practice was both weighty and relevant, and that consequently the state had good reason to finance and organize advanced education for these occupations.

Competition and restrictions on competition

Competition is a phenomenon which is intimately associated with capitalism. Free competition and free markets are even used as criteria for defining an economy as capitalistic. The transition from feudalism to capitalism is often described as a question of the dismantling of obstacles to competition and to the free movement of capital, goods and the labour force. In Sweden, the possibilities of competition increased markedly through, for example, parliament's deregulation of the economy in 1846 and 1864. From about 1870 a real international market for mass consumption goods and means of production also developed. During the last decades of the nineteenth century the economic actors in Sweden thus increasingly learned the advantages and disadvantages of competition.[2] This also applied to areas of activity within the professional occupations. The situation of dentists in the county of Småland prior to their attaining a professional organization has been so described by a chronicler:

> Envy, suspicion, and fear of competition prevails easily amongst those who isolate themselves from contact with colleagues. . . . Before the arrival of the organization, a lamentable lack of solidarity and understanding of our occupational and our group's interests prevailed . . . There were places where colleagues did not even know each other. It is not strange then that the consequences of this were unsound competition and all sorts of discord.[3]

Thus free competition did not only have advantages, but also disadvantages which sometimes could be considerable. Free competition between relatively equal partners could lead to common ruin. At the time this sort of competition was not called 'free' but 'disloyal' or 'dirty'. To cope with the disadvantages of competition, the economic actors – companies, workers, free practitioners, property owners, tenants and so on – developed a series of different methods.

One important method of restricting competition is what I have termed 'open cartel'. Such cartels were first formed in Sweden as organizations to limit the competition between producers of goods (and in certain cases, producers of services, such as the Swedish Railway Association, formed in 1876). They were often traditional industrial branch organizations, such as the Swedish Paper Mills Federation or the Convention of Welders, which effectively controlled conditions for sales within metal manufacture. In other cases, cartels and trusts arose and became common after the turn of the century – for example, the oat-producers' trust and the sugar trust. These were often misleadingly described in the literature as monopolies; I would claim that the term 'open cartel' is much more fruitful in the context.

Open cartels could work with several different tasks. Their basic principle was that prices and other sales conditions were regulated through agreements between independent producers. The cartels were open – that is, everyone who wished to could become a member – since agreements on price regulations functioned better the more numerous the companies that respected them. Other important areas involved credit and conditions for loans as regards capital and the regulation of prices, and other conditions as regards purchasing of raw materials and so on. Various kinds of standardization may have had a similar restricting effect on competition as regulation of prices.

The closed cartel is totally different. Through the closed cartel certain actors agree to divide up the market between themselves, at the same time as other actors are excluded. The secret tendering cartel is a typical example of this.

The open cartel seems to have been very common in Sweden during the period from about 1890 to the 1940s. The organization of companies as sellers of goods occurred normally before they organized themselves into employers' organizations as purchasers of the commodity of labour, and many employers' organizations grew out of commodity cartels. Swedish labour unions chose also as one of their primary tasks to limit competition between workers for jobs, a competition which was conducted through underbidding one another as regards wages and other conditions of employment. Collective contracts or bargaining agreements became a central instrument in this battle. In the agreement, or price lists presented by the workers to their employers, piecework prices, wages and other conditions of employment which each member was obligated to demand from his employer were given.

When the employers began to accept collective bargaining and signed under collective agreements at the end of the 1890s, the contract agreements themselves could also become an instrument with which to limit competition between the employers over labour – which of course assumed that the agreement was equally binding among several companies. By about 1905, this function of the agreements was a decisive cause of employers beginning to pursue the principle that there should be a national agreement for each whole industry. Thus employers decided to exploit the advantages which the collective agreement system gave them: peace (with their workers) and good possibilities of being able to calculate longer-term costs of labour. This meant that the Swedish Employers Association (SAF) gave priority to being able to predict and calculate – according to Max Weber, the most important basic principle of modern rational capitalism.[4]

One pivotal condition for the employers accepting the system of collective bargaining was that LO (the Swedish TUC) in its turn accept the employers' right to lead and distribute work and to employ and sack their employees – the so-called December Compromise between SAF and LO in 1906. With this, a fundamental distinction between labour and work was adopted, and it was agreed that the labour market organizations primarily should deal with conditions covering the purchasing and selling of labour, but not with power over work processes.[5]

Thus open cartels then became the principal method for restricting competition for producers of goods as well as, and perhaps particularly, for the Swedish labour market, even if it was by no means the only method. Other methods, such as monopolization, closed cartels and social closures, were also frequently used.

There are two theoretical bases for my analysis of the restriction of competition. The first is the work of Marx and Engels. In a famous statement Marx distinguished three aspects of the competition which determines fluctuations in the price of a commodity: the competition between sellers, which presses prices down; the competition between buyers, which pushes prices up; and the competition between sellers on the one hand and buyers on the other, in which the former want to sell at as high a price as possible and the latter want to buy as cheaply as possible. Marx adds: 'Industry leads two armies into the field against each other, each of which again carries on a battle within its own ranks, among its own troops. The army whose troops beat each other up the least gains the victory over the opposing host.'[6]

What is central with Marx is that he perceives all three elements of competition and their internal relations, and that he points to internal competition within a group as the most decisive factor. Marx[7] and Engels[8] also contended that the task of trade unions was to abolish the undercutting of the workers' competition, and if this succeeded, it would be a heavy blow to the very core of capitalism.

Hence Marx and Engels depicted, at least indirectly, the open cartel as a method of restricting competition which was of central significance to the working class. However, they did not perceive – neither did they live long enough to experience – capital's own organization for the purpose of limiting internal competition. Like the liberal economists (Marx was clearly influenced by Adam Smith on this point), Marx exaggerated the significance of competition for capitalist economy.

From the foregoing, of particular interest as regards the theory of professionalization are the importance of limiting competition internally, within the group, and the historical experience of Sweden at the turn of the century: that is, that both companies and workers organized themselves using the open cartel as their main form.

The second theoretical basis is the work of the other great social theoretician, Max Weber. In contrast to Marx, Weber maintained that striving for monopoly is a universal factor in all markets. Weber's ideas have been recently developed, especially for use in professionalization theory, by researchers like Frank Parkin, Randall Collins[9] and Raymond Murphy.[10]

Parkin takes up Weber's concept of 'social closure' and declares that classes and social groups arise through one group's ensuring itself a privileged position at the cost of other groups. By means of various methods, individuals or groups wishing to participate and pursue a certain occupational activity are excluded through the formation of various kinds of social closures around the activity in question. Parkin views, for example, the ownership of capital as an exclusion of workers from having power over production, while in their turn the workers struggle to usurp the power of capital. Ruling groups arise, according to Parkin, through their acquisition of monopolistic control over key resources such as land, knowledge or violence. The primary power bases of the capitalist class are ownership and professional knowledge and qualifications.[11]

Thus for Parkin professionalization is primarily a strategy aimed at limiting and controlling the supply of labour within an occupation in order to monitor its market value. Parkin also claims – and in this, according to Murphy, he parts ways from Collins – that the professions are characterized by the fact that they can acquire a legal monopoly in the pursuance of their occupations. Measures taken to accomplish this are, however, not directed towards exploitative employers but towards clients' possibilities of choosing professionals in occupations where limits have been set through occupational monopolies.[12]

On this point I think that Parkin has a too finite definition of the concept of profession. I am more inclined towards Collins, who considers 'credentialism' in general a typical professional strategy.[13] The idea of a social closure becomes more usable if one accepts that the closure can be formed by a number of different methods and that diverse types of measures are accessible to different occupational groups.

While Marx and Engels discussed the necessity of limiting competition within the group, Parkin and Collins – with assistance from Weber – discuss the possibilities of demarcating and controlling one's own occupational area. Hence different aspects of the same fundamental problem are discussed, that is, the collective's methods of limiting competition on the market in which they themselves are active. The Weber-inspired idea that it is an occupational and knowledge monopoly which the actors strive for, is, I think, too narrow: restriction of competition is the universal goal of the actors on the markets, especially for organizations of professions, while a true monopoly is difficult to attain and less often a concrete goal for the actions of organizations.

Two further points should be made here. All restriction of competition requires that there actually exist markets on which to restrict the competition. This was far from self-evident for (for example) the few Swedish dentists in the early nineteenth century. During their development phase, the creation of markets played an important role for many professional organizations.[14]

Different types of competition-restricting strategies are not the only means which those in professional occupations can use to improve and protect their positions. Sometimes a completely different kind of strategy appears, which can be called a 'political reform strategy'. The principal goal is then not to improve the occupational group's position, but rather to develop and improve the professional area itself.[15] Such a strategy can often come into conflict with competition-restricting strategies.

The development of organizations

Among those occupations which were, or claimed to be, professions there developed from the mid-nineteenth century a lively organization movement. The first modern organization was the Swedish Physicians' Society, founded in 1807. From the beginning it was a private and closed society, based in Stockholm, with a limited number of members. The society had several functions – social, supportive and charitable – but its most important function was to develop and spread medical knowledge (see Appendix, p. 112).[16]

From the middle of the nineteenth century, further similar organizations were formed, such as the Society of Dentists, the Veterinary Surgeons' Association and the Association of Technologists. An important aspect shared by these organizations was that the development of knowledge and the establishment of advanced academic education were central issues for the organizations.[17]

From the 1880s onwards, more economically oriented organizations began to appear; for example, the Barristers' Society, the Society of Accountants, the General Swedish Association of Physicians (later the Medical Association), and the Dentists' Union. These organizations dealt especially with independent practitioners' economic problems. From the turn of the century, organizations arose with more purely union ambitions, particularly among salaried groups such as pharmacists, teachers, journalists and ships' captains.

However, it was not before new legislation, put through by the Social Democratic government in the 1930s, that trade-union organization among higher salaried groups and academics began to develop in earnest. Thus a change in the power system was a decisive cause of changes in the professional occupational groups' strategies for ensuring their interests. This is in accord with the idea professed by Michael Burrage; namely, that political and cultural factors are critical for both workers' trade-union behaviour and professional occupational groups' actions, and that political conditions are shaped by large political upheavals such as the revolutions in England and France.[18]

Characteristic of the organizations' development was that it was among their younger members that efforts to unionize first developed – organizationally, through particular associations for younger members of the profession. One important reason for this were problems in the career system. For example, young assistant doctors had to work under very inadequate working conditions and at extremely low wages in the belief that their employment was in fact training. However, it seemed that the base of the career system became bottom-heavy, which meant that the younger doctors, lawyers and teachers remained longer and longer in these 'trainee' positions. In such a situation closure strategies were of no help; instead, a trade-union struggle along the lines of the open cartel seemed necessary. During the 1940s the broadly based associations of younger professionals became straightforward union organizations.[19]

Another important reason for this development towards trade unions was the specialization of scientific knowledge, which led to the creation of more and more narrow, specialist organizations, alongside of or within the broader scientific societies and professional organizations. The content of knowledge and education common to all members of the profession consequently became an increasingly narrow and weaker field for purposes of organizing, at the same time as society placed increasingly greater demands on the breadth and weight of interest organizations.[20]

Specialization needs not only be an expression for the development of scientific knowledge; it can also be a result of a closure strategy. This means that competition is restricted through the formation of enclosure within a broad area. Within the enclosure, specialists are left in peace by many of their competitors as regards careers and resources.

Education

Looking back on the early history of professions, one usually begins with the organization of universities into four faculties – theological, medical, juridical and philosophical – and to their associated occupations – priest, doctor, lawyer and teacher. Many other occupations which would later become professions or semi-professions either did not exist or were practised as skills. In principle, the development of occupational areas during the first phase of capitalism followed three different paths. The first involved the transformation of a previously existing profession into a modern, scientific profession – medicine, for example. The second path proceeded from a previously existing skill, with education through the apprentice system, to developing professional strategies, the educational content and the content of knowledge into a profession, such as surgeon, pharmacist, veterinarian and dentist. The third path involved creating whole new occupations without historical continuity: journalist, sociologist and psychologist are examples of this.

In Sweden, the first advanced theoretical education for dentists was begun as late as 1897 with the Dental Institute in Stockholm which was awarded university status. At the same time dentists were forbidden to take on students and examine assistants, which meant that the step from apprentice training to academic, theoretical education was taken.

The technical education which was developed in Sweden during the nineteenth century was established on two levels. The Technological Institute in Stockholm and Chalmers in Gothenburg were founded at the end of the 1820s and were developed into institutions for higher education, with university status awarded in the 1820s. From the mid-nineteenth century a number of technical secondary schools were founded in order to provide education on the advanced secondary level.[21]

Thus, characteristic of Swedish development was that special advanced schools for various occupational areas were created alongside the universities: the Dental Institute, the technical colleges, schools of business (for economists), the Forestry Institute, the Agricultural College, the Institute for Veterinary Science, the Institute of Social Work, the Military Academy and so on.

Although there might be private or local authority influence on higher professional education, especially in the developmental phases, the role of the state was of pivotal importance as regards financing, dimensions of the education, entrance requirements and course content. It would seem that the strong state influence gave the professional organizations a great deal of influence over the dimensions of their education. Investigations conducted by the state also provided comprehensive estimates of the long-term need for academic occupational practitioners in order to avoid over-production and unemployment. (The debates concerning unemploy-

ment among academics were particularly lively during the 1930s.)
However, statistics show that the number of doctors and dentists
in relation to the population was considerably lower in Sweden
than in other comparable countries. In the United States in the
1920s the proportion of doctors was three times as great as it was
in Sweden; in Norway, twice as great from the 1880s to the 1950s.
The situation was the same with dentists.[22] It is difficult to find any
explanation for this other than in the dimensions of the education
and the powerful influence exerted by the professional organizations in Sweden. Typical, and probably special, for Sweden was
that the professional organizations used their power over the labour
supply in cooperation with the state, and not against it.

Certification as a closure strategy

Higher education can be used in two ways in a closure strategy: to
regulate the number in a given occupation, and to control who has
the right to pursue the occupation and to exclude the 'unentitled'.
In chronicles and histories of professional occupations and their
organizations the struggle over rights and suitability to pursue these
occupations is a constant theme.

Mistrust of dentists, for instance, was great for a long time. In
1882 it was claimed that there were more quacks than dentists in
the country. One problem in this context was that in the end the
dentists charged such high fees that few people could afford to go
to them. The high fees were made possible through the effective
control over the output of certified dentists. Also, the scarcity of
dentists rendered the market easily accessible to the 'quacks' and
to the dental technicians who could claim to carry out the work of
dentists.[23] The strict limitation of education thus created a conflict
between control over access to the supply of labour on the one
hand, and control of the pursuit of the occupation on the other.

Accountants did not avail themselves of this sort of certification
to protect their occupational area; instead they used authorization.
For a long time this was carried out privately and by the clients
under the auspices of chambers of commerce, which began to be
formed at the turn of the century as open associations for everyone
involved in local business, trade and industry. To become a char-
tered accountant it was necessary to take an examination in economics with special emphasis on accountancy and bookkeeping, as
well as to have five years' experience. Hence a smaller social closure
for economists was formed within the greater occupational area.[24]

Civil engineers did not use the method of special certification for
the right to pursue their occupation. They had another method of

obtaining guarantees for professional competence: to control the products instead of the producers. The problem arose during the decades after 1850 in the debates about steam engines, which had an unpleasant tendency to explode unexpectedly. The Association of Engineers early on took up the question of checking the steam engines, but the question was controversial. The basic idea of product control, however, would gradually win ground and be developed into an advanced system of regulations and instructions concerning nearly everything. It was precisely this issue of steam engines which prompted demands for certification from the state – not directed towards the engineers, but towards the workers who performed the most important tasks in the production, the welders.[25]

Thus in the history of professions there is a lively and extensive struggle for rights and competence to pursue occupations. Doctors and dentists fought against quacks; pharmacists were pitted against herbalists and paint dealers for the right to sell medicines; lawyers fought against pettifoggers and lay advisers; journalists against newshounds, and so on. In these struggles can be found several different methods for creating social closures around the occupational areas: low and broad closures such as the examination requirements, membership in interest organizations and Swedish citizenship requirements, as well as high and narrow closures such as certification, authorization and experience in the occupation.

Among large groups, such as teachers, engineers, economists and social workers, there was no method for certification beyond the requirement of an examination, which was considered sufficient for entitlement and for competence requirements for public posts and as a guarantee of a certain amount of knowledge or competence in private employment.[26]

I find Parkin's claim that the legal monopoly constitutes a criterion for professionalism too limiting, since this would exclude groups which should be included in the theory of professionalization, and embrace occupations which can hardly be accepted as professions. For instance, in Sweden the latter would include actuaries with insurance companies, ships' officers, lorry and bus drivers, electricians, and welders.[27]

Hence attempts to restrict competition over the right to pursue an occupation were widespread among people in academic occupations. Both methods and successes varied greatly from occupation to occupation and from one period to another. Such attempts were not exclusive to the professions, nor to closely related occupations. Demands for certification existed for other occupations in circumstances where the state and society demanded guarantees of effective work.

Open cartels

The measures pursued by professional organizations to restrict competition dealt with so far were Weberian: they strove to build up social closures using a number of methods of exclusion, directed downwards in the social and knowledge hierarchy, but also directed laterally, not least towards foreigners. This type of social closure method is well known from international literature. However, what was the picture regarding the methods referred to by Marx – namely, restricting competition within the group? Although this problem is given relatively little attention either in the literature or by historians and chroniclers, several examples can be pointed out.

Initially, we should expect to find an open cartel strategy in the form of a trade-union struggle for collective agreements. However, as pointed out by previous research, it is striking that neither those with professional occupations nor other salaried employees conducted direct, collective campaigns for wages, nor did they demand collective agreements until after 1930. By excluding purely trade-union questions from the agenda, the employer and employees, managers and subordinates, free practitioners and wage earners could be combined in the same organization. An unusually clear example of the problem of keeping together people with very different positions in the work process can be obtained from journalism. In 1874 the Publicists' Club was formed for all publicists regardless of their positions. The club was patterned after the Physicians' Society, among others. However, in connection with several acute conflicts over security of employment around the turn of the century, the club split, and an employers organization, the Newspaper Publishers' Association, and a union organization, the Journalists' Union, were created.[28] Thus, in this instance employer–employee conflicts proved stronger than occupational loyalty, and threatened to break up the professional organization.

However, there are examples of various recommendations or stipulations, from the organizations or the state, which regulated the rates and fees which people in a number of professional occupations were to charge in private practice, regardless of whether this was carried out independently from or together with a public post.

Doctors are one example. Purely private practitioners were in a clear minority – constituting about one-third of all doctors in the first decades of the twentieth century; but many doctors combined private practice with some sort of public duties. An important issue for hospital doctors concerned their right to receive private remuneration from patients who were treated in hospital. The hospital statutes of 1901 declared that doctors did not have such a right, but that they could receive remuneration offered voluntarily. In 1928 this passive right was restricted to applying to patients in private or half-private rooms, and there was a list of suggested rates to charge. Only as late as 1959 were hospital doctors prohibited from receiving renumeration from patients.

These regulations applied to hospital in-patient care; however, out-patient care connected to hospitals was considered to be the doctors' private sphere, and there they were paid by their patients. But even in this sphere, rates of remuneration were a major issue. Charges were affected to a degree by the regulations applying to the privately organized but state-supported national health insurance. Hospital doctors and the publicly employed provincial doctors received a large part of their income from public duties of one sort or another. The differences between the private doctors with public duties, and the publicly employed doctors receiving payment for services and fees for open health care under private management as well as from purely private patients in hospital, were actually not very great.[29]

The Swedish Association of Technologists, formed in 1861, quite soon organized a rate and contract committee. This committee concerned itself with (for example) general regulations covering contracts by tender within the building and construction industry through recommending contracts for rates charged in construction of buildings, and rates for consultant engineers and architects. There are records of these rate recommendations dating from the 1890s.[30] Thus the Association of Technologists functioned as an open cartel for entrepreneurs and self-employed engineers.

The Bar Association also paid a great deal of attention to the question of charges, which were closely associated with legislation and, consequently, with state regulation, as the courts could award renumeration for court costs to the winning party. However, the Bar Association made its own recommendations in rate questions in order to obtain a better agreement between the actual amount charged and the lower charges levied by the courts. Like the accountants' organizations, the Bar Association also dealt with disputes in the matter of charges.[31]

Networks of organizations

How are rates for fees and a standard contract seen in terms of restrictions on competition? To start with, let us look at the collective agreement, which was a collective restriction of competition as regards the buying and selling of labour as a commodity. The standard contract is a mixed form, combining the personal contract, which according to liberal theory was used early on, also for workers as a contract agreement between two individuals – the individual worker and the individual employer – and a collective agreement.[32] The general regulations of the contract have the same wording – 'standard' here meaning 'standardized' – while the form leaves open (for example) questions of wages and hours, or remuneration for products such as an architect's drawing or writer's manuscript. Thus the standard contract could be used in several different circumstances – for instance, in the selling of labour, in going out to tender, in the sale of artistic products.

Charge rates involve more than the buying and selling of goods and labour; they also involve what Marx would call the 'work product' – that is, not labour as such, but the finished results of work including all fringe costs. Someone who goes to a lawyer or doctor in private practice not only pays for the labour costs of the lawyer or doctor, but also a proportion of his expenses – his working quarters, equipment, staff and so on. Someone who buys a work product does not retain the right to control how the work is done, unlike the purchase of labour.

How do rates for fees and charges function for people in various occupations? Contemporary Swedish research gives very little information on this, but a recent debate in the Writers' Union provides an interesting insight into the problem. The Writers' Union has issued a unilateral recommendation concerning charges or fees for lectures which its members are expected to follow. The recommended sums are high. Many cannot or will not pay such fees, especially for less known writers. Thus there is no doubt that the union recommendation affects the less known writers who anyway tend to have the worst incomes, while it favours successful writers with high status.[33]

Consequently, the effect of regulation of fees could be that the price (fee charged) rises as underbidding is eliminated, while the market (the number of transactions) diminishes, which particularly affects those with low status. Thus it is the price of selling the work product which is regulated by fee rates. The open cartel is one of the main mechanisms for effecting this regulation, and professional organizations fulfil this function in varying degrees. The organizations of dentists and lawyers tried to control the fees of the practitioners. A medicine charge rate controlled the prices of the medicines sold by the pharmacies. The journalists' and authors' organizations worked for a standardized contract for employment for the sale of manuscripts to book publishers.

The regulation of rates through open cartels should exemplify how the professions use their power against clients through the few and organized being pitted against the many and unorganized, as Parkin expresses it. For him this is an important argument for including those in professional occupations in the capitalist class.[34]

However, Swedish realities have not been so unequivocal, because there have been more organized counter-parties to the professions than one might at first have thought. Within the health services, the opposition has lain with the patients' collective spokesman, the state/county and health insurance during the long period when they were privately organized and exerted an active influence on fees charged by doctors. The same has applied to pharmacists and lawyers. In the case of writers, the Publishers' Association has performed as opposing party.

So far we have identified five important functions or interests around which professional occupational groups have organized themselves: (1) the development of knowledge and education; (2) the sale of work products; (3) the sale of labour (for employed professionals); (4) political action; and (5) social contact and economic support. The fifth interest was normally present in all organizations, regardless of other functions they might have fulfilled. The other four functions and the organizations that developed around them may be found in Figure 6.1, where I have used the distinction between the sale of work products and the sale of labour. Free practitioners, who sold their work products, organized themselves in typical professional organizations (item 5 in the table), which not only included an economic policy on their programme but also knowledge-related activities such as programmes for standardizing work tasks. The free practitioner has no employer, but he himself employs secretaries, nurses, cleaning staff and so on. The dentists' and doctors' unions established special employers' organizations (6) to be responsible for these tasks.[35]

Among the purchasers of work products are the ordinary client (7), the individual person, and also the company such as the construction company which purchases the services of architects (8). Thus clients consist of two main groups: direct customers and consumers of the final products (9). The latter may very well organize themselves into consumer organizations (10) – for example, tenants' associations.

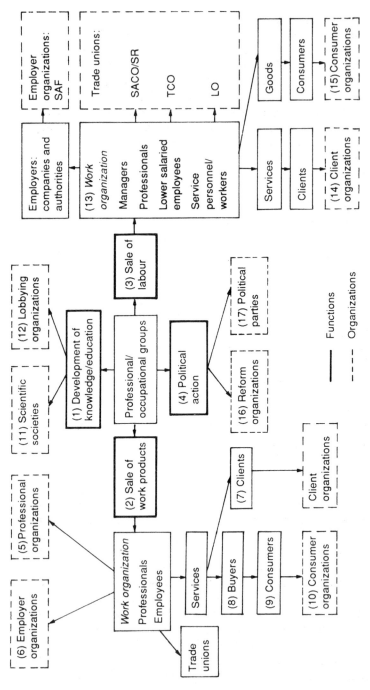

Figure 6.1   *Network of organizations – a flow chart*

In the table knowledge and education (1) stand for efforts to develop that status and knowledge upon which the pursuance of the occupation rests. Around this function are created not only the academic or scientific associations and student organizations (11) which were often the historical antecedents of professional organizations, but also what I would call various kinds of 'lobbying' organizations (12). An example of the latter is the National Council for the Improvement of Oral Hygiene, which devoted its efforts to dental hygiene under the auspices of dentists. There are many such organizations, ranging from those fighting various popular diseases to associations supporting public libraries, and to the Swedish Historical Society.

These lobby organizations are, in contrast to academic or scientific associations, generally open to the public. From the point of view of professionals, their most important function is contributing to the creation of markets, raising the status of the occupation and even channelling resources to the area.

Selling labour assumes that conditions for employment exist. Professionals also enter into work organizations (13), with directors, subordinates and service staff or workers. Many professionals work with the production of services – such as teaching and care professions – and thus services are produced in relation to clients, such as students, patients, social services or clients. Over the last decades these clients have organized themselves (14) on a relatively broad front.

Engineers, economists and company lawyers are often members of work organizations which produce goods as in the manufacturing industry or in agriculture or forestry. Commodity production does not have clients; it has consumers. And it is here that the state requirements for safeguards are expressed through product control instead of through certification of the people working in the occupation. Consumers can organize themselves in consumer organizations (15) and the state can protect their interests through consumer information. For employed professionals a union strategy – a special form of the open cartel strategy – should have been at hand, but it was not developed to any degree until after 1930.

Political reform strategies have only been treated in passing in this chapter. An interesting example may be taken from the area of social work where the Central Union for Social Work (CSA) played a significant role from the turn of the century until about 1920 (CSA was equivalent to Verein für Sozialpolitik). Political strategy can also be an alternative for the individual, as a politically engaged civil servant or as party politician (17). There are also isolated examples of organized solidarity with clients initiated by professionals.[36]

In the literature on professionalism one occasionally comes across the expression 'the professional organization', as if there existed one organization for every occupation. Such is not the case – at least not in Sweden. Organization according to function was common – for example, according to the type of product sold by professionals in an occupation. Special types of organization according to forms of employment – for instance, the District Medical Officers' Association and the Association of School and Public Dentists – and particularly according to occupational speciality became widespread. All these organizations in turn became part of a comprehensive network of other organizations: lobby organizations, political pressure groups, client and consumer organizations, industry and employer organizations, health insurance and state and municipal authorities. The typical situation which Parkin discusses, in which the organized free practitioner meets the unorganized client, comprised in fact a very small element in Sweden.

To a certain extent professional occupational groups' economic interest organizations could combine monitoring of those interests related to sales of work products and those related to labour. However, this occurred under the condition that it was totally clear which of these two tasks was foremost and would be given priority when conflicts arose. Monitoring of interests concerned with selling work products was often given priority until the 1920s, while union work became dominant from the 1940s.

Conclusion

The professionalization theory inspired by Weber has proved fruitful when analysing professional strategies aimed at occupational and knowledge monopolies; that is, restricting the occupational markets to include only those considered entitled to pursue the occupations in question. However, it does not provide sufficient theoretical understanding of phenomena such as rates for fees. Concerning this aspect, a Marxist-inspired analysis of what I have called open cartels has proved more far-reaching as regards understanding and theory formation. For instance, it forces us to analyse what professionals sold, and such analysis in its turn illuminates important bases for the formation of organizations within knowledge-based occupational areas. I have not been able to deal with the many other methods, such as standardization of work tasks, the strict regulation of advertising professional posts for free practitioners, patent and copyright laws, codes of ethics and disciplinary boards and so forth. But in principle, all these concrete methods for restricting competition are expressions of an open cartel strategy, not of a social closure strategy.

This means that researchers working in the Weberian tradition look too much for closure strategies and therefore overlook a different kind of strategy, such as the open cartels or the frontier strategy to which Staffan Selander points in his chapter in this volume.

Thus, open cartels and social closures are the two most important strategies used by professional organizations. Swedish history shows that they can be used together, but one of them was dominant. In the 1920s, the dentists kept the quacks outside their professional organization, even if this meant less efficiency in controlling prices. As long as social closure was dominant, open cartels could be used, but only within the framework of social closure.

In the 1960s and 1970s, the teachers' unions accepted as members persons without the university degrees which were required for positions in the schools and at the universities. This weakened their argument that a certain knowledge was essential for performing the job and therefore should be rewarded with higher salaries. Even if social closure methods can be used by the modern trade unions in their professional strategies, they are limited by the framework of the open cartels.

In order that a strategy restricting competition of the type under discussion might function, the normal requirement in practice is that it is accepted mutually or by several parties; that it is agreed to by the opposite parties as well. The trade-union movement's struggle for collective agreements could not be successful before the employers decided to accept the fundamental principle and organize themselves and negotiate accordingly.

The choice of strategy by those in professional occupations also was dependent upon other parties, on the economy and the state, on clients and consumers. The social closure strategy seems to have developed in conjunction with representatives for private business and the state, who saw in professionals a necessary resource for rationalizing and rendering their own enterprises more effective. On the other hand, for some time the professionals seem to have had difficulties convincing clients and consumers of the advantages of engaging their services instead of those of uncertified competitors, or instead of doing without the particular service entirely.

A successful social closure strategy can make itself superfluous if the 'unentitled' competitor is beaten. However, it tends to leave another problem unsolved and unattended: wage development for employees in professional occupations. The idea should be that their wages will be increased by creating labour shortages; however, instead the opposite problem arose. The expansion of the base of the enterprise led to many professionals landing in lower positions with poor wages and working conditions. The union strategy which started among younger professionals in order to tackle this problem soon won support not only from the Social Democratic government, but also from SAF. Thus the transition to a dominant union strategy was carried out in conjunction with its most important opponents.

Appendix

Organizations among Professional Occupations and Occupations with Higher Education

Scientific societies and/or professional organizations	Trade unions and economic interest organizations
1807 Swedish Physicians' Society	
1821 Pharmacist Society (for Stockholm, 1663)	
1848	Society of Machinists
1849 Swedish Juridical Association	
1851 The Military Society (in Stockholm)	
1857	Society of Steamship Captains
1860 Society of Dentists Veterinary Surgeons' Association	
1861 Swedish Association of Technologists	
1863 Engineers' Association	
1871 Artillery Club	
1874 Publicists' Club	
1880	Sweden's General Elementary School Teachers' Association
1881	District Medical Officers' Association
1884 Swedish Teachers' Society	
1886 Association of Inventors	Midwife Union
1887 Barristers' Society	
1892 Swedish Association of Artists	
1893 Writers' Union	General Swedish Association of Physicians
1894	Actors' Union
1899 Society of Accountants	
1901	Journalists' Union
1903 General Swedish Association of Priests	Union of Higher Civil Servants Dispensers' Union Certified Foresters' Union

1905	Swedish Association of Psychiatrists	Agricultural Teachers' Union
	Swedish Museum Officials'	Swedish Extraordinary
	Association	Teachers' Association
		Steamship Captains' Union
1907		Musicians' Union
1908	Pharmacists' Union	
	Dentists' Union	
1910		Social Workers' Association
		Nurses' Association
1912	Association of Economists	
1915	General Library Association	Secondary School Teachers' Union
1920	Society of Librarians	Metal Trades Employees'
		Association
1921	Association of Agronomists	
1923	Association of Chartered	Association of School and Public
	Accountants	Dentists
1932		Swedish Industrial Employees'
		Association
		Association of Officers
1936	Swedish Association of Architects	Association of Local Government
		Officers
1942		Union of Assistant University
		Teachers
1947		Lawyers' Association
1948	Society of Psychologists	Natural Scientists' Union
		Association of Priests
1954		Association of Civil Engineers
1955		Association of Psychologists
		Social Scientists' Association

(*Note*: It has not been possible to complete the list, because of lack of research in this field.)

Sources: S. Carlsson, *Yrken och samhällsgrupper* (Occupations and Social Groups), 1968, ch. 5.
B. Åhlund (ed.), *Svenskt föreningslexicon* (Swedish Dictionary of Associations), 1954.

Notes

1 See, for example, Torstendahl, this volume, and Jarausch, Siegrist and Burrage, this volume; Hellberg, 1978, ch. 2; Murphy, 1990; Murphy, 1986:21–41; Parkin, 1979:57f. See also Collins, 1979:134f, where professions are defined as Weberian status groups.

2 See Åmark, 1986:20–33; Åmark, 1987:12–18; and Åmark, 1989, ch. 1 (forthcoming).

3 Havland, 1958:15, 64.

4 For the interpretation of Weber, see Collins, 1986, ch. 2; and Weber, 1963:207ff.

5 Åmark, 1989, ch. 1.

6 Quotation from Marx, 1982:75. See also Åmark, 1986:20f.

7 Marx, 1972b:669f; and Marx, 1972a:177–182. See also Åmark, 1986:21. Weber

also points at the regulation of competition within groups, but not with the societal perspective of Marx and Engels; see Weber, 1983:31ff and 54ff (*Economy and Society*, part I, chs 1:10 and 2:8).

8 Engels, 1972:306ff; and Marx and Engels, 1972:470ff.

9 Collins, 1979; Parkin, 1979.

10 Murphy, 1988. See also Torstendahl in this volume and Larson, 1977/1979, chs 4 and 5.

11 Parkin, 1979:48.

12 Parkin, 1979, ch. 4.

13 Murphy, 1990; Collins, 1979.

14 See, for example, Larson, 1977/1979, ch. 2; and Selander in this volume.

15 See also Larson, 1977/1979:59.

16 Lennmalm, 1908; and Bergstrand, 1958.

17 Havland, 1958; Hellberg, 1978; Indebetou and Hylander, 1936; and Runeby, 1976.

18 Burrage in this volume; Sandberg, 1969, ch. 4; Torstendahl, 1984b; De Geer, 1986, ch. 15.

19 Sandberg, 1969, chs 3 and 4; Nilsson, 1985, ch. 10; Torstendahl, 1982; Baumgarten and Corneliusson, 1986:25ff; Johansson, 1971; Åmark, 1948.

20 Hansson, 1981; *Svenska Läkaresällskapet 175 år: dess tillkomst och utveckling*, 1983; Hellberg, 1978; *Sveriges Tandläkareförbund 1908–1958*, 1958; Carlsson, 1968, ch. 5; and Larson, 1977–1979:43, on specialization and restriction of competition.

21 Torstendahl, 1975:38–46; Runeby, 1976.

22 SOU, 1935:52, p. 170, on the ratio of population to doctors in 1927; Berg, 1980:24; Havland, 1958:76.

23 Havland, 1958.

24 'Formerna för auktorisation av revisorer mm. 1971', H 1971:3.

25 Larson, 1977–1979:29, on control of products; Runeby, 1976:92ff; SOU, 1954:15, pp. 257ff.

26 Torstendahl, 1975, ch. 7, on the engineers; see also Collins, 1979:159–171. On social workers, see SOU, 1944:29; and SOU, 1962:43.

27 SOU, 1954:15, ch. 6; See also Björnhaug, 1986, on Norwegian lift mechanics, who developed a fully fledged professional strategy with success.

28 Arnö, 1964:4; Hellkvist and Wingqvist, 1926:13.

29 Bergstrand, 1962; Heidenheimer, 1980; Kock, 1963; SOU, 1947:23, pp. 30–45; and SOU, 1958:15, pp. 235ff.

30 Hansson, 1981:48; Svensson, 1988.

31 Wikland, 1962.

32 Adlercreutz, 1954.

33 See the debate in the journal *Författaren* during 1987; and Larson, 1977–1979:74ff.

34 Parkin, 1979:47ff, 57ff.

35 Carlsson, 1968:124, 126.

36 Boalt and Bergryd, 1974; Wirén, 1980. Examples of organized professional solidarity with the clients are the organization Motpol (see the journal *Motpol*, 4–5, 1986); and the early history of Riksförbundet för Mental Hälsa, see C. Åmark, 1976:28f, 29ff, where the difficulties of combining therapy and politics are discussed.

7

Professionalization: borderline authority and autonomy in work

Svante Beckman

The rising volume of sociological and historical work on professionalization has provided the field with an increasing variety of conceptual approaches, bringing refinement as well as confusion as to what professionalization is about. More concerned about confusion than refinement, I have formed two simple, even simplistic, conceptual tools providing elementary mapping of professionalization in respect of what I take to be the two basic assumptions guiding studies in the field: that professionalization relates to the organization of work and to the role of expertise. Both tools are taxonomic. One conceives of professionalization in terms of four different modes of offering work to a market in modern societies. In that perspective it is coupled to rising *requirements of formal training* and to relative *autonomy in work*. The other relates professionalization to four conflicting types of authority, as defined by a two-dimensional model. Professionalization is here taken to signify an increase in the relative importance of *socially sanctioned expertise* in the authorization of social interaction in general and of work relations in particular. Sanctioned expertise emerges as a borderline type of authority between formal bureaucratic and non-formal expert authority. I will contribute very little by way of proper definitions; namely, extricating a reasonable denotive meaning of 'professionalization' from its seemingly excessive burden of connotative meanings. Whereas the ideal scientific statement denotes exactly something and connotes nothing, the ideal poetic statement denotes exactly nothing and connotes everything. Many statements about professionalization seem in this sense rather poetic.

On defining professionalization

Literally 'professionalization theory' is about processes whereby something grows more, and by implication less 'professional'. A more precise meaning evolves when you decide upon the rather open-ended conceptual problem:

1   which things vary in degree of being 'professional'
2   which are the criteria for assigning varying degrees of 'professionalism' to these things.

In the Aristotelian sense of definition, settling the first issue means pinpointing the *genus proximum* of professionalization; that is, singling out that class, or those classes of things which can properly be labelled 'professional'. Deciding on the second issue involves pinpointing the *differentia specifica*; namely, attributes setting professional things apart – in degree or kind – from less or non-professional things of the same class. Definition is thus a taxonomic procedure in two steps. While Aristotle thought that things had 'essences' in the sense of having *one* true *genus proximum* coupled to *one* true *differentia specifica*, few modern makers of definitions follow him in this. It is obvious that many types of things are legitimately called 'professional' – from the specific practices and traits of specific occupational groups to such nebulous phenomena as 'work', 'knowledge', 'organization', 'power', 'authority', 'culture' and 'society'.

Anyone acquainted with the habit of defining professions in terms of a long list of typical traits must be aware of the folly of maintaining that there is one true *differentia specifica*, or even one true set thereof, for things professional, though students dramatizing one certain attribute of professions as *the* attribute (like a particular strategy of excluding competition, or a particular relation of trust to a client, or a particular type of knowledge), sometimes invite the feeling that the Aristotelian hunt for true essences is not over yet.

Major conceptual difficulties stem from terminological conventions. Many studies labelled as 'professionalization theory' do not deal with things varying in degrees of professionality at all, but with things which are unvaryingly professional by English linguistic convention, such as doctors and lawyers and some other academically trained occupations. This suggests that 'professionalization' is about the historical rise and fall of these specific groups, or by abstraction, how lawyer-like or doctor-like occupational structure and behaviour grow. Typical traits of conventional professions and the contrast with non-professional occupations come to the foreground. The *genus proximum* here is 'occupation' and by implication 'labour'. The *differentia specifica* is a set of traits, unfortunately seldom consistently shared by '*the* professions'. In several languages 'profession' means 'occupation in general'. Accordingly professionalization connotes almost anything connected with the rise and reproduction of market labour. Contrasting market work with non-market work becomes central. The *genus proximum* here is 'work', and the *differentia* is 'market organization'. According to the Latin root, 'profession' is the explication of secretive texts and dogma to laymen by authorized experts. The contrast to laity and to other forms of authority is central. The *genus proximum* is 'status of authority' and by implication 'knowledge' and 'authority'. The *differentia* is 'sanctioned expertise' and 'expert knowledge'. The dominant meaning of 'professionalization', as the term is used in current non-academic Swedish, is raising the social standing of an occupational group mainly by means of higher requirements of formal training, not necessarily academic. This usage falls somewhere between terminological conventions focusing on *the* professions and conventions focusing on occupation in general. There are several other terminological conventions of less importance, some of them formed by various brands of professionalization theory itself. This means that a variety of things can be 'professional' on two, only partly overlapping counts: (1) fulfilling a variety of abstract definitional criteria, regardless if conventionally called 'professional'; and (2) being according to a variety of partly overlapping linguistic conventions 'professional' regardless of whether any abstract criteria of professionality are fulfilled.

To insist that there is an Aristotelian essence to professionalization would be quixotic. On the other hand I think that the essence of Aristotle's theory of essences is a sound one; namely, that grasping a phenomenon is basically a matter of developing handy taxonomies.

The professionalization of work

In this first section I will take 'work' as the basic category of things that may turn more or less professional. More specifically I will relate professionalization to different conditions of offering work to a work market. This market includes both the labour market, as legally defined by work for an employer and work without legal subordination to an employer. Roughly, it is only activities within households which fall outside of the work market, while (for example) unpaid voluntary community work is taken to be in it. The work market is thus defined by work for the 'public' in a wide sense. This implies that I will not recognize a shift of work from households to the work market as a case of professionalization, though the term is sometimes used to cover such changes. It also implies that professionalization may, but need not, entail changes in the legal relations to an employer. Taking the last fifty years in Western countries to be a period of massive de-professionalization, on the sole ground that professionals increasingly cease to be legally self-employed, seems unwarranted.

Autonomy at work

Legal self-employment, however, enters the picture as part of a more general dimension that I take as central to the degree of professionality in work: relative autonomy versus relative heteronomy. This is understood as a complex variable composed of legal, social, economic and cultural indices of relative social independence/dependence in work. When professions, traditionally, are said to work for 'clients' rather than for 'employers', the substance of this is that it expresses a difference in autonomy in the social encounter. When, to take another example, professionalization sometimes is set in contrast to 'proletarianization', this makes little sense if the latter term is taken in the quasi-legal Marxist meaning, but, however vague, it makes substantial sense if this pair refers more generally to degrees of social freedom and subordination in work. That professional work somehow connotes the exercise of expert authority is a third indication that autonomy is central to professional status, while not connoting any particular legal relations.

Social life entails more or less radical heteronomy of an extremely complex kind, so the empirical meaning of 'substantial autonomy' will never be fully clear. Chronic philosophical and ideological conflict over 'freedom' is proof of that. Nevertheless professionalization theory cannot dispense with an idea of degrees of freedom in work. Consequently I interpret many of the traits traditionally used to typify a profession as elements and signs of a social standing of relative autonomy and of a general occupational group strategy trying to realize high degrees of autonomy.

Requirements of formal training

A second indispensable dimension of professionalization concerns the requirements of formal training one has to fulfil in order to be able to offer a kind of work efficiently on the work market. Linking professionalization with the rise of formal educational systems, of universities, of 'meritocracy' and of barriers to work consisting of educational requirements and so on, is indeed what professionalization theory typically is about.

How you choose to explain the tremendous expansion of formal education at all levels during the last 150 years is of central importance to professionalization theory and to the normative attitude towards this process. Stressing (for example) functional adaptation to an increasingly scientific and skill-demanding social system may yield a progressive view of professionalization. Stressing (for instance) a self-reinforcing spiral of competition over power and privilege by means of educational credentials yields a more disillusioned picture. Stressing other factors yields further perspectives. Whether or not the professions possess real skills of real functional importance, or just fake credentials of functionally irrelevant skills engineered for purposes of social monopolization, is not at issue here.

In order to stay clear of this, I will not differentiate between formal training which constitutes a legal requirement for offering work and that where the requirements are of a functional or of some other non-legal kind. By implication, the difference between, say, doctors and engineers is played down. In many countries you cannot efficiently offer certain medical work to the market unless you are legally admitted to it on the ground of certain formal educational credentials. That you cannot offer certain engineering work to the market without certain educational credentials is, by contrast, not typically due to legal restraints. It is thus increasing *actual* requirements of formal training for the efficient offering of work which indicates professionalization. Whether these are *legal* barriers to the work market or not is not directly relevant. The legal monopoly of chimney sweeps in Sweden to sweep chimneys based on credentials of proved skills does not qualify this group as a profession.

I will also play down the importance of the exact nature of formal training. The difference in respect of 'professionality' between engineering work which requires, say, five years of training, mainly in abstract knowledge, in universities and similar work which requires five years of apprenticeship, mainly of practical knowledge under the guidance of a master technician in industry, seems to me of less importance to professionalization than the similarity in the amount of training required, before you are admitted to do the work. So while the rise of university training programmes for an increasing number of jobs is an important piece of empirical evidence of professionalization, such programmes should not be taken as definitional of it. Similarly, the moving of training programmes from workplaces to public educational institutions, conspicuous in the last hundred years, is not in itself indicative of professionalization. The recent trend, conspicuous in Sweden, to move advanced training programmes back to the workplaces, is consequently not indicative of 'de-professionalization'. Rather, it indicates the opposite, as an expression of generally rising training requirements and of the demand for education-based career options within workplaces.

Four types of work

Drawing from mainstream ideas of central characteristics of professionalization, I have so far picked out degrees of autonomy in the social framing of work, and the amount of formal training required. Drawing from the wealth of other 'traits' suggested as typical of professions, one could easily add more dimensions. There are, however, good reasons to stop at these two and see what they tell us about professionalization when combined. If one dichotomizes the two and runs them against each other, one gets Figure 7.1. In the figure four major types of work are defined. Names of the types are given in quotation marks to indicate an element of arbitrariness, as conventional uses of the terms employed vary and do not always comply with the definitions given in the figure.

If work is offered to the market under conditions of little or no autonomy in work combined with little or no requirements of formal training, it is called '*Proletarian*'. The term is of course chosen as it tallies, at least in spirit, with the kind of conditions of work Marx had in mind when he wrote about the proletariat – people with little overall social autonomy on the work market, hired to do jobs requiring no particular skills, having nothing to bargain with but their capacity to offer time spent in manual activity.

If work is offered under conditions of little autonomy combined with substantial requirement of formal training it is called '*Skilled labour*' *work*. Low- and medium-level administrative work in modern highly industrialized societies is typically of this kind. The prestige and bargaining position of work is increased relative to proletarian work in proportion to increased skill requirements, while freedom in and control over work is low.

	Little or no formal training required	Substantial formal training required
Heteronomous work	'Proletarian' work	'Skilled labour' work
Autonomous work	'Vocational' work	'Professional' work

Figure 7.1   *Four types of work*

'*Vocational*' *work* is the label chosen for work of the kind exemplified in community activities, political work, work in various kinds of voluntary associations like trade unions or relief organizations and so on. 'Lay work' could be an alternative term, suggestive of the traditional distinctions between laity and profession and between amateurs and professionals. Such work involves ethical and honorary commitments to ideals, traditions, movements or causes of a kind implying personal autonomy, if not always (or typically) of the strong kind required by Immanuel Kant for morally valid action. This kind of work is essentially 'called' on to the market by the culturally organized standards for individual ethical and honorary status. Though the successful performance of such work may require substantial skills, there are no requirements of formal training. The idea that the scope and volume of this kind of work has been fatally damaged by professionalization loomed high in the wave of anti-professionalist debate in the 1970s. Ivan Illich, in books like *Medical Nemesis* and *De-Schooling Society*, gives a well-known example.

If, finally, high degrees of autonomy in work combine with high requirements for formal training the type is called '*professional*' *work*. The higher the average training requirements and the higher the average degree of autonomy in work, the more professionalized is average work on the market. The work of traditional professions could indeed be used as the typical case, if one bears in mind that many of the traits associated with a profession are ignored here. Engineers and economists doing managerial work in bureaucracies therefore belong here too.

The significance of the typology of work
In order to be useful this typology must first of all be shown to make some empirical sense in the context of professionalization theory.

One way to sustain such a claim is to make sure that the conflicts over the diagonals, which automatically arise from constructing diagrams in this way, make sense. We should, on the one hand, expect to find evident empirical relevance as to the difference between work of the proletarian and the professional kind. We should find that the polarization of these two makes up a natural and convenient dimension for the description of general conditions of work and for describing major differences in the strategies of the two types of labour pursued to improve their conditions. That this is actually the case is pretty evident. An example discussed in several of the contributions to this volume is the polarization between inclusionary (proletarian) and exclusionary (professional) strategies of occupational groups to gain some control over the supply of work to the market. Including as many as possible in your occupational organization makes good sense if your only bargaining resource is restricting your supply of labour time. The higher the skill requirements of the work, and the more autonomy in its exercise, the better sense – from the point of view of collective self-interest – is made by exclusionary strategies, denying as many as possible entry to the market. If setting 'proletarian' against 'professional' strategies makes sense, the typology suggests that 'skilled labour' work must be a problem, as it will be ambiguous in such a dimension, behaving like 'professional work' in some aspects and as 'proletarian work' in others. Also 'vocational work' ought to be difficult to fit into such a frame.

Over the other diagonal we should expect significant conflict between 'vocational work' and 'skilled labour work' in matters relating to professionalization. The conflicts within nursing provide a good example. Historically emerging out of household and voluntary community work, nursing reveals a longstanding tension between a definition of their work as 'a calling' and the ambition to get it accepted as an ordinary skilled job. The negative consequences for collective bargaining strength has made Swedish nurses (for example) keen to get rid of the 'vocational' label. Collectively organized pride in nursing has shifted from the ethical and honorary status of community work to the pride in particular skills of qualified labour. A similar recurrent conflict along this diagonal was highlighted in the 1970s by the outburst of 'neo-amateurism' of the Ivan Illich kind, deploring the general appropriation of ethically significant lay work performed in communities by skilled labour in market bureaucracies. Both the subordination of work – particularly as related to family care – to bureaucratic structures and the claim that formally trained skills were necessary for these tasks were attacked.

Another test for empirical relevance is that borders between the four categories in the table should correspond to meaningful 'semi-categories'. For the conventional groupings 'semi-skilled labour' (on the border between 'proletarian' and 'skilled labour' work) and 'semi-professions' (on the border between 'skilled labour' and 'professional' work), this is quite evidently so. But what about the two other borders? Is there a shady area between 'professional work' and 'vocational work' where empirically significant types of work can be placed?

This seems so if you consider the stress put on 'vocation', 'ethical standard', 'public-spiritedness', 'altruism', 'disinterestedness', 'trust relations' as central features of a profession in traditional 'trait theory'. The idealized profession is expected to stay very close to what the table calls 'vocational work'. In this sense there are 'semi-professions', not of the conventional kind located between skilled labour work and professional work, but between lay community work and professional community work.

A good example of an occupational group on this borderline is the clergy, which sometimes is denied, sometimes admitted to the status of a profession. (Denying them this is slightly ironic considering that they, in a historical sense, are the original profession – those authorized to profess Christian dogma to the laity). Priests are expected to perform their work literally as a calling, and to work in a disinterested spirit alien to a modern labour market. While nurses can ignore the 'vocational' label, priests certainly cannot. In a highly unionized labour market such as Sweden's, this has eventually contributed to a wage disaster. Few unskilled jobs pay, at the present, less than a priest in the Swedish Church when he (now, rather, she) enters the work market after five years of university training.

Another group in modern societies an important one (not least in Sweden) on this borderline is what one might call 'the political semi-profession'. This consists on the one hand of 'professionalized politicians' – performers of what both in a legal and customary sense is lay community work as a full-time paid job, acquiring expertise as professional 'decision-makers'. On the other hand it consists of academically trained experts entering public service and party offices on a professional basis, while eventually turning into politicians, in the sense of acquiring a mandate from parties or corresponding political community bodies. In trade unions and popular movement organizations, similar patterns can be found.

That the borderline between vocational work and proletarian work also contains groups of importance in the context of professionalization is, finally, also quite clear. Particularly within the care sector there is clearly an historically important flow from unpaid vocational work into proletarian service work. Large groups of women in care work are still locked up here, prevented by a lingering sense of community and pride attached to vocational work, from developing hard-nosed proletarian labour strategies. One can even find examples of idealization of this 'semi-category' as in the case of the traditional Catholic notion of the priest-worker, at once a man of the highest calling and the humblest of proletarians.

But what about the centre of the table? Are there empirically meaningful categories of work (and occupation) bordering on all four types of work, containing elements of vocational, proletarian, skilled labour and professional work? The historically most important example which comes to mind here is that of artisans and handicraft work. As vividly depicted by E. P. Thompson[2] and other historians of labour, the onslaught of industrial capitalism squeezed traditional market work, on the one hand between the old quasi-professional status of the guild organization and evolving proletarian status. On the other hand, it was caught between a traditional pattern of work regulated by the ethics of calling to craft and family tradition and the rise of new conditions of work forcing artisanry into the framework of skilled but legally subordinated labour.

Discussion
In these two tests for empirical meaningfulness – relevant conflicts over diagonals and meaningful borderline categories – the suggested typology seems to do well. It has some fair degree of both the internal logical consistency and the external empirical descriptiveness required from any theoretical construct.

Technically, the table could legitimately be turned into a two-dimensional field model, by changing the two dichotomized variables into continuous bi-polar coordinates. It then becomes a map of the work market structure, on which real events can be plotted. Hereby the position and historical movement of types of work and different occupational groups can be depicted. By distributing the workforce over the map according to the value of individual jobs on the coordinates a simple device for describing work structure at various points in time is arrived at. By positioning similar values for a particular job referring to different years' trajectories for the direction of change will be discovered. Movements towards higher values on the training requirements axis and the autonomy axis will of course signify professionalization. Such descriptive use is the primary target of my taxonomic scheme. But it is also useful for the generation of hypotheses about conflict patterns on the work market and about occupational strategies.

Examples have already been hinted at. An occupational group moving from proletarian to skilled labour status can be expected to turn ambivalent over the inclusion/exclusion strategy of wage policy. Moving towards higher training requirements an occupational group can be expected to turn ambivalent whether following an 'involvement minimizing', 'cash-nexus' strategy of proletarian work, or an 'involvement maximizing', 'status-nexus' strategy of professional work. Such groups will face a choice between scaling up skill requirements to realize substantial ground to bargain for higher autonomy in work, thereby leaving traditional 'inclusionary' union strategies behind, or to keep to the latter and use skill requirements essentially for pressing wage claims. Due to the overall increase in formal requirements in modern industrial societies, this dilemma faces growing proportions of the organized labour force. While professional groups in highly unionized Sweden have increasingly combined traditional exclusionary behaviour with the strategies of skilled labour, the trade-union strategies as a whole seem to move slowly towards more professional patterns. Abundant rumours of an impending 'information society' help to sustain these movements. The traditional difficulty of the trade-union movement in bridging the conflicting strategic interests between unskilled and skilled members, will grow increasingly complicated as the proportion of near-professional members rises.

I will here leave the matter of further uses of my taxonomic scheme to the reader, and go on to the issue of expertise.

Professional expertise and authority

The centrality of *expertise* to the idea of professional status need not be elaborated here. At the core of the autonomy in work that professions to a varying degree enjoy and aspire to, is not directly high skills and high training requirements, but the position of expertise in social relations such skills and requirements sustain. Experts exercise authority based on the belief of others in the existence of particular skills held by them. The point of educational credentials typical of professions, is to sustain such beliefs in authority grounding skills. Professions represent socially sanctioned expertise. The purpose of this part of this chapter is to represent professional expertise in its conceptual context as a kind of authority. Once again a typology which eventually can be turned into a mapping device will be constructed.

Defining authority

Over any modern discussion of types of authority hovers the spirit of Max Weber, and his famous three 'ideal types' – traditional, charismatic and legal-rational (bureaucratic) authority, forming the leitmotiv of his *Wirtschaft und Gesellschaft*. Though I will accept Weber's 'subjective' concept of authority, and though I will keep to a similar level of aggregation, I will disregard his three types, primarily because expert authority fits badly in his scheme. Assuming that his typology – at his chosen level of aggregation – is exhaustive, expertise ought to be viewed as a sub-type of legal-rational authority with some elements of the charismatic type. But this is awkward, and blurs the important distinction between compliance to expertise and the compliance to bureaucratic authority. Explicitly, Weber couples his types to *'Herrschaft'*. Though the exercise of expertise connotes some sort of rule over other people, it hardly connotes '*Herrschaft*' in the quasi-political sense of this term. In constructing an alternative typology I will, however, let myself be guided by some of the conceptual rules for differentiation which Weber seems to follow when extracting those clusters of traits which define his three 'ideal types.'

I define 'authority' as that property of instructions – for action, belief, valuation and being – given by individuals, organizations or by systems of rules (such as laws, institutions, roles and customs), to other individuals, which explains why the latter *voluntarily* comply with these instructions. By extension people, organizations, roles, institutions and so on are said to have authority when instructions issued or contained by them are voluntarily followed. They have authority in terms of the probabilities of being willingly obeyed. In some cases they also have *formal* authority in the sense that attached to them are special rules obliging people to follow them. This somewhat complicates the situation as it admits of cases where an institutional rule has authority in the formal sense, while it lacks authority in the sense defined. People are formally obliged to follow it, but actually they do not. The empirical criterion of authority is thus a compliant attitude in the minds of those whose actions and so on are instructed by it.

A difficulty with the proposed definition is its reliance on the distinction between voluntary and non-voluntary compliance – partly because such an attribute of subjective attitudes is not easily observed in others and is difficult to grasp firmly even in introspection, partly because the distinction voluntary/enforced compliance connects the concept of authority with the extremely tricky concept of 'power'. If the function of the concept of authority is to account for voluntary compliance with instructions, a corresponding function for the concept of power is to account for non-voluntary compliance. But this restricted, 'coercive' concept of power is only one of many intricately related power concepts, many of which conceive of authority as an integral aspect of power. In some common usages, having power means first of all having authority over others. In the cases of expert authority this connection to 'power' relates to an ambiguity in 'knowledge', both conceivable as a source of authority and a scarce resource allowing for coercive power. The distinction between voluntary and non-voluntary compliance is destined to be fuzzy in the power-ridden world of a rule-following animal aspiring to self-direction. By far the easiest way to preserve a sense of dignity and self-direction under the spell of more or less coercive forces is to grant these forces authority by voluntary compliance, thereby unwittingly increasing dramatically the ruling capacity of coercive resources.

Dimensions of authority in Weber's typology

Let us first look for conceptual dimensions making sense of Weber's differentiation of authority into three types. There are several.

On the one hand 'traditional' and 'legal-rational' authority differs from 'charismatic', as the two former are varieties of *institutional* authority clinging to institutional systems of rules and roles, while the latter denotes *personal* authority clinging to persons. The authority of, say, a chief in a tribal society or the boss in a modern factory, goes with his role as given in institutional rules, while the authority of, say, a charismatic leader of a popular movement goes with his person. So here is a personal-institutional dimension of authority. Expertise is at first glance clearly of the personal kind as it clings to the skills and knowledge personally imbedded in the expert. When, at a second glance, one considers *professional* expertise the role of institutional sanctions of these presumed skills by means of (for example) an educational credential, it becomes less evident that expertise is a purely personal form of authority. Out of this arises a distinction between 'free' and 'socially sanctioned' expertise, to which I will attend shortly.

On the other hand the basic conceptual difference between 'traditional' and 'bureaucratic' authority may be seen in several seemingly parallel dimensions. One relates to degrees of explicit formalization of an institutional structure. 'Traditional' authority has low values in this dimension, 'bureaucratic' has high. Talcott Parsons' 'pattern variable' 'diffuseness–specificity' is a sub-variety of this dimension covering one aspect of it.[3] Expertise has an unclear standing in this dimension. In the case of professional–socially sanctioned expertise, explicit formalization of the ground of authority is entailed, and the scope of authorization is specific. In the case of non-sanctioned expertise the relations of authority are not so specific and the authority of 'free expertise' is by definition not formalized. While the authority of professions on the one hand is efficient on the ground that the followers assume it to be 'specific' in the sense of being rooted in demonstrable knowledge and confined to the area of action covered by that knowledge, it is at the same 'diffuse', as the follower is typically unable to check its specificity and boundaries.

This 'incompetence' on the part of the follower of expert authority, can on the one hand be understood as a reason why such expertise which is difficult to check by common experience, needs social sanctions to be effective. Sanctions are guarantees of specificity of the authority of the professional. On the other hand, such incompetence is at the very heart of expertise. It is the only type of authority that relies wholly on the personal incompetence of its followers. This explains why relations of trust are rightly thought to be central to professional status. The function of credentials is to inspire trust. Secondly, the authority of the professional is not efficient unless it it trusted by those incompetent to judge it. Thirdly, the professional is entrusted with the interests of incompetent followers. The centrality of incompetence to professional authority has inspired many observations concerning the self-interest of professional groups to preserve incompetence in others, and to keep the alleged specificity of presumed expertise hidden from inspection. When Illich speaks of professionalization as 'disabling', he may be right or wrong in the sense that the clients of a profession become less able to pursue their interests, but he is quite right in the sense that the extension of the area of professional authority necessarily corresponds to extended incompetence.

Another conceptual dimension relating Weber's traditional authority to bureaucratic is akin to Parsons' ascription–achievement distinction. 'Traditional' authority is rooted in what people (or other carriers of authority like laws) *are*, while bureaucratic authority is rooted in what people *do*. More importantly, it relates to Weber's own distinction *Wertrational–Zweckrational*. The instructions of the traditional type carries value-rational authority because those actions, beliefs and so on which they instruct are considered right (or good or true) in themselves, while the ground for bureaucratic authority is goal-rational in the sense that it serves a task or purpose. Involved also is the distinction between *obligations to tasks by contract* and *obligations to rights by status* originated by Henry Main in his *Ancient Law* of 1861.

As a form of authority, expertise is clearly based on achievement rather than on ascription, it is goal-rational rather than value-rational and the nature of the obligations it imposes is contractual rather than based on status. In the case of the institutionally sanctioned expertise of professions, a superficial element of ascription crawls in by the very act of authorization. That which is authorized is, however, at least supposed to be dependent on proven skills of some kind, and professional status is certainly an example, perhaps even the paradigmatic example, of achieved status in the Parsonian sense.

The rest of Parsons' *pattern variables* can be brought to bear on various constellations of Weber's three authority types. One essential dimension distinguishing the 'charismatic' type from the 'bureaucratic' is, for instance, that they represent opposite ends of the 'affectiveness–affective neutrality' variable. Charismatic authority depends on emotional bonds and the affective identification of the followers with the leader personally. The authority of the 'bureaucratic' type, on the other hand, is described by Weber as impersonal in an austere, machine-like fashion. Expertise belongs clearly to the affectively neutral kind, and as in the case of the bureaucratic type this impersonality is part of the conditions for its efficiency. It should be noted that the affectiveness–affective neutrality dimension is not parallel to the institutional–personal dimension mentioned above. Expertise is a personal, affectively neutral type of authority.

Four types of authority
To define my types I have chosen (1) the dimension person-based/ institution-based authority, and (2) goal-based/status-based authority. The latter is derived from that cluster of dimensions mentioned above to which the distinction *Zweckrational–Wertrational* belongs. The centrality of these two polarities to social philosophy in general and to the sociology of modernization in particular needs no elaboration here. The combination results in Figure 7.2.

Four basic types of authority are defined in the figure. 'Expert authority' is goal-based and clings to the presumed performative skills of persons. People in any field from fortune-telling to fiscal policy, offering expert advice and services to the market, are examples of people typically entering into relations of expert authority with others. The motivational ground for accepting such authority is self-interest coupled to beliefs in special skills and abilities of the expert. Such beliefs may be rooted in experience or hearsay. Institutional authorization of professional skills represents a particular mode of sustaining such hearsay.

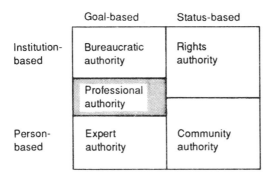

Figure 7.2 *Four types of authority*

'Bureaucratic authority' refers to institutionally defined rules and roles relating to goals and contractual tasks. It depends on the acceptance of task obligations either directly, as in a task contracted by an employee, or indirectly, as acceptance that someone has the lawful task to instruct one's behaviour in certain respects. The authority of managers over employees in modern private and public administrations is a typical case. The authority of a commanding officer over a soldier is another, where the soldier's acceptance of his task, his perception of the task of the officer, and ultimately his understanding of the task of warfare form the obligational ground for authority.

'Community authority' attaches to person and status. The authority of political leaders over their followers, of modern 'pastors' over modern 'sheep', and the authority of friends over friends are examples. Instructions from these sources carry authority by force of a sense of community. Much of the authority of tradition and the rules of games is of this kind. I follow the tradition of having a Christmas tree, not out of a sense of being formally obliged to any tasks or rights, not because it serves my self-interest, but out of a sense of community with people cherishing this habit. Community authority is at the heart of Weberian charisma, connoting the ability of an individual to take on personal identifications from his fellows by force of his personification of the community, its values and aspirations. The infringement of the domain of community authority by professional groups claiming expert authority, and by the expansion of relations of bureaucratic authority, is a major source of discontent with professionalization in particular and modernization in general since the days of Ferdinand Tönnies' heralded distinction between *Gemeinschaft* and *Gesellschaft*.

What I have called 'rights authority' depends on accepted obligations to the rights attached to owners of institutionally ascribed status. Obligations to the constitutionally or traditionally conveyed rights of political governors, to the civil rights of citizens, to the rights of honorary status and to the rights of property owners are four important examples. If my demand that you should leave my house carries the kind of authority it is supposed to have according to current politico-ethical fictions, it is not because you are obligated to any task, not because you comply with my expertise in house-leaving, not – at least not directly – out of a sense of community with me, but out of obligation to my rights as a house-owner. As institutional obligations to tasks and rights typically go hand in hand with coercive powers sustaining them (including coercion by withheld gratification), it is frequently impossible to say whether rights carry proper authority or if they are complied with in view of retaliation. But reducing the motivational forces of adaptive social behaviour to the interplay of power and self-interest in the mode of radical methodological individualism seems to be a case of quite bad psychology. Obligations to rights are psychological realities.

The chronic troubles of rights authority in political philosophy concern how such rights ultimately arise. Some derive them from the superior rights authority of transcendent entities like God, nature or history. Some derive them from obligations agreed in a fictitious contract. Modern democratic theories typically derive the rights of governance from the community authority of the people. But the rights of governments may also be thought to stem from their expertise in the furthering of collective goals like economic growth and military strength. In modern Western societies the authority of the property rights of capital, is frequently thought to be based on a kind of free expertise of entrepreneurs in relation to the collective goal of economic growth. So rights authority can be thought to be derived from any other of the three basic types of authority, as well as from transcendent sources of rights.

As entailed by the mode of distinguishing the four types, maximum conflict can be expected to obtain over the diagonals of the table. Rights authority is radically alien to expert authority, and community authority is radically alien to bureaucratic authority. This fits well with recurrent empirical patterns of ideological conflict in the West.

Borderline types of authority
Professional authority is shown in Figure 7.2 on the borderline between expert authority and bureaucratic authority, containing elements of both. Whereas it clearly belongs to the 'modern' goal-based type, it is ambiguous in the person–institution dimension. Authorizing a professional is to provide him with institutional acknowledgement, while that which is acknowledged is a particular personal ability to perform actions conducive to certain goals. In this middle position, professional groups should empirically be expected to be squeezed into a two-front battle for authority against their neighbours, on the one hand against the wholly institutionalized, role-bound authority of the bureaucratic position, on the other against the wholly person-based authority of 'free expertise', which is not institutionally boosted by credentials and authorization. Take, for instance, doctors fighting both the authority of administrative directors of hospitals and the unauthorized expert authority of 'quacks'. Another example is scientists fighting on the one hand university and state bureaucrats and on the other 'ideologists',

'journalists' and self-styled science experts peddling unauthorized theories to the public. The middle position also allows professionals to alternate between stressing the merits of institutionally guarded authority as against agents on the 'free market' of expertise, and the merits of personal quality and institutional independence as against bureaucratic structures. This ambiguous standing between the authority of formal positions and the market-evaluated authority of personal skills is essential to professional authority and it contributes to certain chameleon-like features of behaviour of professional groups.

'Professional authority' is not the only important category of authority standing on the border between two principal types as defined by Figure 7.2. On the border between rights authority and community authority there are several types, the most important at which is the authority exercised in families and kinship systems of parents over children, spouse over spouse, and older over younger members. Let us label it 'kinship authority'. On the one hand these relations are regulated by the rights of (formal or informal) institutional roles with corresponding obligations. On the other hand, these 'roles' are in a strong sense rooted in personal traits. Being someone's 'father' is both legally and by tradition a highly institutionalized role conferring rights of commanding obedience, and a relationship of biological and psychological community, carrying personal authority to a varying extent. This middle position of kinship authority is expressed in the drift of family ideologies in Western countries in latter centuries. Family relations are ideologically 'de-institutionalized', substituting stress on rights for stress on community. For example, modern children are required to 'love' their parents' persons, rather than to 'honour' and 'respect' their rights.

'Professional authority' and 'kinship authority' share a similar ambivalence over the personal–institutional dimension, while representing opposite types over the goal–status dimension. This squares nicely with the clash between family and professional values, particularly over children typical of the welfare state. Family care by goal-oriented, authorized expertise in schools, nurseries and kindergarten is posed against the rights of parents and the values of community. To bridge this conflict the Board of Social and Medical Care in Sweden (*Socialstyrelsen*) was on the verge of recommending compulsory parenthood education in the mid–1970s.[4] The hailing of biological motherhood as entailing natural expertise in child rearing is an example of a more traditional attempt to resolve this clash.

An important type of authority bordering on community authority and expert authority is that represented by leaders of modern political movements in the eyes of their followers. On the one hand, such leaders carry authority by personifying the values and patterns of the collective identities of the group. On the other, they are felt to represent freely chosen expertise in telling what is the best thing for (as an example) the party to do. One might label this 'movements authority'. In some modern political ideologies, particularly in Leninism, the expert authority of leaders is heavily stressed at the expense of community authority. In his doctrine of the communist avant-garde, Lenin derives its authority from its expert knowledge of historical laws stemming from training in the science of Marxism. The nature of authority of Communist Party leaders is thus very close to the professional kind, providing Leninism with a strong flavour of technocracy, so appealing in early twentieth-century Europe.

Looking for important types of authority bordering on bureaucratic authority and rights authority we find, for example, the ambiguous authority of public officials. On the one hand they represent institutional rights of command conferred from legal statutes, corresponding to the legal obligations of citizenship, and on the other they represent task-specific authority relative to goals given them by the owners of political governing rights. Their authority resides both with obligations to rights and obligations to tasks.

This middle position allows for conflict and drift. Government officials in Sweden, long since accorded more independence than in many other countries, can be expected to defend their domain of authority on the one hand against enterprising bureaucrats by stressing the value of formal lawfulness over that of goal-efficiency, and on the other hand against what they feel as undue interference from political masters. In this they can use the statute law against enterprising politicians. Alternatively, they can defend their domain against political authority in terms of the demands of the goals given to them. As shown by Antoinette Hetzler et al., the latter strategy becomes increasingly important as the current Swedish mode of law-making turns from detailed regulation of the formal conduct of authorities, to open-ended stipulations as to which goals and values a particular public administration should strive for.[5] An ideology of 'goal-direction' is superseding the traditional 'legalistic' ideas of the '*Rechtsstaat*', whereby the authority of officials turns increasingly bureaucratic, in the sense of the typology.

Mixed authority, professionalization and
bureaucratization
It is seldom altogether clear why people ascribe authority to the instructions given to them. An instruction – or the source of an

instruction – may carry several types of authority simultaneously. Also a person may have different kinds of authority to different people and in different social contexts.

In relation to his students and to the general public a university professor may have professional authority. That is what he expects to have as the purpose of institutional sanctions of expertise is to create a deferential attitude in others. If specialists in his field of study comply with his views, it is hardly because he is a professor with formal credentials. In this context he may enjoy the authority of freely evaluated expertise. Towards his department staff he exercises the bureaucratic authority of his administrative role. Swedish professors are still typically appointed as state officials by royal decree, and enjoy in some of their doings what I call official authority, neatly defined by legal statutes of which the right to confer formal educational status to students is one. A Swedish professor may be an honorary professor and is then, at least in principle, entitled to the rights of deference connected with institutional honour status. In certain respects, he may enjoy the community authority of the academic brotherhood, or of his friendly colleagues. So virtually all types of authority may be exercised by a typical 'professional' in his work.

This mixing of authority relates to the issue of 'bureaucratization' as debated in professionalization theory. While for a long time professions have tended to lose formal legal autonomy on Western work markets by becoming employed in private and public bureaucracies, it is, by this fact alone, far from clear that professional authority has lost relative importance. The exercise of expert authority is not directly dependent on such formal conditions. On the other hand, members of groups with the typical academic credentials of a profession, like civil engineers, may only marginally exercise professional authority in their work, while predominantly exercising bureaucratic authority due to management positions. In the perspective of my typology the question of 'professionalization' or 'bureaucratization' is a matter of changing relative social efficiency of different types of authority in the overall pattern of authorization in a society. It is not directly a matter of formal organization.

This 'relative social efficiency' of professional authority – or for any type of authority – has four main aspects.

1   The share of professional authority in the totality of events where people voluntarily comply with instructions given them.
2   The relative consequential importance of those actions guided

by professional authority, as compared to actions guided by other types.
3 The competitive efficiency of professional authority when clashing with instructions given by agents of other types of authority.
4 The exchange value of professional authority for the acquisition of other types of authority.

Seen from the point of view of authority, the question if modern societies, or segments of them, are 'professionalizing' or 'de-professionalizing' can be defined by the movements of these four indices. They can obviously move in different directions. The share of actions guided by professional authority may go down, while the consequential importance of these actions may go up. The competitive efficiency of professional authority when clashing with other types may go down, while at the same time its exchange value goes up. Though such movements are intricately related to changes in the legal structure, the importance of the latter is easily exaggerated.

That the proposed indices can move differently is in a sense unfortunate, as it narrows the scope for getting unambiguous empirical evidence of professionalization. If, for example, the economic policy of a government is increasingly guided by the advice of a few professional economists, the consequential importance of this advice is of such magnitude that it would be misleading to insist that an overall tendency of de-professionalization is at hand, on the grounds that thousands of formerly self-employed doctors are turned into hospital employees. If, to take another example, credentials of professional authority plays an increasingly important role for the acquisition of positions of bureaucratic authority or even rights authority in organizations, it is misleading to speak of 'de-professionalization', on the grounds of findings that persons with professional credentials are increasingly found in bureaucratic positions. The increasing exchange value of professional authority – and thus 'professionalization' – is expressed exactly in such findings.

Authority, as a generalized, exchangeable, inflatable social resource for effecting the voluntary compliance of others, shares several important similarities with money. Sub-varieties of authority are like different currencies – partly exchangeable at varying rates. According to changes in conditions in converting one kind of authority into another, agents will change the particular mix they strive for in order to maximize its social efficiency. The honorary status of nobility was a very strong 'currency' in feudal society easily exchanged into other currencies, including the professional authority of clergy and the bureaucratic authority of officers. Trying to convert other types of authority (and money) into nobility was the master strategy of social success for those not born with it. In terms of exchangeability, the strength of professional authority on the twentieth-century 'authority market' is partially expressed in what superficially seems to be the 'bureaucratization' of the professions, but more generally in the steeply rising demand for credentials of professional status associated with meritocracy. As in the case of nobility, this results in inflationary pressures whereby the strength of the professional 'currency' is bound to fall if not guarded by very strong exclusionary practices of already established professional groups. Though the exchange rate of professional authority will fall, simply by over-supply, its exchangeability may still rise. This implies that a highly professionalized work market need not be one where the direct exercise of professional authority is prominent.

The uses of the typology
The proposed typology of authority is intended to be useful for conceptualizing and describing certain aspects of professionalization, as well as for the generation of hypotheses. It provides a simple point of departure for theorizing about patterns of conflict between groups asserting professional authority and groups representing other types, as well as with groups subjected to professional authority. The typology provides a (partial) definition of professionalization in terms of the relative strength of institutionally sanctioned expertise in the overall pattern of authority. This can be elaborated into four indices of professionalization representing aspects of the 'social efficiency' of a type of authority. The dimensional variables of the authority table can technically be treated as coordinates of a mapping device, thereby allowing the description of states and of continuous real movements in the composition of the authority structure of a society or a segment thereof. One can map the trajectories of specific institutions and groups moving from one kind of perceived authority to another.

As for the generation of hypotheses some hints have been given; for example, in relation to the money analogy. Entailed in the approach is also a zero-sum theory of authority, whereby the loss of appeal of one type is the gain of another. Though such an idea must be corrected for changes in the overall receptiveness to authority, it is a good starting-point for questions about the causes of changes in the pattern of authority. Here a 'crisis' hypothesis of the appeal of expert authority may be suggested. Drawing *inter alia* from Weber's discussion of charisma, one could assume that cultural crisis will – apart from creating general turbulence in patterns of authority – tend to move it in favour both of more goal-based and more person-based types. The increasing levels of uncertainty combined with higher pressures for goal-efficiency favours expertise. The often observed differences in career patterns of armies in peacetime and armies in wartime, is an example. The strong appeal of technocracy and expertise at the turn of the last century during the bewildering break-through of industrial modernity in the West, seems a more general example. Periods of ease and cultural self-confidence, as created, for example by the extraordinary economic boom in the West from 1948 to 1972, will – apart from diminishing general receptiveness to authority – tend to increase the appeal of institutional and status-based types. The falling ideological appeal of professional expertise in the 1960s and 1970s illustrates this. Current rumours that a cultural crisis on the threshold of the 'information society' is at hand would then square with what seems to be a rising appeal of expertise and signs of a revival of receptiveness to technocracy in Western social relations at the present, as well as with the revival of trust in free expertise of entrepreneurs.

Concluding remarks

I have suggested two simple taxonomic tools for approaching professionalization at a fairly general level of analysis. Their usefulness is for the reader to judge. To elaborate how to bring them together would require another paper. The starting-point of such a paper could be the assumption that all agents on the work market strive for higher degrees of autonomy in work. Acquiring that autonomy is vitally connected with the acquisition of authority. The latter can, however, be of many kinds. Opting for rights safeguarding labour against exploitation and unemployment has been a classical strategy of labour movements. In Sweden strong unions have enabled the legal rights of employee status to rival that of citizen status.

To opt for legal monopoly rights of work safeguarding against competition was a prominent strategy in the age of the guilds, surviving in a modernized form in a few of the traditional professions. To opt for increasing autonomy by means of enhanced bureaucratic positions is extremely important on the individual level in modern societies, but it is, for obvious reasons, not a strategy that occupational groups can pursue collectively. Everyone cannot be a manager.

To strive for autonomy by acquiring a measure of expert authority in work relations by means of special skills and their credentials is the strategy of professionalization. Ascertaining autonomy in this way is limited by the general level of skills requirements in work, by the skill reproduction capacity, and, in the end, by the fact that expertise by its very nature must either be generally rare, or if abundant, extremely segmented. Only few can enjoy any significant amount of expert authority in the same line of work, but the more lines there are, the more people can opt for this strategy.

If the heralds of the 'information society' are right, significantly higher levels of differentiation of work lie ahead, combined with a general rise in skill requirements. The combination of the two will generate increasing difficulties of skill reproduction. All three factors will pave the way for further professionalization and also for some real dilemmas for traditional trade-union strategies. What will happen to the old-fashioned monopoly-rights strategies of lawyers and doctors is probably of little importance in the context of professionalization.

Notes

I thank members of the SCASSS group on 'Professionalization and conflict' for comments on an earlier draft of this chapter.

1 *Personalutbildning*, 1988.
2 Thompson, 1972.
3 Parsons, 1951.
4 Discussed in my book *Kärlek på tjänstetid*, Beckman, 1981.
5 Hetzler et al., 1985.

8

Associative strategies in the process of professionalization: professional strategies and scientification of occupations

Staffan Selander

The word 'profession' can be used in quite different ways in everyday language. Some occupational groups can maintain that they are professional since they have a practically oriented but unique knowledge which is difficult to access for most citizens, as is the case for air-force pilots, surgeons and engineers. Others can maintain professionalism since they have a complete mastery of academically oriented basic research, as is the case with researchers within theoretical physics, biochemistry of philosophy. And others can claim professional status because they control some of the mechanisms of power in society, as is the case with politicians, legal advisers of companies or specialists in stock-jobbing. In these examples the word 'professional' has quite different meanings and refers to various kinds of praxis and knowledge.

When different occupational groups today strive to professionalize themselves, as do physiotherapists, teachers, educational and vocational counsellors, nurses and other occupations within the middle layers, it is difficult to interpret what this strife entails. Is it a matter of status, specific knowledge, an exclusive, practically oriented competence, or all of these?

In this chapter I shall use the concept 'professionalization' in the following way: the aspiration that an occupational group cherishes to reach exclusive societal advantages and preference of interpretation within their special field of knowledge and praxis. Paradoxically enough, it may seem, we will at the same time state that there is no point any more in talking about new professions in modern society. How can this be understood? We simply mean that the concept 'profession' can be used to identify a typical phenomenon (and thus some typical occupational groups) during earlier periods in the history of the industrialized countries. However, to use that concept for all sorts of modern, practically oriented, occupational groups which have an abstract, systematic or theoretic basis of knowledge will lead to a concept that to an ever-increasing extent gets more slender. This point of view does not exclude the view that the status of earlier professional groups, as well as their control over specific knowledge and a field of work, can be seen as a model by those occupational groups which today strive to be recognized as professional.

In this chapter a differentiation will also be made between professionalization and scientification of occupations, which will be illustrated by two occupations: the journalist and the educational and vocational counsellor. Professionalization can be looked upon as a form of collective, social mobility, and in the process of professionalization two main strategies can be identified – closure strategies and associative strategies. The Weberian concept of 'closure' is well publicized by Frank Parkin and Raymond Murphy, but the associative strategy is new.[1] It has, we believe, theoretically a good potential to explain how modern occupations outline their projects of professionalization. To use an analogy, we can think of the associative strategy as a 'go west' strategy. During the nineteenth century, many people emigrated to the United States and moved westward. On their way, they did cooperate in order to become stronger and to protect themselves, but once there, they made demarcations, enclosed certain areas and thus used a strategy which has been known as 'closure'. Modern occupations sometimes use the associative strategy – they cooperate with others until they are strong enough to make social and occupational demarcations, to enclose a certain area of interest.

The profession as a historic phenomenon

In the sociological research on professionalization, there has been a tendency to construct an a-historical and timeless concept of 'the professions'. However, what have been seen as characteristic for professions in the Anglo-Saxon context (they have clients and not employers, there is a market orientation, and so on) has differed from what has been seen as characteristic for continental, state-bound professions.[2] According to this problematique, we can either choose a vague or a concise definition of 'the profession'.

In modern society, according to Wilensky, professional organizations can be seen as hybrid organizations,[3] which contain professional as well as trade-union interests. This phenomenon also embraces modern occupations trying to become 'professional'. Instead of using a wide concept, referring to too many different forms of social phenomena, I shall, like Parry and Parry,[4] use the concept 'profession' for a specific phenomenon during a period in the development of the capitalist state.

The shaman, the priest and the knight at certain times had a specific status, since they could offer special competence to different groups in society. They had a special knowledge of the religious, symbolic language or of special war techniques. We could call these occupations 'proto-professions'.

When peasant, feudal societies were transformed into industrialized, capitalist societies[5] both the bourgeoisie and the proletariat organized themselves. Trade unions and professional organizations can then be looked upon as two different forms of occupationally based organizations for social control, albeit with different aims. During this period physicians, lawyers and engineers create their professional organizations.

With the welfare state after World War II, new occupations were created; for example, psychologists (the first occupation created from university-based education), educational and vocational counsellors, graduates from schools of social studies, computer specialists and others. An older occupation like the journalistic occupation, is changing with the new mass-media technology and becoming more and more important for the transformation of knowledge and ideology in society. For all of these occupations, except for the computer specialist (as yet), formal education plays a significant role. We could look upon these occupations as 'post-professions'. But to call them 'professions' in the old sense would be to miss the point and the strength of 'profession' as a historical and sociological concept, even if these later occupations are examples of occupations with a practical orientation and a theoretical basis of knowledge.

The scientification of occupations

The term 'profession' also has an ideological bias,[6] and, therefore, arguments have been given that the concept 'profession' should be abolished in favour of the concept 'scientification of occupations'.[7] Of course there is a tendency in modern society that occupations to an ever-increasing extent begin to use a scientific language, that they strive to build up their own research facilities and that the education is transposed to a university level. In Sweden it has been said (since 1977) that university education should 'rest upon a scientific ground'. This acknowledges that more occupations now are getting an abstract basis of knowledge but also that they very actively work to build up their own research competence and thus themselves are able to produce occupationally relevant theoretical and empirical knowledge.

In a way these developments can be seen as 'scientification' of occupations. But the ambition to develop occupationally relevant research can also be seen as an aspiration for professionalization, depending on the concrete context and conditions for the occupation. As we shall see below, there are specific differences between the process of scientification and the process of professionalization. The process of professionalization can include scientification, but scientification does not necessarily include professionalization.

There is, furthermore, a difference between earlier professions which had a specific base of knowledge, working to build up their own organizations (which were not research-oriented, primarily), and the modern occupations which have their organizations but are searching for their specific body of knowledge. However, first we shall look at different strategies for social mobility.

Alliance strategy and other strategies for collective social mobility

The strength of the concept 'professionalization' lies in the perspective of professionalization as being a strategy for collective mobility, not for individual mobility.[8] The strategies hitherto discussed have been 'closure' and 'usurpation'[9] respectively, and 'assimilation' and 'reduction of internal competition'. If it is not possible for an occupation to keep back other organized interests within its own field of work, it is possible to assimilate these organized interests and thus neutralize them.[10] Not only reduction of competition between occupational groups but also internal reduction of competition have been analysed.[11] Finally, there is one perspective that emphasizes the advantages of partnership between academic-oriented education and practical-oriented occupational education from the students' point of view, as they can acquire both theoretical and practical knowledge.[12]

Traditional professionalization as upward, collective social mobility differs from trade-unionist strategies because its purpose is to cross class boundaries, which is not the case for trade-unionist strategies. It is also understandable that an occupational group which has been successful in organizing itself around a body of knowledge uses the 'closure' strategy. But is this a useful strategy for an occupational group which still is in either a subordinate or middle position? We think that it is not. Instead, we will argue that the associative strategy has an explanatory potential. This strategy entails that an occupational group during a period of time makes associations with other occupational groups or (for example) with certain research institutions in society. In Sweden there is one very good historical example of this strategy: at the end of the nineteenth century primary school teachers used an associative strategy concerning sex role but, later on, the male primary teachers used a closure strategy towards the female primary teachers.[13] The associative strategy is a kind of opening strategy which can be used by an occupational group to strengthen its status. This can be used either before they are strong enough to use a closure strategy, or during periods when they already have been using it but are weakened. The associative strategy is a means of reducing conflicts and mobilizing resources.

As was mentioned earlier, traditional professional organizations differ from trade-unionist organizations as they strive to cross class boundaries. But they also differ because the professional organizations first and foremost struggle to get control over a field of work and a body of knowledge, while the trade-union form of organization has the purpose of gaining strength in, for instance, wage negotiations. However, in the modern labour market these two forms and purposes are mixed, and we can see new 'hybrid organizations', as Wilensky called them.

This makes the picture even more complicated. Occupational groups now trying to professionalize themselves endeavour at the same time to gain control over a body of knowledge, a field of work and strength in their negotiations against their counterparts in the wage negotiations. Furthermore, the professionalization projects within these hybrid organizations aim to reach traditional trade-unionist strength from a class basis, and through upward social and collective mobility cross the class borders with the help of professional strength. Modern projects of professionalization entail different and even contradictory tendencies.

In spite of these tendencies, we think that it is meaningful to talk about 'professionalization' as a tendency in modern society – the aspirations from occupational groups to gain control over certain areas of knowledge (diplomas, credentials and so on) and work (legitimation) as well as social status. The concept 'scientification of occupations' can be used for another societal phenomenon: rationalized and formalized knowledge plays an important role in high-tech society, and the control of the production of knowledge grows more important. The difference between professionalization and scientification is that the former refers to an occupational group which tries to reach both social status and occupational control over its field of work and its basis of knowledge, while the latter refers to the control over the production of knowledge and the language used (the occupational discourse). An occupation can have both status and control over its field of work, though no control over the production of knowledge. In the following this will be exemplified.

Associative strategies in the professionalization process and scientification of an occupation: educational and vocational counsellors and journalists

There are certain basic differences between educational and vocational counsellors (hereafter called 'counsellors') and journalists. One is mainly concerned with providing information about educational and vocational opportunities to young persons individually: the other is mainly occupied with collecting and providing information about news, and so on, to collectives. But there are also differences of more fundamental importance. We distinguish some old and some (relatively) new occupations and, further, occupations within the state (federal) sector and within the market sector. From such considerations the following table is developed:

	Old occupation	New occupation
State sector	Teachers	Counsellors
Market sector	Journalists	Computer specialists

What we want to discuss here is an old occupation within the market sector, and a new occupation within the state sector. These two occupations have been shaped, and shaped themselves, during different historical and societal conditions, and thus we can expect different traditions and ideologies. For a long time journalism was a male-dominated occupation, but during recent years around 50 per cent of the journalism students have been women. The counsellor students, since the occupation changed from 'career teaching' to 'educational and vocational guidance' have been mainly female, and today around 80 per cent or more of the students in Sweden for this occupation are women. The average age of counsellor students is ten years older than the average age of students of journalism.[14]

Professionalization of counselling in Sweden

The emergence of a societal function of educational and vocational counselling can partly be explained by certain structural changes in society, not least within the educational system, partly by those strategies developed by counsellors themselves.

In 1902 an office for a work-related information service was set up by the authorities for employment exchange in Munich, and this year is seen as the birth of vocational guidance. In Switzerland, Holland and France this initiative was repeated, but it was in Britain that vocational guidance was legalized for the first time (in 1909). In Sweden regular vocational guidance was established by the Federal Labour Market Commission only in the 1940s. Advisers within the primary and secondary schools were trained as careers teachers, and the responsibility was divided between the National Labour Market Board and the National Board of Education.

The new nine-year compulsory comprehensive school, when the former elementary school and the former lower secondary school were combined, also led to a great many new options and voluntarily added subjects (Lgr–62, the official school curriculum from 1962). The educational part of educational and vocational guidance increased. The individuals' own interests and their aptitudes were seen as the most important factors, and aptitude tests were used by the career teachers. This was motivated by theories of individual capacities.

At a Nordic seminar on vocational guidance in Finland in 1967 emphasis was laid instead on the possibilities for individuals to realize their ideas and hopes. Private interviews became more important than tests, and this was motivated by therapeutic psychological theories (Rogers' ideas of guidance in therapy were applied to educational and vocational guidance).[15] The new municipal adult education also increased the numbers of the students.

In 1971 an integrated upper secondary school was founded (an integration of the former upper secondary school, continuation school and vocational school), the career teachers were to become counsellors and a new organization for educational and vocational counsellors was formed. Increased student rolls and growing youth unemployment were factors in transforming vocational orientation and preparation into working-life orientation, a much broader concept. The societal problems and the political radicalization led to a greater emphasis on sociological theories about the relation between education and the labour market and working life.

With the university reform of 1977 the training for counsellors was changed. Counsellors' training, which had formerly been 40 weeks at most, was now 60 or 120 weeks. At the end of the 1970s a continuation course of 20 weeks was instituted as a preparation for research work within counselling. This was done in association with the institutes of education at the universities.

During the 1980s the conditions for the counsellors changed again. As the expansion of the school system became the most important task (the integrated upper secondary school had twenty-five different lines of education and around 400 specialized courses in 1984), counselling for education became more important than counselling for work. The rate of youth unemployment reached its climax in the beginning of the 1980s, but has now declined. However, during the 1980s the counsellors' own organizations fought for full employment for a counsellor at one school, and also sought for counsellors to be allowed, and educated, to teach different subjects. In 1983 parliament legislated along these lines, and counsellor education was transformed to one single education for all counsellors (120 weeks over three years). Thereby the circle seems to be closed; pedagogical ideas are today emphasized and the counsellors' competence is once again to be based on educational competence as was the case for the older career teachers.

Three dissertations on counselling have been presented, albeit not written by counsellors. There have been different attempts to develop further the ties to research. First, this aim was to be effected by means of association with pedagogical institutes, but later also attempts were made to associate with sociological institutions as well as with psychological institutions in order to achieve this goal.

The development of counselling has been dependent on the changing nature of relations between education and the labour market and on the expansion of the educational system. A new field was opened up by the state in Sweden, and the counsellors' own organizations have been very active in strengthening their positions. Up to now the counsellors have been subordinated to teachers as to status at schools, and education as well as research have been seen as important tools for the counsellors to take control of their field of work, their knowledge basis and their own production of new, occupationally relevant knowledge. In this process the education departments for counsellors have tried to associate with different research institutes and different disciplines within the social sciences. The counsellors have used both an associative strategy and a closure strategy: they have tried to associate with others, and they have built up their own (occupationally more or less relevant) education and succeeded in reaching some kind of indirect legitimation (which can be seen in advertisements for counselling jobs), and they have finally tried to enclose a field of work and a specific knowledge basis – called counselling and choice of career. It is, however, doubtful that they have succeeded in this (and we will reconsider it below in the summary).

The scientification of journalism in Sweden

The occupation of journalist is an old one. For a long time journalists were educated in the craft through apprenticeship. Though this was the case for most of them, some were academics with specialist competence within a specific field. During the last two or three decades the journalistic task has changed profoundly through the new mass media (radio and TV). The journalist is more visible today than he was before, and plays a dominant role in many different areas where information is to be transmitted to the public.

In 1959 an institute for journalism was created in Stockholm. It offered a one-year, post-secondary education. In 1962 another institute opened in Gothenburg. To be admitted to the course, one term of pre-training practice was required. In 1967 the institutes were reformed into institutes of higher education, and the training was prolonged to two years (80 weeks), including one term of practical work. The students were admitted after selection through tests.

As a consequence of the university reform of 1977, journalistic education became a function of the universities, and selection through tests was replaced by selection from examination results. Today journalists can also be trained at other kinds of institutions: at the Dramatic Institute, at the College for Higher Education of Photographers, at a university course of cultural education or at other institutes of higher education dealing with information. In the year 1987/1988 there were also twenty-three adult residential colleges which offered different sorts of education, from common media education to a one-year course in journalism. A government commission suggested in 1987 that the selection tests should be used again in the university-based journalistic education, instead of marks from the integrated upper secondary school, in order to increase the quality of the students.

Another road leading to the occupation of journalism was re-opened in 1985: the so-called 'trainee education'. This form had existed before, and was then named 'volunteer education'. A continuation course at the institutes for higher journalist education was also created in 1975 (20 weeks). This was open to all students who had the basic education in journalism (80 weeks) and had one year of practice, as well as for those who did not have any higher education but who had four years of practice. However, very few journalists chose this course, and it was closed (in Gothenburg in 1982, in Stockholm the year after). Instead, different forms of special courses were offered by the university institutes.

In line with the ideas presented in the government Bill of

Research,[16] a chair of journalism was created in Stockholm in July 1988 and the first professor was appointed early in 1990. The professed motive was that, in spite of journalism's profound function in modern society, there was a great lack of knowledge concerning the conditions of journalism and the journalistic means of expression. With this chair, a basis for a research done by journalists has been created. Before this, mass media research was mainly carried out by the institutes of political science. There is also a proposal that higher education for journalists should offer a course on research of 20 weeks (comparable to the continuation course for counsellors).[17]

Counselling and journalism – a summary of strategies

When comparing counselling with journalism as regards the acquisition of knowledge, we can find certain similarities. In both cases the educational institution plays an important role. It seems that the educational institutions have taken over the role that the traditional professional organizations had in protecting the knowledge basis and in discharging and developing the professionally relevant knowledge, which is not very surprising seen from the point of view of a very active state.

But this (too short) overview also pinpoints some important differences. The journalists have managed to acquire a chair, which is intended to give an opportunity for journalists to do their own research. They have been successful in using a closure strategy to enclose this area from others. Counsellors, on the other hand, still have to rely on other research institutions and therefore have had to rely on an associative strategy and cooperate with these research institutions to build up their own specific knowledge basis. Further, journalists nowadays have a relatively high status in society, while counsellors still have a relatively low status.

There is also another difference worthy of note. The occupation of journalist is an old occupation which has developed its specific competence within the market sector for more than a century. The counsellor's occupation is a new one, shaped and developed within the state sector, and has developed over four decades, with different aims and directions. Journalists have managed to enclose a field of knowledge, something which counsellors have not been able to do. This is mirrored in their education: the education for journalists consists of 80 weeks of education (one term being 20 weeks), of which 40 weeks include 'journalism'; that is, 50 per cent of their total education.[18] The education for counsellors takes 120 weeks, in which the specific field of knowledge – choice of career and guidance – comprises 23 weeks: that is, 17.5 per cent of their total education. If we include here also public administration and the organization of counselling (4 weeks) and a continuation course (4 weeks), we will still only reach 25.8 per cent of their total education.[19] Thus the evidence indicates that counsellors have not yet found their specific competence, their own specific field of knowledge.

We can the interpret the counsellors' ambition as a project of professionalization: they are trying to achieve status; they are seeking their specific knowledge basis; they are trying to establish research and trying to get control over their field of work. Journalists, on the other hand, have already got a status position and control over their field of work as well as their knowledge basis.[20] Their ambition can best be understood as scientification of an occupation. The journalists have been successful in using a closure strategy, but the counsellors have had to use both associative and closure strategies.

In this chapter some basic ideas have been formulated and exemplified from Swedish material. Of course, they have not been tested in a stricter sense. But the ideas could be looked upon as attempts to sort out some modern phenomena, which differ from earlier conceptions of professionalization processes, and as an outline against which to analyse these phenomena. There is much more work to be done, but the evidence presented indicates that it is fruitful to analyse the occupations within the middle layers of society and that the developments in these layers signify the beginning of radical changes within society.

Notes

1 Parkin, 1979; Murphy, 1988.

2 Rueschemeyer, 1980:311–325.

3 Wilensky, 1964:137–158.

4 Parry and Parry, 1976:78.

5 In the years 1800–1945, after which the welfare state and corporative capitalism are developed (Torstendahl, 1984a).

6 Saks, 1983:1–21.

7 Gesser, 1985:246–247.

8 Parry and Parry, 1976:76–79.

9 Parkin, 1979.

10 Parry and Parry, 1976:78.

11 Wilensky, 1964:145; see also the chapter by Klas Åmark, though he has a different theoretical perspective from that of Wilensky.

12 Becher, 1990.

13 Florin, 1987. Florin does not use the concept 'associative strategy', but she describes the process very well.

14 See SOU, 1987:50, *Högskolans journalistutbildning*.

15 This is clearly expressed in Person, Lindblom and Odmark, 1980.

16 Government Bill of Research, 1986–1987:80.

17 SOU, 1987:50.

18 It includes: mass media knowledge, law, ethics, psychology/social psychology, criticism of the sources, radio, TV, practice (7 weeks), language, theory of style and rhetoric, elementary journalism, reportage and interview, research and news service, sources and information through data storage units, news hunting, editing, graphical representation, modern history and novels. The rest of the education includes social sciences (20 weeks) and a deeper course – media (20 weeks) (SOU, 1987:50, p. 99).

19 The first-mentioned 23 weeks include: cultural patterns, socialization, qualification and choice of career (5 weeks), theory, models and methods for guidance (8 weeks) and practice (10 weeks). Then there is commerce, industry and occupations (20 weeks) and the rest is: education, information and teaching (20 weeks), didactics and methods of teaching (8 weeks) (Lindh, 1988:39). There are of course different kinds of problems in this kind of comparison – where to draw the demarcation line? However, I think that we can accept these figures if we concentrate upon the main core of the knowledge as it is defined by the respective occupations.

20 Journalists are now also penetrating ('usurpating') the traditional work of typesetters, and the two occupations are involved in borderline fighting (how to make demarcations between their occupations).

9

Beyond a sub-set: the professional aspirations of manual workers in France, the United States and Britain

Michael Burrage

The separation of an elite, a word and a discipline

Throughout Europe, all occupations were once corporately organized, in similar ways, for similar purposes. In England, in the late seventeenth century a few elite occupations which thought themselves more learned, more honourable, more independent than the rest began to distinguish themselves as professions. Over succeeding generations, the English word 'profession' came to be used less as a synonym of occupation and instead came to refer only to this sub-set of occupations.[1] At the same time, it began to accumulate certain distinctive, evaluative connotations, referring to one or other of the ways in which this sub-set were thought to be, or claimed to be, distinctive.

When, much later, the professions became the subject of academic investigation, these connotations stymied sociologists' attempts to define a profession. They could not agree on which one deserved priority in an objective scientific definition of the term. Some could not accept that the claims of professions should be allowed to define their field of enquiry and yet could not bring themselves to ignore them entirely since, if they did, the field of enquiry would itself have disappeared.

De facto therefore, they came to work with three categories of occupations; a select minority whose claims to professional status are never disputed, a larger group of occupations that claim professional status and may in some circumstances be accorded it, and the vast majority of routine non-manual or manual occupations which have never claimed professional status and never been offered it. Despite the rather vaguely defined intermediate category, students of the professions agreed at least about routine non-manual and manual occupations. These they felt sure were outside their field of interest and properly belonged to labour historians or sociologists who were interested in class formation and stratification. A sharp disciplinary boundary therefore developed between the study of professional occupations and non-professional occupations.

There has been virtually no communication across this boundary and no relationship therefore between the study of organized labour and the study of the organized professions. In recent times students of the stratification have, it is true, often sought to identify the class position of professions, but more, one suspects, because it would have been embarrassing to exclude the ever-expanding number of professional occupations from their analyses of the class structure than from any interest in the actions, institutions or strategies of the professions. Obviously, there are important differences between the organized professions and organized labour, and this disciplinary boundary is therefore often a useful one, but for several reasons it seems doubtful whether a permanent demarcation between these two fields of enquiry can be justified.

To begin with, the ways and means of the divergence of professional and non-professional occupations from a common institutional framework presumably has much to tell us about both. Moreover, this divergence did not proceed uniformly. In some countries manual workers evidently preferred to remain organized as occupations, and sought, just like the professions, to control admission to, and training for, their occupation, to demarcate and defend what they considered to be their work jurisdiction, to enforce their trade rules and to defend and enhance their status. In any case, even when they organized on an enterprise, industry or class basis rather than as members of an occupation, they often displayed the same occupational loyalties and aspirations that motivated the collective action of lawyers, doctors and engineers. There is, in short, a kinship between professional and non-professional occupations that merits investigation. In recent times this kinship has become more noticeable as professions have adopted trade-union strategies and forms of organization while more and more non-professional occupations have sought recognition as professions.

This pattern of divergence and convergence rather suggests that the differences between professional and non-professional occupations are not differences in kind at all but historically contingent differences of strategy. There is a case therefore for looking beyond the professional sub-set, and periodically at least, comparing the two kinds of occupation and tracing their divergent or convergent paths and seeing what they may have in common.

This chapter is an exploratory step in that direction, a feasibility study. It outlines the history of the professions in these three countries alongside that of occupationally based trade unions. By so doing, it hopes to trace what one might call 'the professional theme', or 'professional project' in the histories of three labour movements, when trade unions have organized as occupations and, like the professions, sought to control admission to their ranks, to defend their work jurisdiction, to regulate the work behaviour of their members and collectively to defend the status of their members against neighbouring occupations.[2] This chapter attempts therefore to provide a sketch of a comparative history of occupations and ends with a discussion of some of the leads it might provide for future research.

France: the realization of Le Chapelier's ideal

The history of professional and manual worker organization in modern France starts from a common point since the corporate institutions of both were swept away between 1789 and 1793. When the Constituent Assembly abolished the guilds, some of their journeymen assumed that the Revolution intended to free them from the control of their masters. They therefore organized quite openly as independent brotherhoods and societies, and continued to meet to preserve their trade rules and defend their collective interests. The carpenters of Paris, in fact, used the same hall as the Jacobin Club. On 14 June 1791, however, by passing the *loi Le Chapelier*, the *constituants* made it clear that the abolition of the corporate institutions of the professions and the guilds, also applied to any form of organization which sought to organize and govern members of the same occupation, including the journeymen societies.[3]

This law has frequently been described as a piece of class legislation. Soboul, for instance, considered it 'one of capitalism's master strokes', as though the bourgeois leaders of the Revolution were specifically attacking the infant trade-union and working-class movement.[4] In fact, it was merely a reiteration of the revolutionary ideals of equality and the sovereignty of the people, and for this reason obtained immediate, and virtually unanimous, support, including that of Robespierre and the *montagnards*. Moreover, as the experience of the legal and medical profession demonstrates, the law was entirely consistent with the previous decisions of the assembly. The journeymen societies were exclusive and therefore deemed incompatible with the principle of equality, and they had their own form of government and were therefore also found to be incompatible with the sovereignty of the people. One can be sure that these considerations were uppermost in the minds of the *constituants*, because they did not prohibit other forms of worker assembly or organization and did not interfere with the clubs or sections or, for that matter, with street meetings and demonstrations.

After the passage of the *loi Le Chapelier* there were, supposedly, no organized or regulated occupations in France. The practice of law and medicine were, as the saying went, 'free', and manual workers were similarly 'free'. However, after a very short interval, the state began to reconstruct professional institutions. In 1792, the Legislative Assembly established an Ecole des Travaux Publiques for the training of engineers, which shortly thereafter became the Ecole Polytechnique. In 1794 the Convention created three *écoles de santé* to provide *officiers de santé* for the revolutionary armies. Private medical practice, however, remained entirely unregulated until 1804, when new admission requirements, new medical school curricula and the entirely new division of medical labour were written into law. Medical licensing and medical practice were henceforth to be controlled by the Ministry of the Interior and the police.[5] These reforms pre-empted any professional or regulatory role for practitioners comparable to that performed by their corporate institutions under the *ancien régime*. Although medical discussion groups and learned societies were tolerated, any form of association which sought to represent or regulate the profession as a whole remained illegal.

The reconstruction of the law differs from that of engineering and medicine for, though the revolutionary regimes recognized the need for tribunals to settle disputes and punish criminals, they did not believe that these required specialist legal experts and hence sought to laicize legal proceedings and made no attempt to revive legal education. Napoleon as First Consul and Emperor did not share his predecessors' belief in the possibilities of a law without lawyers and therefore revived formal, hierarchical systems of courts manned by trained legal experts. He shared, however, their dislike of trained, specialist advocates and therefore made no provision in his new system for any corporate body of practising advocates. The state might need trained lawyers, its citizens did not. Thus, despite the reconstruction of courts and law schools, private legal practice remained unregulated and unorganized.

The abolition of the orders of advocates and the years of unregulated practice had not, however, eliminated all sense of professional loyalty and obligation. Surviving members of the Paris order still regularly met in the Marais district of the city – indeed, had begun to do so, informally and covertly, immediately after the abolition of their orders and under the Directory had even organized their own schools. After the reconstruction of the legal system these *avocats du Marais* began to petition the Emperor to allow them to re-establish their orders, along with all the other institutions by which they had once controlled the practice of law, the *bâtonnier, tableau* and *stage*. In 1810 the Emperor finally relented, and allowed the orders to be re-established, though they remained under strict state control.[6] The three reconstructed professions were therefore all state-controlled; the difference between them was one of degree and of form. Engineers were trained and employed (and thereby controlled) by the state. Doctors were trained by the state, an elite employed by it and the unorganized majority supervised by the Ministry of the Interior and the police. Advocates were trained partly by the state and partly by their own apprenticeship system; none were employed by the state and they were controlled by their revived orders, acting under the surveillance of the *procureurs généraux*.

Some of the old guilds responsible for the supply of food to the city of Paris were also revived by Napoleon, so the advocates were not strictly speaking unique. And there is a further, more interesting parallel in that journeymen societies also survived, as the advocates had initially done, as underground organizations. They, however, did not immediately 'go public' and petition for legal recognition because the provisions of the *loi Le Chapelier* had been reinforced by the Napoleonic criminal code, and such an action might itself have provoked investigation or severe punishment. In any case, the journeymen did not want a restoration of the *ancien régime* since that would merely have restored the authority of their former masters over them. They preferred therefore to remain underground. In the later years of the restored monarchy, however, they began to emerge informally and their more innocent functions – their mutual benefit funds, their processions and masses – received informal approval from both the church and the state.[7] Their other activities, such as collective action in defence of their professional interests and, of course, their political activities, remained secret.

There is evidence, however, that they operated as professional bodies effectively and on a very wide scale under the restored monarchy and subsequently under Louis Philippe. In particular, they enforced rules of apprenticeship, of *compagnonnage*, and routinely administered the oaths and performed the initiation ceremonies that they had inherited from the guilds. It is also evident that their former masters often negotiated with them and routinely made use of their corporate institutions, such as their *mères* who were responsible for sheltering itinerant *compagnons*, and *rouleurs* who checked their credentials and found them work. Moreover, masters and men had a common interest in identifying, and if possible destroying, those who sought to practise the trade without regard to its rules, such as the *confectionneurs* of the apparel trades who made low-quality, standardized products and the *marchandeurs* or sub-contractors in the building trades.[8]

Some idea of the strength and solidarity of their occupationally based journeymen societies under the two monarchies can be gauged from the police reports of their strike activities. Their strength and solidarity were visibly demonstrated in February 1848 when the massed membership marched in orderly procession, behind their trade banners, through the streets of Paris. This spectacle is sometimes thought, more than anything else, to account for the loss of nerve of the personnel of the July Monarchy, including Louis Philippe himself, and therefore for the collapse of his regime. In any event, the protests and the demands of the organizations of skilled workers dominated the early days of the Second Republic.[9]

Once, however, they were ensconced in the Luxembourg Commission under the chairmanship of Louis Blanc, they were preoccupied with their primary concerns; that is, with negotiating collective agreements with their employers on matters of day-to-day interest to their members such as job placement, hours of work, price lists and the like. The representatives of the trade societies in the commission appear not to have been concerned with larger, revolutionary issues at all, with the new form of government, with educational reforms, with the condition of those who were not members of their trades, so much so that Louis Blanc was obliged to remind them that 'you are not here as blacksmiths, joiners, machinists, you are here as men of the people, who are brothers and who wish to carry out the liberation of the people'.[10]

This appeal evidently fell on deaf ears and thereafter the active, popular support for the Revolution shifted towards other kinds of organization, to the political clubs, to street demonstrators and to immigrants to the city seeking employment in the newly created national workshops. The 'glorious' June days seem to have belonged more to these groups than to the journeymen's societies, though after Louis Napoleon's coup every kind of worker organization was suppressed. The journeymen or skilled worker societies could not however be eliminated as readily as political clubs, since they were, so to speak, being revived and reconstituted every minute of the working day. In a short while, therefore, they were once more performing their traditional functions. In the later, liberal phase of the Second Empire they again received a degree of official recognition and support. In 1864 trade unions were partially legalized and these societies therefore once again became half public, respectable and law-abiding organizations and half secret and subversive.[11]

The 1864 legislation, however, also encouraged the formation of another kind of trade union, one that had little interest in enforcing trade rules or defending trade interests and instead sought to recruit all workers and to emancipate them all by revolutionary action. Thus, there were two rival forms of worker organization in France; the professional, whose institutions, strategy and ideology were rooted in the *ancien régime* and the revolutionary syndicalist, a product of the Revolution. This division was implicit in the *loi Le Chapelier*, had appeared briefly in 1848, and had now, in the later years of the Second Empire, re-emerged. The division was evident during the Paris Commune, in which revolutionary, class organizations took the lead while trade unions remained passive bystanders. It continued during the early years of the Third Republic though, since both kinds of labour organization were still subject to various legal restraints, they seem to have recognized their common interests and worked reasonably harmoniously.

As soon, however, as trade unions were fully legalized in 1884, the two kinds of organization went separate ways, and competed with each other openly and often bitterly, for the support of the workers, in particular for the support of the skilled workers.[12] This struggle continued for two decades, and to the overwhelming majority of French workers the revolutionary, class form of organization proved more popular than the elitist, self-interested professional form. The victory of revolutionary syndicalism was finally confirmed by the Confédération Générale du Travail which, at its congress in Amiens in 1906, prohibited future affiliated unions organizing on an occupational basis.

In a curious and belated manner therefore, the ideal implicit in the *loi Le Chapelier* was finally realized by the workers themselves. Thereafter, apart from some sections of the print trade, occupation has rarely been the basis of organized collective action for French manual workers. Their trade unions have never been particularly interested in professional matters, in upholding apprenticeship rules, for example, in dealing with shop-floor grievances of their members or in protecting the jurisdictions or improving the status of particular occupational groups. Everything they have gained in the workplace, up to and including the Auroux laws of 1982, has been by the grace and favour of the state and indeed often on the initiative of the state rather than the trade unions.[13] They, and more certainly their leaders, have concerned themselves with the interests of the entire working class and for this task they were inspired by the tradition of revolutionary action rather than by the customs and institutions of their craft predecessors.

The freedom of association granted by the Third Republic also had significant consequences for the professions. Under the previous repressive regimes, the orders of advocates had served as a refuge for the political opponents of the regime, a sort of functional equivalent of an opposition party. Once political parties were legalized, however, they lost this heroic role and in the process seem also to have lost some of their status and legitimacy. At any rate, in the early eighties, a number of attempts were made in the National Assembly to abolish the orders altogether.[14] They survived but as isolated anomalies, nostalgically hoping to restore the degree of self-government they had enjoyed under the *ancien régime*.

The other professions had no such option since the state had long since assumed the functions of their professional bodies. They could therefore only organize to defend their economic interests and for this reason adopted a trade-union form of organization. The doctors were the first to do so in order to counter the threat from mutual benefit societies and insurance companies, which acted like surrogate employers by fixing rates for medical treatment. The doctors responded by organizing trade unions for collective bargaining purposes. In the early twentieth century engineers also joined trade unions,[15] and in 1926 some advocates formed a national association which, though not a trade union, was, in contrast to the professional concerns of their orders, intended to represent and defend advocates' collective economic interests.[16]

Freedom of association under the Third Republic did not therefore lead to association on an occupational basis, either among manual workers or among professionals. Manual occupations participated in national politics by discarding and transcending narrow professional loyalties, much as lawyers, doctors, pharmacists and others during the great Revolution had expressed their commitment to revolutionary ideas by inciting the destruction of their own professions. No profession sought to imitate the orders of advocates. Some like the engineers, *notaires* and other *officiers ministériels*, were, one way or another, comfortably organized 'within' the state. Others adopted trade-union forms of organization. The occupational form of collective action, which had seemed acceptable under the authoritarian regimes, in other words, became under the Third Republic increasingly identified with the anti-republican, extreme right.[17]

It remained a part – indeed, the central part – of right-wing ideology, until the catastrophe of 1940. It was then adapted by the apologists of the Vichy regime who blamed France's defeat on the excessive egalitarianism and individualism of the great Revolution, which they claimed had undermined the moral unity of French society. As part of its 'national revolution' in 1941, the Vichy regime tried to revive occupational self-government and arranged the entire labour force into self-governing professional families.[18] This forced professionalization included the creation of an Ordre des Médecins to regulate medical practice, and a number of similar orders to regulate other professions.[19] These were, however, state agencies in a corporate dress, and merely assumed the professional functions once performed by the Ministry of the Interior and the police. They have continued to perform them to the present day.

The United States: suspects in a new democratic order

The spirit, though not the exact form, of English professional association and self-regulation was carried to the American colonies, and since there were no formal declarations or enactments against them during the revolutionary period, bar associations and medical societies continued to develop their representative and regulatory functions immediately thereafter. The legal profession, however, was the subject of much popular criticism as 'aristocratic', 'elitist', and 'undemocratic' and this criticism continued until the state legislatures, one by one, removed or reduced to insignificance their admission requirements. Massachusetts, the bastion of bar organization in the colonial and post-independence period, finally did so in 1835. As elsewhere, the bar associations then collapsed.[20]

Starting somewhat later, a similar movement led to the repeal of all medical licensing legislation between 1817 and 1850. Some medical societies survived, though only as elite, voluntary learned societies rather than regulatory, professional associations.[21] In the present context, however, it is sufficient to note, first, that right through the middle of the nineteenth century there was no form of professional regulation among either American lawyers or doctors.

Very few craft or trade societies had established themselves on a permanent footing by the 1820s and 1830s. None had obtained statutory support for their rules. In Boston in the 1820s, the mechanics, coopers and housewrights had sought legislative support for apprenticeship and other trade rules, but their applications were rejected, in the face of opposition of merchants who argued to the city council's satisfaction that 'such rules would be of no benefit to the community'.[22] Consequently there were no grounds for political attacks on the organizations of manual workers comparable to those being made on the legal and medical professions. These organizations were, however, subject to repeated attacks from rival forms of trade-union organization, which sought to unite workers on some basis other than that of occupation and to generate a loyalty other than that centred on trade or professional interest. This inter-union rivalry is a more or less continuous theme in American labour history, but there were four major forms of rival organization.

The first arose in the 1820s and 1830s, and they may be described generically as workingmen's associations, though in fact they operated under a variety of names, and even, which is rather confusing in the present context, called themselves 'trades' unions'. There is, however, a clear difference in the aims, methods and composition of the two kinds of organization, since the workingmen's associations or trades' unions sought either to federate or merge existing trade societies and to recruit all kinds of workers irrespective of the trade to which they belonged. The first such body, the Mechanics Union of Trade Associations, was established in Philadelphia in 1827, and initially depended almost entirely on the support of craft or trade societies, but then decided to appeal to factory operatives, day labourers, farmers and all who are exploited by 'the rich who never labor . . . the possessors . . . the idle capitalists'. The secretary of General Trades' Union, a similar kind of organization, founded in New York in 1833, declared that 'true unions should embrace every citizen whose daily exertions from the highest Artist to the lowest Labourer, are his means of subsistence'. The secretary of the Boston Trades' Union, formed in the following year, likewise argued that 'there are but two parties in our country . . . all who labor whether as boss or journeyman and the rich men, the professional men and all who now live, or who intend hereafter to live without useful labor, depending on the sweat of their neighbour's brow for support'.[23]

To begin with, therefore, the workingmen's associations depended on, and cooperated with, the trade societies, but they soon demonstrated that they had little interest in the ordinary business of trade societies such as apprenticeship and demarcation rules, organizing black lists and conducting collective bargaining. Instead, they were concerned with a wide range of reform issues – among them, the extension of public education, temperance, the abolition of slavery, penal reform, public ownership of utilities and the election of public officials. They also, incidentally, joined the attacks on the privileges of the professions. In promoting these causes they were mainly engaged in propaganda activities, publishing newspapers and manifestos, organizing demonstrations and mass meetings, and endorsing or even nominating political candidates. Their influence and success is difficult to judge, but the important point here is that they were all ephemeral bodies that soon lost the support of the trade societies and disappeared. When they had gone, the trade societies continued in their old ways and sought to protect the professional interests of their members in their town or city. In the decades before the Civil War, led by the printers, the locomotive drivers and the cigar makers, they began to establish rudimentary national organizations and occasionally held national conventions.

The second major alternative to the craft form of labour organization was the Knights of Labor which was founded in 1873 and which grew into a mass labour organization in the seventies and eighties. Like the workingmen's associations, the Knights initially depended on the support of trade societies, and benefited from the collapse of many of them in the depression of the seventies. Many of the Knights' first 'local assemblies' were, in fact, confined to the members of a particular trade. Soon, however, the Knights authorized mixed assemblies whose members were drawn from many trades or from no trade at all – indeed, they would enrol anyone other than 'lawyers, gamblers, bankers and liquor dealers'. Initially, this indiscriminate recruiting policy proved successful and the Knights grew rapidly. In 1885 they had reached 111,000 and, after a dramatically successful strike against the Gould railroads, zoomed to 700,000 in the following year. This was their high point. Subsequent strikes were often ill-advised and poorly organized, and the relationship between the mixed and trade assemblies proved an uneasy one, since the former were often indifferent or hostile to the interests of the latter and resented what they perceived as their privileged position in the organization.[24]

At the same time, the craft unions had begun to recover from the calamitous defeats of the seventies. In 1881 they held a national convention to consider the formation of some kind of federal, coordinating body. In 1886 they met again, provoked largely it seems by the spectacular growth of the Knights whom they had come to see as the enemies of trade unions, bent on their destruction. After this 1886 meeting, they finally established an enduring national organization, the American Federation of Labor (AFL), and then successfully appealed to the disaffected trade assemblies of the Knights. The counter-attack, along with further unsuccessful strikes organized by the Knights and the anarchist bombing in the Haymarket, Chicago, in 1886, with which the Knights were unfairly but indelibly associated, precipitated a decline from which the Knights never recovered.

In the first decade of the twentieth century, a third challenge came from the Western Federation of Miners, which spurned any form of association with the AFL and created the Western Labor Union for all workers in the West 'irrespective of occupation, nationality, creed or color'.[25] This led in turn to the formation of the Industrial Workers of the World (IWW), the Wobblies, which was divided into thirteen 'departments' which recruited members according to the industry in which they were employed regardless of trade, skill, race or ethnic origin. In contrast to the craft unions, the Wobblies deliberately kept subscriptions low in order to encourage mass recruitment of workers. After a brief and turbulent career the IWW collapsed.

The fourth rival, with the help of the state, finally dispossessed the craft unions and succeeded in organizing American labour on a new basis. Like the workingmen's associations and the Knights, it began within the ranks of the crafts unions themselves. In the early thirties, the leaders of several AFL unions, conscious of the fact that they and other members had thus far only succeeded in recruiting a tiny skilled elite of the labour force and unhappy with the plans of the AFL to recruit workers in the mass production industries, established a Committee of Industrial Organization (CIO) for this purpose. Realizing that the recruiting efforts of this committee would inevitably trespass on craft jurisdictions, the AFL issued an ultimatum to those who had subscribed to it to withdraw or be expelled from the Federation. The rebels, including the Mine Workers, Clothing Workers, and new unions recently organized by the AFL for auto and rubber workers, refused to do so.[26]

State intervention in the form of the National Labor Relations Act of 1933 and the Wagner Act of 1935 enabled the breakaway industrial unions to recruit large numbers of semi- and unskilled workers. Most craft unions, apart from those in the building trades, then abandoned their occupational jurisdiction and began to organize on a plant or industrial basis to compete with their CIO rivals. In the 1960s the remaining craft unions faced a further political and legislative assault on their rules and exclusiveness by civil rights activists and civil rights legislation, in particular the Civil Rights Act of 1964, and as a result occupationally based labour unions have become a rarity in the American labour movement.

The conflict over the proper form of labour organization in the United States therefore resembles the earlier conflict in France. After coexisting in varying states of cooperation, suspicion and competition, state intervention in both cases prompted a bitter, dramatic and relatively brief confrontation between the two forms of labour organization which ended in both cases with the rapid decline of the formerly dominant, occupationally based association. Thereafter, unions in both countries became highly competitive, recruited promiscuously without much regard for any union's occupational jurisdiction. Both have depended on continuing state support and, though they have enjoyed brief periods of mass support, both have been vulnerable and weak in the face of determined employer opposition.

However, while the occupational organizations of manual workers were approaching their demise, it might appear that those of the professions were entering an unprecedented era of power and success following the reorganization of the medical and legal professions in the last decades of the nineteenth century. Over the first two decades of the twentieth, the American Medical Association (AMA) organized its successful campaign to raise the standards of medical education and thereby reduced the number of medical schools and the numbers admitted to medical practice. Shortly thereafter the American Bar Association (ABA) began a similar campaign against the proliferating law schools. Is there a sharp contrast therefore between the failure of occupational organization among manual workers and its success among professionals in twentieth-century America?

To begin to answer this question, we must note that the AMA never exercised any direct power over the medical schools or over admission to medical practice. It exercised power only indirectly by organizing an alliance to support the accreditation of medical schools, an alliance which included the elite medical schools, state medical examiners, state legislatures, the Carnegie Foundation along with the press and, as far as one can judge, public opinion.[27] Thus it was power in a specific context, for a specific purpose and for a limited period. State support for the AMA was therefore limited and conditional and did not extend to their campaigns against homeopaths and other unorthodox practitioners, or to defend the general practitioner against further specialization.[28]

American commentaries on the AMA, from both the left and the right, often convey the impression that it is the most powerful professional organization the world has ever seen. Although it may well be the most powerful professional association the United States has ever seen, in a comparative context it seems more like an energetic, and at times ruthless, lobbying organization which performs rather few professional functions. It became a mass organization of medical practitioners only after World War I and since 1960 has represented only a minority of the profession and has had to compete with a number of other medical associations which are often at cross-purposes with it.[29] Moreover, it occasionally fails to persuade its own member societies to follow its policies. It exercises no 'ethical' disciplinary authority and has been remarkably unsuccessful in protecting medical practitioners against malpractice suits. In recent decades the courts have considered many of the rules of its local societies 'in restraint of trade' and have accordingly struck them down. It has not been able to resist the controls of medical practitioners exercised by hospital management nor those attached to federal medical aid programmes, nor to prevent the emergence of physician assistants, though initially it strongly opposed them.[30] All these facts throw doubt on the conventional American view that the AMA is an especially powerful professional body.

The ABA has exerted still less influence over the legal profession. Its attempts to create an 'accreditation alliance' like the AMA failed, and there is little evidence to suggest that it has been able to exercise any control on admission to legal practice.[31] The manifest failure of bar associations to regulate the behaviour of lawyers within their jurisdictions after World War I led twenty-eight states to create so-called 'integrated' bars, meaning mandatory compulsory membership of a state bar association.[32] Several states later created lay-dominated regulatory commissions attached to the state supreme court for the same reason.[33] There is therefore no settled system of professional government of American lawyers and still much disagreement about the scope and substance of lawyers' ethics.[34]

Since the AMA and ABA are generally regarded as the two most powerful professional bodies in the United States, it seems unlikely that we will find others that have been more successful in regulating admission, training or practice. There are therefore some resemblances between professional and craft organizations in the United States. Both seem to have had difficulty retaining the loyalty of their own members. The early bar associations were attacked by lawyers. The revived ones often competed with one another and even with anti-bar associations.[35] The early medical societies were riven by internal disputes, the later ones by inter-association quarrels.[36] Rival labour organizations were similarly often supported by deserters from the craft unions, and once the state intervened to legalize and support another kind of union, they quickly abandoned the occupational principle. In this nation of 'joiners', occupational associations, controlling the admission and training of new members, exercising regulatory authority over their members and protecting their jurisdictions and status, have never been securely established.

England: homeland of organized occupations

The history of the professions in France and the United States begins with their revolutions and so, in a manner of speaking, does the English. The legal and medical professions were subject to popular attacks during the interregnum comparable to those in revolutionary France and post-revolutionary America, and both Charles II and James II had attempted to exert greater state control over them and all other 'lesser governments' in the kingdom. The threat to their corporate independence was brought to an end by the Glorious Revolution, the return of confiscated and amended charters, and William and Mary's promise to protect the liberties and privileges of the English people.[37]

Thus the English revolution was, from the point of view of the professions, no less significant than the French or American, though its effects were exactly the opposite. Instead of destroying the existing systems of practitioner self-government, it left them intact. Instead of providing an anti-professional ideology, it ended by reinforcing the customary rights and privileges of corporate bodies, such as the Inns of Court and the medical corporations. The modern English legal and medical professions are not therefore, like their French or American counterparts, reconstructed professions. They are medieval institutions whose basic powers and institutions have remained much the same, despite the Industrial Revolution, despite the scientific revolution in medicine of the late nineteenth century, despite mass democracy, and despite the establishment of the National Health Service and the extension of state legal aid.

The legal and medical professions are not, moreover, isolated exceptions. On the contrary, their forms of government, their use of apprenticeship to control admission and training, their collective defence of their work jurisdiction and of their status have been imitated by dozens of other non-manual occupations in England. The first to do so were the surgeon members of the United Company of Barber-Surgeons who left to form their own company, which later became the Royal College of Surgeons. The next to do so were those legal practitioners who were excluded from the Inns of Court, the attorneys and solicitors, who subsequently formed the Law Society. In the nineteenth century they were followed by engineers, architects, accountants and many more.[38]

Not surprisingly, these later professions could not reproduce exactly the circumstances and institutions of the great originals. The solicitors, for instance, relied far more on statutory support for their rules than the huddled communities of the Inns of Court. Moreover, many of the later professions could not afford to be quite so dismissive of the status and market advantages of a university degree, while the newer professions or semi-professions dependent on public employment were more disposed to university qualifications from their beginnings. None of the newer professions, of course, could protect their jurisdictions as effectively as the Inns of Court or the Royal College of Physicians. Nevertheless, when all these and other variations are taken into account, it seems clear that we are describing the diffusion of a model form of practitioner self-government that was first embodied in the corporate institutions of barristers and physicians. The question to consider now is how far such an ideal of practitioner self-government has also influenced organized labour in Britain.

Historians of the labour movement have shown little interest in the Puritan or Glorious Revolutions, since neither led to any significant change in worker organization or ideology. In a comparative context, however, the 'silences' of these revolutions assume considerable significance. Since neither generated a popular ideology of equality or individual rights, English workers have never subsequently been able to claim indigenous revolutionary legitimation for their protests and demands. Neither of them, moreover, provided any grounds for questioning the traditional, exclusive, elitist, craft form of worker organization, and as a result this never became a political issue except for a brief period following the emergence of socialist-inspired trade unions in the late nineteenth century. The legacy from the Glorious Revolution to the trades therefore resembled that to the professions since it legitimized, or failed to de-legitimize, their established rights or practitioner self-government. Hence, just as the peculiarities of the English professions can only be understood by reference to the revolution so also, I would suggest, it is a key to understanding the peculiar continuity, and the peculiar strength, of occupational ties and associations among manual workers in Britain.

To document this continuity from the late seventeenth century and through the eighteenth as 'masters' gave way to employers and entrepreneurs, as the 'shop' was transformed into the factory, as journeymen who had 'served their time' were forced to work alongside 'foreigners' and 'illegal' workers, is no easy task. One reason for the difficulty is that members of the journeymen societies, fearing the reprisals of employers, were usually sworn, not merely to secrecy, but also not to 'write, or cause to be wrote, point, mark, either on stone, marble, brass, paper or sand, anything connected with this Order'. The other reason is that the Webbs decided that, since there was no documentary evidence of a journeymen society or trade union which had descended directly from a guild, there was no continuity at all between them, and that trade unions were therefore a new form of collective organization coeval with industrialization.[39]

This legalistic and tendentious argument subsequently became part of the conventional wisdom of British labour history. In recent times, however, more attention has been given to the continuity first documented by Brentano, of beliefs, institutions and interests, a cultural continuity, that does not require the transfer of property, or a succession of officers and does not preclude adaptation and amendment.[40] In this cultural sense, there appears to be an unbroken line of descent from the yeomanry of the guilds of the revolutionary period, to the journeymen's societies and trade unions of the late eighteenth and early nineteenth centuries. As the Webbs themselves showed, these early trade societies were organized on an occupational basis and concerned almost exclusively with occupational protection.

In the second and third decades of the nineteenth century, several attempts were made to form another kind of union, which seems, at first glance, rather like the contemporaneous workingmen's associations in the United States, especially as Robert Owen had a hand in both. There is, however, one significant difference between these movements in the two countries. All of the 'attempts at general union' in England, the Philanthropic Society of 1817, the Philanthropic Hercules of 1818, the National Association for the Protection of Labour of 1830, the Society for Promoting National Regeneration of 1833, and the Grand National Consolidated Trades Union of 1834 were unions of trade unions; that is, they were intended to federate occupational loyalties, not to replace or transcend them.[41]

The most persuasive evidence of the strength of occupational loyalties at this time is to be found in E. P. Thompson's account of various kinds of protest and collective action among English workers in the late eighteenth and early nineteenth centuries. Journeymen, of course, took part in these protests, indeed a major part in many of them, such as the campaign for parliamentary reform and Chartism. Thompson includes all of their activities are part of 'the making of the working class', but there is no evidence to suggest that they were ever disposed to abandon their trade loyalties and trade interests in favour of wider, class loyalties. In fact, Thompson provides not a single instance where trade loyalties were superseded or abandoned in favour of class action.[42] Occupation was therefore the enduring basis of collective organization and collective action of British manual workers right through the first three-quarters of the nineteenth century. The major change of the third quarter of the nineteenth century is not, as is often supposed, the emergence of a 'labour aristocracy', since such an 'aristocracy' had long existed, but how this labour aristocracy formed national organizations, the so-called 'new model unions', and how these collaborated in 1868 to establish a trade-union congress to express their collective views to the government.[43]

The first real attempt to create an alternative form of manual worker organization in Britain therefore came in the late 1880s and early 1890s as a result of attempts to organize unapprenticed workers or, in Tom Mann's words, to organize that 'portion of the working community' that is not 'called upon to keep one occupation for life'. These so-called 'new unions' sought to recruit members regardless of occupation, ignored the jurisdictional claims of the new model unions and saw themselves engaged in a crusade against 'craft and sectional prejudice'. They professed contempt for the new model's mutual benefit activities which were derisively referred to as 'coffin clubs', and looked primarily to the state to improve the conditions of workers. They were therefore quickly converted to socialism. Some of the new model unions responded to the challenge of these new unions by recruiting neighbouring semi-skilled workers in industries in which they were strongly entrenched, though these new recruits were not allowed to dilute the occupational unity of the union and were given a separate, second-class category of membership, with inferior rights and benefits.

Thus the confrontation which we have observed in the other two labour movements had its counterpart in the British, but was resolved not by the elimination of the occupationally based unions but by a compromise: to put it briefly, the 'new model' or craft unions triumphed organizationally, while the new unions of semi- and unskilled workers triumphed politically. In the present context, the political aspect of this compromise – that is, the conversion of the new model unions to socialism – need not be pursued. It is the organizational aspect which is all-important, since it meant that occupation became the legitimate basis of mass manual worker organization in Britain.

Of course, the conflict between the two kinds of union had muddled the occupational demarcations, but from the turn of the century the new unions began to reorganize themselves on an occupational or trade basis, and began to defend the occupational interests of their members. They retreated from the streets, so to speak, to the factory floor, declared their willingness to respect the occupational jurisdictions of the new model unions, even withdrew from sectors where they were thought to have trespassed, and turned away skilled workers who applied to join them. At the same time

they began to work out their own jurisdictions, for their heterogeneous semi- and unskilled membership, and to help this process
often reorganized themselves internally on a trade basis. Simultaneously they became much more concerned with petty, shop-
floor issues – professional issues, one might call them – and adopted
the shop steward as their front-line representative.[44] To describe
them as 'general' or 'industrial' unions is therefore somewhat misleading. They might be more accurately described as multi-occupational unions.

The survival, and indeed the growth and development, of occupational ties within British trade unions can be demonstrated by
two concerns which they long shared with the English professions.
The first, and perhaps most important, is their support for apprenticeship, or some form of practitioner-controlled training, and their
indifference or hostility towards formal vocational training.
Apprenticeship long remained the only form of professional or
technical training in Britain,[45] and the state only began to intervene
in the training arrangements of manual workers and to define the
rights and responsibilities of educational institutions and employers
in 1964.[46]

A second distinctive concern of British trade unions is their
determination to protect their jurisdictions collectively and therefore to control or regulate the division of labour,[47] a matter of
much less concern to American unions and none at all to the
French. The behaviour of British trade unions in this respect once
again resembles that of the professions. English lawyers and doctors
have both retained, and even reinforced, the jurisdictions they first
marked out in the seventeenth century. The jurisdictions of manual
occupations have never been documented in the same way, but we
can indirectly demonstrate their peculiar concern with this issue
by describing the distinctively 'professional' pattern of inter-union
relationships found among British trade unions.

Since the turn of the century British trade unions have rarely
competed for members in the labour force at large, in the manner
of French or American unions. They have argued instead about
their jurisdictions. For them it is not therefore a question of how
to recruit a particular group of workers (who are unorganized or
organized by some other union), but rather, which union does the
work these workers perform belong to? Since most jurisdictions are
already in the possession of a union and not in dispute, there is
much less inter-union competition than in either France or the
United States. Until 1988, this has been resolved amicably, under
the auspices of the 1938 Bridlington Agreement, by which unions
recognized one another's jurisdictions and set up procedures to

handle disputed cases as well as new and marginal kinds of work. There is a close analogy here to professional associations, since they also acknowledge one another's core jurisdictions and compete only at the margins. Institutes of accountants, for instance, do not organize recruiting drives among barristers, or engineers or doctors.

There are no aggregate statistics to document the survival of occupation loyalties as a basis of collective action in so-called general or industrial unions. As there is no space to review the relevant case studies, I turn to consider a single contemporary work setting, the National Health Service. The NHS is not, it need hardly be said, a typical employer, but it will illustrate the way in which occupational organization has developed among all kinds of British workers, from the least skilled to the highest professionals, and has formed a distinctive 'system' of representation and bargaining. By 1979, its staff numbered well over a million, and forty-three organizations were recognized for collective bargaining purposes, it being hardly possible to distinguish professional associations from trade unions. Names and past history are uncertain indicators. The British Medical Association is, in fact, a registered trade union. A willingness to use the ultimate weapon of collective bargaining might be a better indicator, and associations sometimes use this criterion when distinguishing themselves from one another, though since some indubitably professional bodies have taken collective action which might be described as a partial strike (by limiting hours, for example), one has doubts. This difficulty is, of course, itself a good illustration of the convergence and confusion of professional and trade-union strategies. In the present context, however, the important fact is that the service is organized from top to bottom on an occupational basis.

A map of these associations, which is all I can provide here, may begin with the British Hospital Doctors Federation, a recent merger of the Hospital Consultant Staff Association and the Junior Hospital Doctors Association.[48] Alongside, and partly overlapping with these, is the British Medical Association, which is best seen in the NHS context as a federation of occupational associations, since it is internally divided into a series of 'craft committees' for hospital consultants, junior medical staff and general practitioners, which, in fact, negotiate with one another as well as the Department of Health and Social Security. Beneath these are more than a dozen semi-professional associations for physiotherapists, radiographers, midwives, health visitors, nurses and others, and then various associations for managerial and administrative staff, including two multi-occupational unions, Manufacturing, Science, Finance (MSF, formerly ASTMS), the National Association of Local Government

Officers (NALGO) and others which cater for single occupations, such as the Guild of Medical Secretaries. Beneath these, if that is the word, are a cluster of unions – the lineal descendants of the 'new model' unions – representing the skilled electrical, engineering and building workers, and finally a number of multi-occupational unions – the lineal descendants of the 'new' unions – for nursing auxiliaries, catering, laundry and other manual workers. These are the National Union of Public Employees (NUPE), the Confederation of Health Service Employees (COHSE), the Transport and General Workers Union (TGWU) and the General and Municipal Workers Union.

In this complex network there is, not surprisingly, a degree of overlap, of dual membership and of competition, a reminder that the process of demarcating occupations, of finding appropriate representation and expression of occupational aspirations and alerting and mobilizing members of the occupation is a continuous one. Thus, to give a specific example, ambulance personnel have in the past been recruited by four multi-occupational unions (NALGO, NUPE, COHSE, TGWU), but these are currently being challenged by an outsider, which is not among the forty-three recognized bodies, the Association of Professional Ambulance Personnel. This association argues that unions have failed to recognize or further the collective interests of ambulance personnel and now claims to have recruited about 5,000 of the 17,000 engaged in this kind of work, both manual and non-manual, from all levels of the service other than chief and deputy chief.

The uses of cross-occupational studies

Whatever disagreement there may be with specific arguments in the preceding sketches, they may at least be said to identify certain points of resemblance between the organization of manual workers and that of professionals. In France, neither have been able to organize freely and continuously as occupations. In the United States, the occupational form of organization of both has similarly been threatened and checked, though in quite different ways, while in Britain, both professional and manual workers have been able to organize on the basis of their occupational membership, over a much longer period, and with far less opposition, than in either France or the United States.

Much more research is needed to specify these distinctive national patterns of collective organization, let alone to explain them. Nevertheless, there is sufficient evidence to suggest that the form of organization adopted by either manual workers or professionals cannot be a product of the kind of work they perform, cannot therefore be inherent in the occupation itself, since the work itself is common to these societies while the form of organization differs markedly. Nor, for similar reasons, can it be the product of changes in the economic system as a whole. The evidence therefore strongly suggests that, in order to explain variations in the extent to which either manual workers or professionals were able or willing to organize effectively on an occupational basis, we must refer to political factors.

In the case of the professions alone, this is perhaps not such a surprising conclusion since it is difficult to see how the varying forms of state–professional relationship in France, the distinctive American brands of conditional and pressure-group professionalism and the powerful 'lesser governments' of Britain could be explained in any other way. Manual worker organizations, however, can be explained, and usually have been explained, in another way. The abandonment of occupational forms of organization is commonly attributed to changes in methods of production, in particular to the growth, first, of the factory system and later of mass production.

The evidence suggests, however, that changes in manual worker organization do not follow the sequence one would expect if these economic factors were decisive, for then, surely, Britain would have been the first to abandon occupational organizations, followed by the United States, and finally by France. In the event, France was first, was followed by the United States, while Britain, if it is following at all, must be at least half a century 'behind' the United States and a century or more 'behind' France. And it is hardly credible that there was a simultaneous transformation of the production systems methods of most French industries in the 1890s or that there was a subsequent analogous transformation across American industry in the 1930s. In any case, the very fact that there were bitter struggles among workers in both these countries to determine the proper basis of their collective organization, beginning in the United States in the 1820s and in France in 1848, throws doubt on the notion that the move away from occupational forms of organization was economically or technologically determined and suggests that political and cultural factors were of greater importance.

The history of the professions suggests that the great revolutions of these three societies are the most plausible starting-point for an analysis of these political and cultural determinants of occupational organization since the relationship between the state and the professions was first re-defined during or shortly after them. The three revolutions also appear to have largely determined the political and cultural environment in which such organizations had subsequently to survive by undermining, or in the English case reinforcing, the legitimacy of occupational self-government.

Many of the subsequent turning-points in the history of occupational associations of all kinds also appear to coincide with political rather than economic transitions. In France, for instance, the establishment of freedom of association under the Third Republic had a decisive effect on all the professions. The orders of advocates lost their political functions and almost immediately came under attack. Doctors began to adopt trade-union forms of organization, while manual workers abandoned occupational associations and turned to revolutionary syndicalism. Defeat by Germany and the creation of the Vichy regime constituted a further landmark, a futile attempt to revive occupational self-government. In the United States, the reconstruction of the professions seems to have been intimately related to the progressive movement and the emergence of mass industrial organization of manual workers to their political mobilization within the Democratic Party. In England the attacks on new model unions coincided with the enfranchisement of a large proportion of male manual workers and accompanied the formation of the Labour Party, while recent attacks on the professions have followed the adoption of a distinctly 'new' Conservative philosophy.

One of the advantages of looking at occupations in this broad comparative perspective therefore is to open up questions about how and why manual workers or professionals organized in a particular way and to alert one to the way larger political events may have shaped their collective aspirations, capacities and institutions. And by breaking down the wall that has separated the study of professionals and manual workers we may formulate better explanations of their corporate institutions. Thus, in attempting to explain the commitment of English barristers or doctors to practice-based professional training, it is relevant to note that English manual workers have been similarly attached to apprenticeship. Or in trying to explain professional codes of ethics, it is worth noting that when French trade unions under the July Monarchy required government approval for their constitutions and rules, that they gave these rules a pronounced 'ethical' tone, stressing the quality of workmanship expected of their members.[49]

Such a broad, comparative perspective may be equally useful if we wish to consider professions and occupations as an independent rather than dependent variables and to ask in what ways they may have shaped other institutions and the rest of the social structure rather than being shaped by it. This point may best be illustrated by imagining two polar, ideal types of society. In the first, every member of the labour force belongs to an organized, self-governing occupation each of which controls admission to its ranks and the training of new entrants, protects an exclusive work jurisdiction, operates its own disciplinary system and collectively upholds its status position relative to other occupations. In sum, it is the realization of the Vichy dream, though to give it a less ideologically loaded name we might call it 'Tawnia', after the most elegant and persuasive defender of the totally professionalized society. In the other society, although everybody in the labour force has an occupation, they are not organized on this basis but on diverse, competing bases of collective action, by the company, plant or industry in which they are employed, for instance, or by their individual political or religious beliefs, by their class perhaps, or by the school which they attended. This society bears some resemblance to Durkheim's image of a society with endemic anomie, so we may call it 'Anomia'.

Given only this information about Tawnia and Anomia one can reasonably, *ceteris paribus*, infer that they will differ in a number of other ways. First, the educational system of Tawnia must be much less developed than that of Anomia, because organized occupations are themselves responsible for training all entrants to the labour force, whereas in Anomia none is. Second, the division of labour in Tawnia must be more rigid and inflexible than that of Anomia since every occupation is organized to defend its jurisdiction. Third, the Tawnian state must have more limited powers than the Anomian because it has been willing to delegate powers to every organized occupation, whereas the Anomian state, unless it has been willing to delegate its powers haphazardly to other agencies, such as companies, churches or schools, must have retained these powers. Finally, the stratification system of Tawnia must be more structured and institutionalized than that of Anomia since everybody belongs to an occupation which is collectively responsible for upholding the honour and prestige of their occupation, whereas in Anomia, however status may be determined – by education, by income, by the nature of work or by style of life – it cannot be institutionalized by the collective action of members of an occupation.

The evidence presented earlier suggests, of course, that Britain is more akin to Tawnia while France and the United States might further be analysed as variants of Anomia, for in both of them self-governing professions are deviants. However, the challenge in utilizing such imaginary societies to illuminate or analyse the real world is to identify the past and present sources and direction of change. In France, as we have seen, the establishment of freedom of association under the Third Republic was a critical period of transition, for then the opportunity for widespread occupational organization finally became available but was quickly discarded in favour of other forms of collective action. However, the present decline of competing forms of collective action, of revolutionary parties and class-oriented trade unions in France, also raises interesting questions. Occupational loyalties are continually renewed in everyday working life, even in France,[50] and we may therefore wonder whether professional interests might not at last find an accepted place both in the labour movement and in French political life.

In the United States the critical historical questions are how the progressive movement helped the professions to reconstruct some of their collective institutions; to what extent, and in what form, occupational ties have been able to reassert themselves during the twentieth century in the face of entrepreneurial and managerial initiatives that seem to be more insistent, compelling and legitimate than anywhere else. In Britain, the 'Thatcher revolution' is easily the most serious threat that both the professions and the trade unions have faced in more than a century, affecting most of their traditional institutions and traditional forms of collective action. This raises the question of how professional and trade unions will resist, survive or adapt to this threat. Since professions and trade unions have long been a secure and integral part of British social structure, and have helped to shape ambitions, careers, authority and social order in Britain in quite distinctive ways, we might also ponder what the effects of Thatcher policies may be on the future of British society – if, that is, they survive and succeed.

Notes

1 These observations are still contested. The evidence I find compelling is presented in Holmes, 1982.

2 Obviously I would also like to record, in each instance, how far they actually got with their professional strategy, but that task is far beyond the scope of the present chapter.

3 Soreau, 1931.

4 Soboul, 1962.

5 Leonard, 1978; Vess, 1975; Ackernecht, 1967.

6 Gaudry, 1864.

7 Sewell, 1980.

8 Ibid.; Festy, 1891.

9 Price, 1972.

10 Blanc, *Historical Pages*.

11 Hubert-Valleroux, 1885.

12 Lagardelle, 1901. The survival of occupational associations of various kinds is documented in Barbaret, 1886. There is also much useful information in Moss, 1976.

13 Smith, 1987.

14 Vasseur, 1900.

15 Boltanski, 1987.
16 Sialleli, 1987.
17 Elbow, 1953.
18 Chaigneau, 1945.
19 Minville, 1954.
20 For the revolutionary period itself the most vivid evidence is to be found in Jensen, 1974. For the subsequent decades: Ellis, 1971. The best single source remains Reed, 1921.
21 Rothstein, 1972.
22 Handlin and Handlin, 1969.
23 The best documentation is to be found among various contributors to Commons (ed.), 1921.
24 Ware, 1929.
25 Dubofsky, 1968.
26 For an introduction to a large literature, see Bok and Dunlop, 1970.
27 Stevens, 1971.
28 For details about the AMA's generally unsuccessful campaigns against various kinds of irregular practitioner, see Rayack, 1967. Rayack, however, believes these show the power of the AMA.
29 Stevens, 1971.
30 Glaser, 1963; Reedy, 1978.
31 Woodworth, 1973.
32 McKean, 1963.
33 Nader and Green, 1976.
34 Burrage, 1988a.
35 Gawalt, 1979; for one example of an anti-bar assocation, see Tierney, 1979:165–166.
36 Rothstein, 1972; McDaniel, 1959.
37 For more details and references, see Burrage, 1988a.
38 Millerson, 1964.
39 Webb and Webb, 1920.
40 Brentano, 1870; Leeson, 1979; Dobson, 1980; Price, 1980.
41 The constitutions of all these unions are given in Cole, 1953.
42 Thompson, 1972.
43 Musson, 1972. Musson, aptly in my view, re-labels the unions involved as the 'old model'.
44 Clegg et al., 1964.
45 Carr-Saunders and his colleagues estimated that in the mid-thirties about a quarter of male school leavers were entering some form of apprenticeship and in 1956 more than a third. Carr-Saunders et al., 1937 and 1958.
46 Apart from special programmes during the two world wars, see Sheldrake and Vickerstaff, 1987.
47 It is impossible to provide comparative data on this point, but some idea of the importance British trade unions have attached to jurisdictional matters may be obtained from Goodrich, 1920; Jeffreys, 1945; Turner, 1962; More, 1980; and Flanders, 1964.
48 Derived from Dyson and Spary, 1979:145–176.
49 Vial, 1895:40; Roux, 1867. The same ethical concerns also surfaced when craft groups sought to gain producer cooperatives; see Lemercier, 1857.
50 Brilliantly documented in Latreille, 1980.

10

Professionalization as a process: patterns, progression and discontinuity

Hannes Siegrist

'Professionalization' signifies a process whereby an activity or occupation becomes a 'profession'. Relevant reference works differentiate this process according to various analytically distinguishable developments which may be either simultaneous or occur in succession.[1] First, the term frequently refers to processes by which an occupation acquires the character of an academic profession evidenced in the fact that relevant expertise as a prerequisite to admittance to a given professional field could only be obtained in higher institutes of learning, professional practice being limited to those who successfully complete entrance examinations and obtain the respective title. Second, some authors treat professionalization primarily with respect to certain policies within established arrangements of knowledge and the division of labour which are responsible for the professional's superior expertise in relation to laymen. A third approach considers professionalization chiefly as a process of separation and exclusion whereby a profession monopolizes occupational opportunities and functions in order to acquire or secure an exalted social and economic status. Finally, from the sociological perspective of organizations, professionalization refers to the development of a specific type of collective consciousness and organization and to a collective representation of interests and approval of strategies. It is the professional organization itself which defines the scope of professional practice, determines norms and values for its members, and strives for general recognition of its fundamental concepts from other social and political groups.

Accordingly, the term 'professionalization' may designate distinguishable divergent processes which occur within institutions of learning, the division of labour, the economic market, and areas of political and social power. The concept also refers to *the sum of all such processes* which are intrinsic to the development of professions. Various types of processes are therefore required in order to generate the end result known as a 'profession'.[2] Common to all these processes is the fact that they lead to a higher cultural, social and economic status and to an increased socio-political power of individual professionals and of the profession as a collective. Furthermore, such processes are promoted by professional strategies which serve as guidelines for specific forms of conduct and activity.[3]

A significant number of authors are more concerned with the structural characteristics of professions than with the dynamics inherent in the *process* of professionalization. Statements concerning the processes of professionalization are frequently derived from a static conception or are limited to deducing subordinate processes from global developments. Structural functionalists, for example, tend to view professionalization in light of modernization in general, describing the professionalization process as an intrinsic developmental component of the latter.[4] Opponents of structural functionalists devote more attention to the dynamics of professionalization by emphasizing its political character and conflict-oriented nature.[5] But it is doubtful whether or not the 'professionalization process' leads to what is implied in the definition of 'profession' and whether the aspirations particular to 'professions' correspond historically to the sociological category of 'professions'. The category 'profession' is by no means a-historical; it is to a certain extent often quite particular to a given society or epoch. The question of what constitutes social esteem and in what ways functional, cultural, political and economic characteristics are valued depends upon the respective historical context. Likewise, the professionalization process is also relative to a specific society and to a particular historical period. Being neither automatic nor linear, the course of development of the professionalization processes is highly complex and dynamic,[6] an important fact when considering the spatial and temporal validity of generalizations, theories and concepts.

Those who emphasize the individualized character of these processes argue that the considerable differences inherent in the growth and development of professions with respect to country and period necessitate divergent paths of progression. Representatives of this approach have also expressed doubt as to whether enough common traits among the learned, professional and academic occupations exist which would allow us to speak meaningfully of 'professions' *per se*.[7] The subsequent step is an individualized, historicist conception of history which views the motives and programmes of historical agents as the only valid standards. They contend furthermore that the sociological model of professions is a-historical and therefore useless as a reference point. This view implies that it is meaningless to speak of a 'professionalization process'. Advocates of this approach include sociologists such as Freidson, who holds that the best solution would be to document and analyse the peculiarities of each profession and not impose artificial models upon them for the sake of simplicity.[8]

The degree to which generalizations are possible and meaningful is dependent on epistemological premises and interests as well as on the theoretician's motives. I opt for an approach to research which aims at meaningful generalizations but which in no way ignores the warnings of the hermeneutical method or the individualizations of historiography. Theories and generalized concepts must heed the historical character of structures and processes; they are only valid within certain strictly defined social and historical bounds. Special emphasis must be placed on the *historical* nature of the concept of professionalization. For that reason, I first examine how relevant sociological and historical references structure the process of professionalization as a process in time. By examining the factors most frequently cited in the construction of periods and disruptions within the historical development of the professions, we can see most clearly which elements are regarded as particularly critical and significant. We may thereby obtain better insight into the extent to which certain processes, structures and models are valid. In the second half of the chapter I shall introduce a historical typology of various *modes of professionalization* based on the assumption that different historical and social types of professions exist and that consequently *different types of processes of professionalization* have occurred which vary according to the kinds of controlling instances and regulatory principles which were dominant in any one historical period of a given society.[9]

Dynamics and temporal structure of professionalization research

Relevant reference works contain very different notions about the structure, logic and periodical character of the professionalization process.[10] This divergence can partially be accounted for by the varying existing concepts of what professionalization is. Authorities for whom specialized knowledge is the central variable in a profession tend to structure its historical evolution according to the development of education and knowledge. They thereby arrive at a concept of a developmental structure different from that propounded by those who are primarily concerned with the history of organizations and institutions. Authors who emphasize the role of the state as the most crucial element in professionalization hold a

still different view of continuity and disruption within the professionalization process.

In addition to these differences based on varying approaches and
interests, we may also note dissimilarities in periodization based on
the comprehension of time as the fundamental dimension of history. Therefore, dissimilar approaches to periodization result from
different notions of time and of the structure of temporal processes.
As such they defy further specification, because notions of time
depend on ideologics, interests and motives which modify our conceptualization of time and temporal structures. This is a fact quite
often encountered in the realm of politics. The revolutionary who
attains state power vigorously proclaims a complete and total break
with the past. The conservative, in contrast, strives to stabilize his
role as sovereign by stressing the historical continuity and legitimacy of his position. For that reason political historiography
always contains a 'conservative' and a 'progressive' school which
operate with different notions of time. The case is much the same
with the history and sociology of professions due to the affinity or
even bonds existing between professional scholars and the objects
of their research. Some are prone to regard alterations – for example, in scholastic knowledge – as a starting-point for revolutionary
change and thereby hope to ratify their own positions. Others are
more likely to emphasize elements of continuity such as in an
established system of certification.

The following modes for structuring temporal developments
appear in professionalization research and must be kept distinct.
First, there is the pattern of continual, linear or exponential progress towards an expressed end; that is, the *teleological time pattern*.
Second, there is the pattern of long duration or Braudel's notion
of *longue durée*:[11] structural characteristics and social mentalities
endure, disregarding temporary fluctuations, for long periods of
time, in some instances for centuries. The teleological concept and
structures of long duration are based upon large periods of time. In
contrast, the third and fourth types reflect deep splits or temporary
changes. The third mode is the conception of *revolution* which is
concerned with changes of a principal type which result from social,
economic, political, institutional or scholastic revolutions. The
fourth way of structuring temporal processes encompasses
sequences, rhythms, cycles, virtuous or vicious circles[12] *and conjunctures*; that is, vertical movements devoid of systemic change.

Sequences, rhythms, cycles
An example of sequential professionalization which may be seen
as a cyclic progression or virtuous circle is provided by Wilensky.[13]

According to this view, professionalization can only be pursued by occupational groups employing principles of higher learning, and the development of professions proceeds in stages. At first, the respective occupation becomes full-time in character. Second, the pertinent group lays claim on certain areas and functions which are relevant to the respective occupation. The third stage of progress provides for places of training which eventually become academic institutions unless the educational programme is not already represented as a university faculty. Teachers at these institutions or leading professionals establish at the fourth stage a professional organization which continues to expand. This organization succeeds in obtaining governmental legislation limiting professional practice to the holders of a mandatory licence, thereby attaining an occupational monopoly. Finally, the rules of professional behaviour and conduct are restated and general codes of ethics are developed which have to be applied by the boards of the professional union.

Wilensky ascribed a temporal dimension to the classificatory models; that is, to the list of features embodied in professions.[14] That is to say, Wilensky really was concerned with the problem of professionalization as a process. His elaborate model of this process suffers from drawbacks which he himself has not failed to notice, one being that the succession of stages may in fact vary – to what degree and for what reasons remains unclear. For our purpose it is important to note that the model was abstracted from the development of professions in the United States during the nineteenth and twentieth centuries where the principle of liberal self-regulation in markets and society was already present and where professions were historical subjects acting to shape society. Wilensky clearly shows that professionalization can be hindered by various factors, but the fundamental dismantling of the professions which has caught the attention of only a few[15] is hardly an issue.

The model of development described by Wilensky is drawn up according to features seen as common to all professions; the initial starting-point of his enquiry is the profession *per se*. The sequence would obviously appear in a different light if the activities of the state had been made the focal point of query.[16] In the case of the bureaucratic centralized states of continental Europe, the process of professionalization was initiated by kings, princes, patricians and states, who attempted to influence the behaviour of barristers, clergymen and, to a lesser extent, also of medical practitioners, by issuing codes of ethical conduct. By the eighteenth or early nineteenth century, the function and operational realm of these occupational groups were state-regulated. This is especially true during a phase of forced state expansion since it is assumed that these areas of occupation were of the utmost importance for the welfare of the state or the 'general welfare'. Preventive measures adopted in order to reform the system of education and to establish qualification standards served to enhance efficiency. The conduct of these professions was controlled and made calculable by implementing official limits on the numbers of admissible members and by fixing a scale of fees. The professional was an isolated individual since his group was forbidden to organize into associations. This pattern of development could be described as a sequence occurring during the professionalization process initiated from above – that is, controlled by the state.

Such occupations fulfil the essential criteria of a profession, exhibiting systematized knowledge and a formalized outline of education and terms of certified qualification, leading, in turn, to a homogenization of the occupational group in question. The expert enjoys a superior position in relation to laymen, and his higher economic and social status are granted security to a considerable extent. However, a central element of all professions is missing, namely the autonomy of an occupational association to determine and settle both internal and external affairs. It is the state, instead of the profession itself, which pursues the professionalization process; the profession is a product of state management policy. If we take the state to be the subject of operation and the process of professionalization to be the object, then the implicit premise in Anglo-Saxon theories of professions is contradicted; this states that the driving initiative proceeds from the members of an occupation and that the autonomy of the occupational group is the most decisive factor in the professionalization process. But the question arises as to whether it might not be more appropriate to view the vertical process of professionalization – that is, from top to bottom – as part of an overall strategy leading to bureaucracy and officialdom – a strategy which would permit the state to structure and control not only the civil service, but also other occupational realms which it deemed of central importance. Under this assumption, a large number of academic and 'free' professions in continental Europe could not properly be treated as 'professions', unless one were willing to exempt them from the given definition.

German research treats these types under the concept of vertical professionalization from top to bottom.[17] This concept is derived from the 'revolution from above', a term employed in German historiography denoting the reforms effected at the beginning of the nineteenth century. Periodization would occur from this perspective according to the cycles of state intervention. Periods of strong intervention, the bureaucratic, centralized state and the modern welfare state, alternate with periods of little intervention which exhibit greater self-management on all social, economic and cultural levels.

These 'state professions' which emerged on the Continent during the late eighteenth and the early nineteenth centuries later developed into professions which correspond more closely to the Anglo-Saxon sociological type. I would like to elaborate on this type of 'state profession' by examining selected German groups. In the nineteenth century, fundamental changes in general needs in a wide range of social areas led to significant modifications in the occupational world of those physicians, engineers and lawyers who were not employed by the state. The importance of professional expertise outside the realm of government and public administration increased dramatically. These professionals sought more power, the maximal demand being autonomy, in order to fulfil their goal of attaining a high status and being respected, by virtue of their expertise, as a superior group which selflessly served the advance of knowledge and the common good. Strategies of professionalism were employed in this pursuit with the objective of acquiring more freedom to develop and a wider margin of occupational activities. Such strategies were simultaneously coupled with methods more typical of civil middle-class movements which were aimed at changing the scope of both occupational fields and social activity. This explains why members of the professions in the nineteenth century continuously held leading positions in liberal organizations.

Around 1870, breakthrough was finally achieved in Germany as physicians and barristers were granted the liberty to exercise their professions. This was clearly an act in opposition to state management and control. It was at the same time a corrective of the traditional professionalization process and an expression of a broad movement within the professions and society at large favouring the principles of social self-determination and professional autonomy. In order to suppress the influence of the state, decisive elements among the professions began to demand something that is in clear contradiction to the established theory of professionalization as a closure strategy, namely the implementation of a measurably increased open market and the suspension of limits on the numbers of admissions to the professions. The fact that a closure policy remained somewhat intact through the continued existence of compulsory state admissions examinations does not substantially contradict this finding. German advocates[18] and physicians were finally granted certain rights of self-management over disciplinary measures and professional ethics. The synthesis of the established tradition of exclusion with the newer, open, liberal concept, is most clearly described by the term 'liberal professionalism'.[19]

The cycle of development nevertheless remains ambiguous, and a different concept is revealed according to the aspect under consideration. 'Liberal professionalism' continued to remain an ambivalent phenomenon, as the system of education and the method of certifying qualifications continued to be determined by the state. The professions had inherited from the preceding period a prevailing mentality of seclusion which surfaced once again under critical circumstances. Ethical issues were no more than a resumption of principles which had already been defined by the state, and which, if at all, witnessed only very cautious further development. Advocates continued to present their profession as serving the administration of justice, whereas their image as service entrepreneurs or as assistants to citizens was slow in finding a foothold. Emphasis was, however, placed on the fact that advocates were independent of the state, and of their clients. A professional conscience and expertise were held to be the highest of assets.

The transition to liberal professionalism signified in this case one step towards professionalization resembling the Anglo-Saxon model, thereby changing the importance of specific aspects of various professions. Education was now important not only for the general welfare of the state, but also for the proper functioning of society as a whole, the well-being of its citizens, and for establishing a solid social foundation for the continued growth of the professions. But the *laissez-faire* social and political policy did not find full acceptance in Germany. Neo-corporate models quickly developed. The preceding period exhibited enormous structural tenacity and historical momentum, with traditional and established structures of thought continuing to exist on or just beneath the surface. I am referring here to longstanding values and attitudes (*mentalités*) which can revive in times of crisis. These mental structures are typified, for instance, by the tendency of a large number of professions to lean on the state for protection in times of crisis, thereby relinquishing the modern liberal principles of self-help. This type of antiquated mentality surfaced during the crises of the 1920s and 1930s. Fascism, as a state organization, perverted the idea that the professions *qua* agents of the state also served the interests of society as a whole, and professions surrendered. Liberal professionalism revived in several variants after the end of World War II. To summarize, we may say that sequences of professionalization retain their individual significance according to the specific context in which they occur; from an intermediate perspective these sequences are more properly characterized as cycles than as uni-linear sequences.

Economic, political, cultural, scientific and demographic develop-ment cycles have all gone into characterizing the history of the professions. The effects of such cycles have often been elaborated on – for instance, in research dealing with development cycles and the labour force in periods of economic slowdown or financial boom. Related arguments tend to be *ad hoc* and arbitrary. Diffi-culties remain in assessing the effects because of the fact that a surge in the system of education, for instance, may overlap with an economic crisis. Institutions of higher learning may turn out an increased number of professionals, having an adverse effect on the income of the professionals. In turn, this may lead to a heavier work-load and greater efficiency on the part of the professional, thereby enabling members of social strata to experience the benefits of professional expertise for whom it would otherwise have been an unaffordable privilege. The professional is rewarded with greater prestige. A critical over-supply is normally correlated with a tend-ency to exclude laymen from the market, and it has been an accepted fact that European professions adopt a closure strategy in times of crisis. As a programme, such closure tendencies among professionals do indeed make their appearance as an anti-crisis strategy, but characteristic features of professionality frequently do not become visible until an economic boom sets in. Demographic and cultural cycles give rise to additional complications.

Questions concerning the effects of short-term or intermediate cycles must, therefore, remain unresolved. Generalizations must necessarily revolve around three points: (1) the various effects of cycles neutralize each other; (2) the positive effects of individual cycles towards professionalization are stronger than cycles having a counteractive, destructive effect on the professionalization pro-cess, and the characteristic dynamic development as a virtuous circle is therefore maintained; (3) stronger factors emerge which counteract the professionalization process and a vicious circle is the result in which de-professionalization in the following key areas occurs: the status of knowledge and expertise; the role of the expert or professional and his position in society; the strength of professional organizations and their ability to carry out decisions.

Revolutionary change
Disruptions caused by revolutions are a central principle in structur-ing history and temporal relations. It is not always easy to dis-tinguish between cyclic fluctuations and revolutionary breaks which affect the entire scope of an area of occupation. And 'revolution'

does not always merely mean an abrupt or violent change such as political overthrow with a total new political and social order. 'Revolution' also connotes an unobvious, but fundamental change.

Political revolutions have frequently succeeded in implementing principles upon which new concepts of occupational activity were based, as was the case in the French Revolution, and in the liberal and democratically motivated upheavals of the nineteenth and twentieth centuries. As Burrage[20] points out, political revolutions of this type made way for new options: the professions, government administration, and the rights and opportunities of citizens as social and economic subjects were transformed.

These revolutions effected principles which serve as the foundation of modern professionalization: the creed of effectiveness, achievement-orientation as well as the principle of expediency, rationality and of organized vocational activity. Clients made new demands, and new modes of action among professionals appeared. A search for a new order began in areas in which revolutions had succeeded in dissolving the traditional institutions which had functioned as refuge to professions. To avoid being pushed into an existence peripheral to the rest of society, professional occupations were forced to partake in this conquest for a new social order.

Much has been said about different revolutions within the history of professionalization, and, for each of the aspects of the professionalization process described above theses have been proposed outlining the abrupt change. Fundamental are the civil, liberal and industrial revolutions. In many European countries, a political-institutional revolution actually preceded the Industrial Revolution[21] and to a great extent contributed more to the shaping of the professions than did the latter.

Research on the history of professionalization has shown only marginal interest in the civil revolution. However, most recent studies show that the status of the professional as expert is entirely dependent on his social and socio-political position in the middle class and within civil society.[22] In some societies, civil society was instituted in a revolutionary act; in others, the development was gradual evolution. As the case may be, this social process had extensive effects on the status of professions as such. Middle-class physicians had found it enormously difficult in an aristocratic society to be an authority for members of the aristocratic estates. Russian engineers of the nineteenth century were forced to resign themselves to a precariously inferior social status in spite of their superior technical expertise.[23]

A top-to-bottom trend towards professionalization did manage to elevate (or merely alter?) the occupational status of professionals in several nations on the Continent. This did nothing, however, to change the fact that in the early nineteenth century most professionals lacked real political rights, power and influence, and were therefore not capable of bringing to bear their own professional interests. Professional associations were virtually impossible in areas where the freedom to freely associate did not exist. Professionals who were neither part of the bureaucratic apparatus nor by birth members of the endowed power elite often felt quite frustrated. Together with entrepreneurs and liberal forces, they strove for political emancipation. Some achieved higher positions in society by participating in revolutionary activities which were committed to the establishment of a new social order. Their political motives aimed at change not only within the scope of their immediate professional fields but also at the structure of society as a whole. This political accentuation only waned at the arrival of civil society and after the full integration of the professions into the dominant middle class. As the (upper) middle-class character of the professions threatened to become proletarian, professional strategies grew increasingly important. The professions retained a definitely political hue in many countries simply because a number of essential questions and issues within a given context could only be approached, and solved, politically.

The effects of the Industrial Revolution and industrialization on the process of professionalization are less central than has often been assumed; in any case they tended to be indirect and ambivalent.[24] At times the advent of the industrial society seems to have threatened the professional status already attained in the preceding process of political-institutional modernization. On occasion, new opportunities emerged which were either seized or missed.

Scientific revolutions have been the concern of a great many studies. A revolution in knowledge or the sciences, which according to some authors is the most central factor in the entire process of professionalization, is frequently directly dependent on a corresponding political or economic revolution. The progress of knowledge none the less often exhibits an individual dynamic character. Most theories of professionalization assume that the superior social status and the autonomy of the profession *per se* are principally dependent on an advanced and systematized scholarship which achieves a general breakthrough in a scientific revolution. Mok's contentions, which are by no means free of problems, involve a distinction based on this assumption and distinguish between old and new professions: traditional professions were founded on correct and proper behaviour towards colleagues and clients; modern professions are based on the dominance of expertise (*Wissens-*

beherrschung) and scholastic orientation.[25] The periodization of the history of the physicians' profession is also based on this assumption. According to Freidson and Huerkamp, the significant monopoly exercised by physicians could only emerge on the condition that safe and efficient medical technology was already in existence.[26] Modern science had only progressed to this level of technology in the latter half of the nineteenth century which witnessed fundamental advances in diagnostic techniques as well as a broad expansion on the research front with the discovery of antiseptics and the establishment of bacteriology as an independent research field.

Periodization of this type implies that a new paradigm in knowledge as described by T. S. Kuhn[27] or revolutionary innovations in science had somehow decidedly contributed to the growth of professionalization, because the relative preponderance of the expert increased and efficiency improved. This is not the same type of periodization as one would expect if the deliberations involved were primarily concerned with the factors of education or the historical development of institutions. Education and the system of certified occupational qualification standards were already evolved much earlier. In some countries, a type of monopoly on the part of examined, licensed medical practitioners and a corresponding institutionalized superior status *vis-à-vis* patients had been in existence for a long time. This superior status was not based on the acquired professional expertise of the medical practitioners, but rather was primarily the result of political motives and culturally based preferences.[28] A comparison of these two types of periodization – the one based on the history of scientific progress and the growth of knowledge, the other centred on the development of political forces and institutions – shows clearly what consequences can result from a set of deliberations from a given approach and what effect that approach can have on our concept of the history of professionalization.

This novel paradigm in knowledge and science came to prevail in general practice; the degree and rate at which this process became manifest were dependent on the innovative capacities of both medical practitioners and clients, as well as their willingness to adapt. The new status that physicians enjoyed is in part to be attributed o the increased theoretical knowledge and efficiency of medical doctors, but also to the fact that greater numbers of groups placed trust in the novel advances of science.[29] Lundgreen supports the demand-side argument with a supply-side one. He postulates that, as a new principle, science and its institutionalization in places of research and learning in the second half of the nineteenth century actually embodied a quasi-revolutionary change. Having its outset in Germany, this change had a positive and lasting effect on other countries, and, according to Lundgreen, on professionalization as a whole.[30]

There are maybe a few paradigmatic revolutions in sciences to be recorded which have affected the status of professions. Most others were devoid of any clear further consequences because higher and systematized learning does not automatically affect professionalization or the division of labour. Legal doctrines and methods might quite possibly be changed without showing the effects on the status of lawyers or advocates that some legal historians have liked to assume.[31] The status of lawyers was particularly dependent on social and political factors; that is, even though legal knowledge and theory were quite similar in many countries, the comparative status of lawyers was not.[32] Not all revolutionary novelties in the natural and engineering sciences have made such a fundamental impact on the development of the professions. Other factors have indeed proved stronger, as the status-consciousness and the activities of professionals cannot be explained by means of the occupation alone, but rather must be considered as dependent on their role as members of the middle class in a social class hierarchy. This also explains why professionals never ceased warning of the dangers of 'proletarianization of the professional' whenever they saw their social position in any way threatened. The argument of the 'threats of proletarianization' has continued to re-emerge periodically in a number of variations from the nineteenth century to the present day.[33] At its roots lies the basic fear of radical social change.

Structures of longue durée *(long duration)*

The concepts of discontinuity which have been discussed mainly thus far may be contrasted to notions which emphasize the element of continuity in development. The history of the professions contains structures of long duration which have been the focus of a number of research studies. Structures of *longue durée* span several cycles and outlast revolutionary upheaval. They are relatively resistant to new forms of influence as well as to cyclic and conjunctural fluctuations.[34]

The chief difficulty lies in the task of distinguishing the *perception* of stability from *factual* stability. Professions which have attempted to find security in organizations or in a secluded niche of the market economy have been incessantly accused of adopting a 'old' corporate mentality. This accusation suggests continuity. At times it may indeed seem that an older tradition is still at work, but originally identical forms often acquire completely different meanings in later societies. The admission restrictions placed on potential members of the professions, first in the historical form of corporate bodies and subsequently in the form of sets of admission standards outlined and enforced by the state, are not identical with the more recent policies of seclusion brought about by cartels and pooling agreements in liberal or neo-corporate systems.[35] Indeed, the forms may appear similar, but they most certainly have undergone change according to the respective historical context.

The appeal on the part of many professions to established tradition, which has occasionally been postulated as an 'eternal' norm, is one more typical example of an element of long duration. Advocates in European countries defended their profession against intrusions with the claim that in their role as defenders not only of the poverished but also of freedom and of individual rights, they were actually carrying out an established historical mission for the good of civilization. From this historical account which spanned the Roman Republic and late medieval townships, a timeless image of the advocate was extracted for use against any attempt on the part of clients or the state to change the profession. An image of the selfless and independent advocate/lawyer was implanted on the minds of people and tenaciously persevered even after external circumstances had changed. This image appears in an anti-cyclic trend to be stronger at times when the status or social position of the professional group is endangered. Factually, not only the site and status but also the attitudes and professional ethics of advocates did change quite dramatically, and considerable conflicts were the result.

The classical example of structures of long duration with respect to occupational fields, mentalities, social roles and status are represented in English professions, most notably in the case histories of English physicians and barristers. As of the seventeenth century, barristers had successfully established themselves as a self-governing guild. The Inns of Court supervised and controlled the training and activities of all members. After the Glorious Revolution royal interventions in their affairs ceased, and they always retained a high degree of autonomy.[36] Recent developments only threaten this autonomy. The type of professional function and organization embodied in the union of organized barristers was later copied by other professional groups, first by the physicians, followed by other legal professions, and subsequently by engineers, accountants and others. The long-term stability of the professions can hardly be completely accounted for by citing the stability of the social and political context, because certain factors underwent radical change. Transformations which occurred between 1770 and 1870 in the judicial system, the organization of the courts, and in general social values have been designated by several authors as 'revolutionary'. But according to Duman, these changes did not appreciably affect the structure of the legal profession.[37] Even the Industrial Revolution did not substantially influence the professions.

On this basis Duman formulated his doubts concerning the accuracy of the established division of old and new professions. Duman does not recognize any process in the nineteenth century which might be described as 'professionalization'. However, Duman does identify processes arising in defence of the status quo, out of resistance to change and in an effort to ward off impending de-professionalization and a resulting impairment of the older model. He says that changes in the organization of the bar and its educational system after 1830 were not directed 'towards the collective upward mobility of the profession – a goal usually viewed as synonymous with the professionalization process – but rather towards preserving the independence, power and status that had *already* been achieved, albeit by some fine tuning and minor concessions where necessary'.[38] The comparison of English case studies with other historical instances confirms that 'any attempt to establish a natural history of the professions or an ideal chronology of professionalisation is doomed to failure'.[39]

Another instance of a mental structure of long duration appears in the description of American professions: the entrepreneur ideal from the middle of the nineteenth century survived in the twentieth century despite the return to a professional association.[40]

Other structures of long duration traverse history in the institutionalized forms of education and qualification, the contents of which however have changed, and in the system of professional entitlement which was based on an older tradition and which came under increasing state control during the course of the nineteenth century. This adopted system of certification standards often remained under state control in spite of a social trend towards greater autonomy.[41] The forms were retained, but the meanings – for example, the value of a diploma – often changed. For an early engineer from the propertied classes or who himself was an entrepreneur, a diploma hardly had the same meaning as for his successor who, like many others, was forced to subsist without means of his own and to earn his livelihood by marketing the only capital he possessed – namely, acquired knowledge.

The assumed existence of structures of long duration has prompted attempts to formulate sociological theories on professions that cover a wider range.

Professionalization as a teleological process

Some of the described methods of structuring temporal processes and history seem to share a supposition which is frequently expressly, at times implicitly, embraced in sociological studies of professions. The essence of that supposition is the underlying conviction that professionalization is an unceasing, goal-directed process, the end of which is the manifest, fully developed ideal profession. The concept of a unilinear or even an exponentially continuous professionalization process appears in two variations; firstly in those structural-functional conceptions which view professionalization (once it has started) as a component of the quasi-automatic process of modernization. In this case, professionalization appears to be part of an overall development towards rationalization, differentiation, and a universal implementation of scientific principles, which are the essential elements of modernization.[42] Interruptions are considered as temporary setbacks; doubt and opposition are regarded as 'dysfunctional' or are ignored entirely when the expressed goal is an idealization of the historical process. Progress and (expert) reason are the sole determinant factors. History is examined from the standpoint of an end result, or is of no interest at all. Conflicts and alternative directions are discreetly filtered out. Such a perspective often endorses the normative concepts of groups which themselves strive for professional status. But these concepts are then reduced to a narrow selection of essential historical aspects, typically the history of production and reproduction of science, or the development of professional organizations.

The second variant of teleological conceptions is found in more recent sociological and historical studies which regard the trait-model as an ideal type or a device for measuring the respective stages of development at different periods in time. This model is in effect a type of heuristic screening process. The closer the general state of a given profession approaches the ideal total of defined attributes at any one time, the more 'professional' the defined occupational field is. New and very important results have emerged from this by no means naïve research strategy, and professions have indeed become more comparable because of the fact that enquiries have become both standardized and more refined.[43]

However, this strategy poses a problem for several reasons, one being that it leads to a teleological interpretation of history. This danger can only be avoided if each time new criteria are established for the evaluation of a specific aspect according to the respective historical context involved. With respect to the educational system, for instance, German advocates around 1840 were professionalized according to a set of criteria. But this caste of advocates was not a 'profession' in the sociological sense of the term because they lacked control over pertinent courses of instruction and admissions policies. It was the state which actually moulded and controlled the profession. An organization of German advocates, as far as such existed at all, bore at most a remote resemblance to a 'modern' professional organization.[44] Thus, problems of interpretation arise consistently according to this variation; the interpretations implicit in this model distort historical meaning. The significance of individual traits within the entire context of characteristics is not deducible from the model or the theory itself.

Should the alternative then be to stop using sets of characteristics and ideal types as guidelines? Or should we recommend constructing ideal types, models and theories for specific socio-historical periods and places? I am in favour of the latter.

Historical types of professions and processes of professionalization

I should like to assume that definite socio-historical types of professions exist, which may be distinguished from one another by (1) the type of control instances and principles dominant in historical periods; (2) the evaluation of all those status dimensions relevant to professionalization; namely, social, cultural, political and economic 'capital'. These briefly described types are genetic in nature; that is, they are specific to certain types of societies but may survive the society in which they form a structure of long duration. First, the corporate type is intrinsic to the guild-societies which existed before the nineteenth century (*corporate profession*). Second, under the control of the centralized bureaucratic state, the process of professionalization from above led to state-defined *office-professions* (or *state professions*) between the eighteenth and mid-nineteenth centuries. The vortex of this development encompassed not only professionals employed by the state; members of older and virtually independent professions such as physicians and advocates were also involved. Third, the modern type of independent *liberal profession* or *autonomous profession* developed in civil, liberal societies in which the principle of social self-regulation began to flourish, irrespective of the individual society, at some time during the course of the nineteenth century (autonomous profession). The fourth type, the neo-corporate professional, achieved an established position in society during the period of social welfare states, at which time the state had a new role between unions and organized capitalism (*neo-corporate profession*). Definite trends towards this development were already visible in the nineteenth century and were intensified in the last decades of the twentieth century. This sort of profession is based on a mixed system of regulation which synthesizes elements of a centralized administration with those of social self-regulation. Whereas the second type of profession is part of a relatively rigid system of coercion, the last two types possess a great deal more operational freedom.

The corporate profession

The colleges of Italian legal consultants, the Inns of Court of the English barristers, and the guilds of physicians and surgeons which existed in parts of Europe before 1800 are all examples of professional corporate guilds.[45] They defined allowances, the type of function and income, and they regulated admission policies and internal order. In reality these guilds were a group of occupational classes which endowed their members with particular political, legal and social rights within the system of estates and graduated privileges. A few aristocratic professions even co-opted their members by virtue of the privileges granted them by birth.[46] The aspect of professional or technical credentials supervised by the corporation was in fact of secondary importance and was often missing altogether. Privileged groups of this kind were upheld most vigorously in circles that maintained close connections to the dominant political elite and in states which for reasons of internal political struggle were unable to adopt or enforce unanimously centralized regulations on the division of labour.

The corporate type of profession belongs to a system of occupational guilds. The allotment of corporate status normally ensued from the decision of a collective elite but was occasionally the endowment of an aristocratic individual. In relevant literature, the guild has been regarded as the most prevailing type of profession; it served as a historical ideal and guideline for subsequent generations of professions. Nevertheless, corporate professions were by no means ubiquitous before 1800, and they were forced to compete with other types which also played significant roles in moulding further development. In many regions of Europe, the decision of who was permitted to practise as a physician, a lawyer, a priest or an engineer, was the sole prerogative of the local territorial authority, whose deliberations were generally purely practical in nature.[47]

The state-defined professional

In the eighteenth and early nineteenth centuries the importance of centralized states increased in continental Europe. Social mechanisms which had traditionally defined the general division and function of labour were repressed by centralized administrations. The state reformed scholastic requirements and the general course of education. During the reorganization of the 'professional' sector into a state-defined system, new forms of legislation were adopted to regulate academic and scientific occupations, which, although acquiring sole control over certain defined functions, were nevertheless subject to state ordinances.[48] In a period extending to the middle of the nineteenth century, continental Europe was marked by a visible professionalization process which proceeded from top to bottom. Access to professions was defined and enforced by state regulations, and the practice of a learned profession was confined to those who were either appointed to a state office or who belonged to the select group holding authorized credentials. In principle, the admittance to professional practice was at this stage more contingent upon ability than had previously been the case.

Because the professions were concerned with central values and issues, particular moral, social and political prerequisites continued to play a leading role in the lives of professionals. These demands were now met by a larger stratum of professionals. Particular birth-rights and the practice of purchasing appointments to official positions were done away with. A pattern of semi-autonomous office professions dominated in academic professions which were caught between the sphere of state and bureaucracy on the one hand, and society in general on the other. From the viewpoint of the absolutist state which enforced its own policies of public welfare on all levels of society, these professions were a type of occupational residue which could not be totally integrated into the state apparatus.[49]

Professions within the liberal self-regulatory social system
The subsequent period is characterized by a marked tendency towards social self-regulation within the framework of civil society[50] and by a liberal economic order. This period began somewhat earlier or later according to the country in question, in some countries commencing as early as 1800. But the last three decades of the nineteenth century actually witnessed the general progression of this trend throughout Europe. In a very ambivalent manner, these tendencies concurred with traditional principles of state control and corporate regulation. Within this new concept of society, various notions evolved as to how 'professional' occupations and their corresponding social functions were to be regulated. I would like to distinguish between the civil-egalitarian model, the model of competence and efficiency, and the model which combines elements of state control with those of a market economy.

Since the end of the eighteenth century, a traditional aristocratic-laity model has reappeared in a civil variety within all concepts of democratic, egalitarian or liberal societies. At the onset of the 1790s, the French Revolution abolished the operational monopolies of advocates and physicians.[51] The de-regulatory movement soon swept the French-dominated regions of Italy and Switzerland. Services which had previously been the exclusive domain of professionals were opened up in order to allow laymen and mature, responsible citizens to perform the respective operations and tasks. Laymen were thereby allowed to represent themselves in legal proceedings or to choose to whom their representation was to be entrusted. Persons who regarded themselves as competent, and as morally, socially and politically reliable, were allowed to earn their livelihood as medical practitioners or as legal advisers; laymen in legal fields were even permitted to become judges. A mature citizen's common sense was as highly esteemed as the professional's specialized scholastic expertise which depended primarily on general trust. Ramsey describes this open array of operational and occupational fields based upon political and social motives as a 'radical free field'.[52]

The civil-egalitarian laity model has had varying degrees of success since the 1830s in comparatively liberal and democratic societies such as the USA and Switzerland.[53] In each case, the central aim of this model has been to weaken the influence of traditional experts and elitist organizations and to abolish the dependence of the client. De-professionalization, or more precisely de-regulation, cannot be explained by examining egalitarian ideologies alone; they are just as much the result of conflicting answers to questions pertaining to the validity and efficiency of paradigms of knowledge (such as a method of cure, a legal doctrine, or a *Weltanschauung*). Problems inherent in the professionalization process came into conflict with concepts of civil society in which citizens reserved the right to define and control operational fields and central social values for themselves. Institutionalized professionalization which ascribed laymen a subordinate role *vis-à-vis* professionals, or which granted special corporate rights to organized professions, was regarded as inimical to the basic concept of civil society. The term 'citizen' signified a 'mature' member of civil society, an autonomous, responsible individual.

The laity model was subjected to a wide range of restrictions during the Consulate and the first French Empire under Napoleon where a social order emerged which was a mixture of state control and a liberal market economy. This social order was not significantly changed by subsequent regimes and administrations, and actually expanded all across Europe during the course of the latter half of the nineteenth century.[54] The state defined both function and duties according to its own discrimination. The state also monopolized the system of education and made it mandatory for candidates successfully to complete admissions examinations before being allowed to practise their respective profession. But, there was real competition among professionals who held the same qualifications; clients thus selected professional expertise at their own discretion. Professionals took it upon themselves to dispute the issue of social rank.

With the legal privilege to form free associations, organizations eventually evolved which began to bargain with other social and political forces over issues pertaining to the status and structure of the respective profession in conflict situations or in instances which called for cooperation. The organized profession in the sociological sense of a model, or autonomous profession, can thus be regarded as a possible, but not compelling, result of bargaining. This developmental pattern became more generalized in the subsequent historical period. It may be said in summarizing that the function and operational fields of 'professions' within the self-regulatory social system may be distinguished according to a few fundamental models or combined types: the egalitarian laity model; the entrepreneurial professional; the organized and to some extent autonomous profession which bargained with other factors or agents over issues of rank.

The neo-corporate profession
The neo-corporate pattern of socio-political regulation belongs to the period characterized by the marked presence of unions and the predominance of the social state (*Sozialstaat*) in which a specific administrative mixture emerged that embodied principles of state control and self-regulation.[55] Education was under the auspices of the state. In the meantime, organized professions acquired 'state' functions such as in supervising professional activity. They considered themselves as autonomous and entered into bargaining processes with the government or organized clients, and accordingly their organizations had a professional or union character. Within the context of a fundamentally liberal society, neo-corporate patterns of regulation describe structures and mechanisms which secure the state a prominent role as guarantor of the common good while bargaining out the various interests of producers, employers and clients. The boundaries between the state/legislative bodies and participant social partners vary, which is the reason why interest groups and associations of professionals were delegated supervisory powers which had previously been a function of the state.

This type of pattern occurred frequently among trade unions and industrialists, and after 1945 it became increasingly influential. Correspondingly, the significance of the established arrangements between professions and the state also changed. Whereas various models of professionalism had previously comprised a separate category of regulations adopted for occupations which were either forced into this pattern (professionalization from above) or had consciously chosen this model, the neo-corporate arrangement now became the norm.

Some societies in which social self-regulation emerged early in the nineteenth century, as a consequence of civil liberal revolutions, have, in contrast, witnessed a marked weakening of the neo-corporate model by older traditions. North American and Swiss lawyers have enjoyed a longer tradition of social self-regulation and individualized strategies. This fact serves to explain why the traditional entrepreneurial mentality tends to assert its presence in the face of all similarity to the modern neo-corporate arrangement.

This clearly shows that the history of the professions is to a great extent determined by the degree to which they have been influenced by specific periods, as well as by the way in which social types succeed one another. Differences between nations and professions may be explained by examining the periodical developments just described. The professions did not change in constant conjunction with the respective type of society, although a certain correlation does exist between a given type of social structure and the corresponding form of profession. The respective successor in the sequence of professions inherits certain aspects from its predecessors, such as its way of thinking, its inner structure or practices. Novelty merges with existing structural and institutional arrangements, forming an intact synchronic unity consisting of elements which are not synchronic. This is exhibited in the fact that modern physicians still cling to an ideology of unselfishness in a highly industrialized and marketed medical profession. In such cases, certain combinations of characteristics emerge which, though not logically linked, are somehow woven together. The elements somehow fit together, although they are derived from different stages of development. Research on professionalization must necessarily reflect on the historicity of pertinent structures and concepts.

Conclusion

I have tried to elaborate on professionalization as a process and the way it is dealt with in relevant research. I have determined that the picture of professionalization varies both according to the research method or approach employed as well as to the underlying concept of temporal development. The concrete nature of the professionalization process renders a pure classificatory approach to long-term historical or sociological studies virtually useless. I would therefore suggest proceeding from a given diversity among historical types of professions and accordingly of professionalization. The remaining problems of interpretation result from a given unit consisting of elements which developed asynchronically.

These problems can only be solved within the context of the most generalized question in professionalization research: what value is placed on competence, and upon what basis is mutual trust achieved between the practitioners of certain occupations, their clients, and those who hold power and exercise influence in particular societies at any given time? The premise of the classical sociological theory of professionalization was that the relationship of trust between experts and clients was founded on the expert's superior subject knowledge. In view of the problems of the approach to professionalization discussed above, this assumption must be interpreted as one specific historical type. Institutionalized arrangements (as is the case, for instance, when an autonomous professional organization is authorized with certain capacities) should be regarded as a specific historical mode of regulating mutual trust. In the case of professionalization instated from above, trust was guaranteed by the state, and as the state itself was highly interested in warranting trust and competence, its administrative control was centralized. There was no room for bargaining here. Within self-regulatory social systems, mutual trust was achieved in a highly complex bargaining process, the study of which has been one of the chief objectives of professionalization theories.

The central issue remains the question of how services which fulfil specific tasks with respect to social utilities and values should be structured. Equally central is the question of the control of central values and critical resources. Processes of professionalization belong to a general species of process in which access to and control over social goods and values are products of shrewd bargaining. At stake is a fair share (and a certain degree of control) of different forms of capital: expertise and skill, cultural, economic, political and social capital. The size of the appropriate share of this capital defines the extent of power and influence which determine the outcome of bargaining arrangements. This accounts for the particular historical forms of transaction, disposition and strategies which have become the topic of professionalization research.

Notes

This chapter was translated from the German by James Polk.

1 Daheim, 1969:1–100, in particular pp. 20f. For examples of the way in which the problem of professionalization is dealt with both theoretically and practically, see the present volume; Johnson, 1972; Larson, 1977/1979; Dingwall and Lewis, 1983 ('Introduction'); Conze and Kocka, 1985, vol. 1; Murphy, 1988.

2 If we describe the various definitions of professions in terms of an ideal type or arrangement, then the term 'profession' would properly signify a particular sort of occupation, the practice of which presupposes a specialized (and possibly scientific) educational background. Specialized education allows the professional to secure practical and theoretical expertise relevant to his field as well as to acquire general knowledge and a sense of ethical values. Knowledge which is utilized 'selflessly' for the common good regardless of person is guaranteed through examinations and licences. Therefore, only licensed experts are, properly speaking, in the position of fulfilling certain functions and providing particular services. The professions demand, therefore, exclusive control over certain areas of operation and service as well as freedom from external supervision. Organized professional groups possess autonomous control over admissions and licensing policies. With reference to competence, ethical standards and the importance of efficiency for society and the common good, professions lay claim to special economic rewards and a more prestigious social status.

3 See, e.g., Siegrist, 1988c:92–123.

4 Parsons, 1968:536–547; Parsons, 1939:457–467. A critical position is offered by W. Schluchter, 1980:185–207; and by Rueschemeyer, 1973.

5 Larson, 1977/1979; Collins, 1979.

6 Siegrist, 1988a.

7 See, e.g., C. E. McClelland's, 'Escape from freedom? Reflections on German Professionalization, 1870–1933,' in R. Torstendahl and M. Burrage (eds), *The Formation of Professions* (Sage, 1990).

8 Freidson, 1983:19–37.

9 There are some attempts on the basis of a structural-functionalist approach to study the relationship between the type of a society (and its principal aims) and characteristics of a profession. See, e.g., Kaupen, 1974.

10 With respect to his research problem which is not followed up empirically, Daheim, 1969:21 suggests differentiating the 'various developments within the professionalisation process' according to whether (a) the process was initiated by those who hold either a particular position and/or an occupation on the one hand, or, by an occupational organization on the other; (b) whether a problem existed at the beginning of the process for which a solution had to be found, or whether specific branches of specialized knowledge existed for which appropriate areas of utilization were sought; and (c) whether interests defined by achievement, reward, and performance expectations take precedence.

11 Braudel, 1969:41–83.

12 Concerning the concepts 'virtuous' and 'vicious circle' both of which are derived from economic theories of market trends, see Kindleberger, 1967:117–120.

13 Wilensky, 1972:198–215.

14 Johnson, 1972:23, criticizes such 'trait-list-definition' of professions.

15 Burrage, 1988b:51–83.

16 I am referring to the discussion papers produced by the standing group 'Pro-

fessions and the State' coordinated by Arnold J. Heidenheimer, of which I am also a member. These papers have not as yet been published. See also Rueschemeyer, 1986:415–446.

17 Rueschemeyer, 1986:20, calls this process state-sponsored professionalization. But the state in nineteenth-century Europe was indeed more than just a sponsor! Siegrist, 1985:301–331, especially p. 314; Siegrist, 1989; Huerkamp, 1985b.

18 The term in German is *Rechtsanwalt* or *Advokat*. It means the legal expert in free practice. I use the term 'advocate' while Americans would maybe say 'lawyers', or, more specifically, 'attorney'. The translation of the term is difficult, because the division of labour and function varies between countries to a certain degree.

19 The term has been used by Jarausch, 1985:379–398; Jarausch, 1986a:107–137; Jarausch, 1988.

20 Burrage, 1988a:225–277.

21 See, e.g., Italy: Meriggi, 1988:141–159, vol. 2; Siegrist, 1988b:11–48.

22 Lepsius, 1987:79–100; Rueschemeyer, 1987:101–120; Siegrist, 1988b.

23 Späth, 1988:84–105.

24 A number of authors over-estimate in my view the connection between the Industrial Revolution and professionalization. One such author is Huerkamp, 1985b:17. The connection is certainly more evident among technical professions than with physicians or lawyers.

25 Mok, 1969:770–781.

26 Freidson, 1970a; Huerkamp, 1985b.

27 On the topic of paradigm revolutions see Kuhn, 1974.

28 See Ramsey, 1984:225–305.

29 Braun, 1985:332–357.

30 Lundgreen, 1988:106–124.

31 Max Weber, in particular, was one who shared the view that immanent legal factors and techniques, and externally, class-based legal motives were a central element in the development of the legal profession and administration of justice. Weber, 1972:387–513. See also Rottleuthner, 1988:145–173.

32 Rueschemeyer, 1973, sees the differences in the legal profession in an international comparison as lying mainly in the legal role or in their particular type of expertise. In 'Comparing Legal Professions' (1986), where he examines a broader spectrum than merely German and American societies, Rueschemeyer minimizes the significance of this factor. For arguments against an over-evaluation of the factor of legal technique see also Siegrist, 1986:267–298. Bertilsson, 1990, holds a different viewpoint.

33 Murphy (1988) offers a survey of newer variations. The meaning of 'proletarianization' varies considerably among relevant texts.

34 Braudel, *passim*.

35 See Åmark, 1990.

36 Burrage, 1988b; Duman, 1983; Prest, 1981; Prest, 1984:300–319.

37 The contradictory thesis was introduced by Atiyah, 1979.

38 Duman, 1983:206.

39 Duman, 1983:205.

40 Burrage, 1988b.

41 Exemplary articles on this topic are provided in Conze and Kocka, 1985.

42 For the most important works of that type, see the selective bibliography in Johnson, 1972:33–38.

43 See the relevant contributions in Conze and Kocka, 1985.

44 Weissler, 1905; Ostler, 1971; Siegrist, 1989.

45 Burrage, 1988b; Prest, 1981; Brambilla, 1982:79–160, vol. 3; Braun, 1985; Huerkamp, 1985a:358–387; Waddington, 1985:388–416.

46 Brambilla, 1982.

47 For further details see Siegrist, 1990 (forthcoming).

48 Cf., e.g., Wehler, 1987:210, vol. 2; Siegrist, 1988b; as well as Conze and Kocka, 1985; Rueschemeyer, 1986.

49 See, e.g., Wehler, 1987:210ff; Meriggi, 1987.

50 On civil society: Grimm, 1987; Kocka, 1987c:7–20; Kocka, 1987d: 21–63; Kocka, 1988a, vol 3.

51 Ramsey, 1984:230f; Boyer Chammard, 1976; Gaudry, 1864/1977.

52 Ramsey, 1984:230f.

53 Burrage, 1988b; Siegrist, 1986:267–298.

54 Ramsey, 1984:230f, calls this model a 'modified free field, with strict certification'.

55 Jarausch, 1988:124–146, vol. 2, applies the concept of neo-corporate professions in reference to Germany after the late nineteenth century. Further examples of neo-corporate professions in the sense I employ the term are presented in this volume and its companion, Torstendahl and Burrage (eds), *The Formation of Professions*, for instance, in the contributions of R. Torstendahl, A. Elzinga and M. Bertilsson.

11

An actor-based framework for the study of the professions

Michael Burrage, Konrad Jarausch and Hannes Siegrist

During the last decade or so discussion of the professions has been shifting its ground. The critical debunking that began during the 1960s to 1970s of the functionalist, somewhat normative, early contributions to the subject is more or less exhausted. Moreover, the Anglo-American literature on the professions has begun to attract the attention of historians and sociologists on the Continent, and social scientists have begun to realize that their early theorizing rested on narrow, ethnocentric evidence. At the same time, historians have started to understand that merely chronicling the rise of professional institutions fails to convey adequately the role of professional loyalties and aspirations in the life either of their subjects or of the societies of which they are a part. There are moves therefore towards a theoretical analysis of the professions that can accommodate both historical and comparative evidence.[1]

These are, however, still early days. Taxonomies, typologies, theories of short, medium and long range, inductive versus deductive approaches all compete with one another. This volume has brought a few more to the lists. In spite of some promising beginnings, however, it is not at all clear how a historical professionalization theory is to be constructed nor how one might extract generalizations from the rapidly accumulating empirical evidence. It may therefore be useful to try to bring some order to the discussion by mapping its parameters, identifying the key actors engaged in the struggle of occupations to establish themselves as professions, noting the varieties of their interrelationships and indicating, wherever possible, areas of emerging agreement as well as points of continuing dispute.

Such a map or framework has few ambitions in its own right, but it may help to clarify further debate by suggesting parameters essential for a theory. It might also aid the description of particular cases, identifying the minimum requirements for analysis of the professions and facilitate their use in comparative analyses, across both occupations and countries, by identifying critical variations in the institutional relationships in which they are involved. The format of our discussion is first to consider briefly the concepts used in the analysis of the professions, next to identify the actors involved in the establishment and transformation, or the destruction, of professions, and to assess the resources at their disposal. We then introduce the analysis of the interaction of these actors, an enterprise which lies at the heart of any attempt to construct an historical and cross-cultural theory of the professions, and conclude by commenting on the priorities and limits of this exercise.

The troublesome concept

There can be few areas of social enquiry that have become so involved, distracted and perplexed by matters of definition than the study of the professions. The reasons for these difficulties are fairly clear. Both the meaning of the term, and the occupations that might be described as professions, have changed over time, and members of professions have energetically propagated their own definitions of what they are, what they are doing and what it is that entitles them to be called a profession. The difficulties of the term are compounded when it is used in comparative analyses beyond the English-speaking world.

Much of the literature on the professions can side-step these difficulties and avoid giving a precise definition of a profession because it consists of case studies. It therefore needs to refer only to a single occupation and has no reason to define the generic characteristics of professions. However, any analysis of the professions collectively cannot circumvent the problem and must provide a clear definition about what constitutes a profession and what are its essential elements. One observer, weary of disputes about the term, recently suggested that we abandon the term altogether.[2]

To do this, however, and invent a new term would detach analysis from the self-consciousness of actors, from their notions of what they are trying to do or what they are proud to have become. This seems a rather high price to pay, even though part of the unease with past definitions is that they rested exclusively on the self-consciousness of the actors. Like many others, the most recent edition of *Webster's Dictionary*, for instance, defines a profession almost entirely in terms of professionals' own claims as:

> a calling requiring specialized knowledge and often long and intensive preparation including instruction in skills and methods as well as in the scientific, historical or scholarly principles underlying such skills and methods, maintaining by force of organization or concerted opinion high standards of achievement and conduct, and committing its members to

continued study and to a kind of work which has for its prime purpose the rendering of a public service.

Historians and sociologists now try to avoid incorporating any of the claims of the professions to special knowledge, to distinctive ethics or public service ideals into their definitions on the grounds that these reproduce professional rhetoric or ideology rather than describe reality. However, this reticence creates further difficulties, since one of the ways in which a profession is commonly recognized is that some at least of its claims have been accepted either by the state or by the public, or sectors of the public, or by both. Thus it seems that a satisfactory definition will have to include both the institutions and the claims of the professions. Some such distinction lies behind Collins' neat formulation: professions are 'socially idealized occupations organized as closed occupational communities'.[3] The first part refers to the actions by which some occupations have claimed, and somehow obtained some special power or recognition and become 'socially idealized', while the second half refers to specific mechanisms and institutions. However, rather too much is left unsaid and too many questions are left begging.

One recent definition that draws on the Anglo-American discussion, but broadens it to include also the continental experience, is Kocka's suggestion:

> Profession means a largely non-manual, full time occupation whose practice presupposes specialized, systematic and scholarly training . . . Access depends upon passing certain examinations which entitle to titles and diplomas, thereby sanctioning its role in the division of labor. . . . [Professions] tend to demand a monopoly of services as well as freedom from control by others such as laymen, the state, etc . . . Based upon competence, professional ethics and the special importance of their work for society and common weal, the professions claim specific material rewards and higher social prestige.[4]

Although not very elegant or economical, this formulation has the makings of a satisfactory working definition in that it distinguishes between the characteristics that describe professional occupations and the demands and claims that they make and provides clear criteria for recognizing both; criteria that can, moreover, be operationalized and measured. In the absence of any agreed suprahistorical or cross-cultural definition that can be applied with a consistent meaning to various historical and cultural settings, it is probably best to work with a definition that can be disaggregated and operationalized in this manner. At least, it ensures that we are aware of the shifts in meaning or emphasis as we move from one environment to another and identify those elements that tend to be constant and those that are more variable.

By spelling out the defining characteristics of a profession, we have, so to speak, brought the discussion of the traits of a profession in by a back door. There has been so much criticism in recent times of attempts to identify these traits that it may seem perverse and retrograde to insist that they are, after all, a vital part of any analysis of the professions. However, the impatience with this approach stems from a number of incidental assumptions that often accompanied the compilation of the list of traits: the idea, for instance, that a single, authoritative list would eventually emerge, as well as the implied acceptance of the claims made by professional bodies, and the notion that the list itself constituted a significant discovery about the nature of the professions.

There is, however, no reason to embrace any of these assumptions and a tentative list of the defining characteristics of a profession may therefore be used simply as a research aid: as a yardstick for the inclusion or exclusion of occupations among the professions, as a means of classifying professions or of measuring historical change. A list of traits is, moreover, indispensable if one wishes to analyse the process of professionalization or de-professionalization, rather than work with some vague, evolutionary notion of 'less' or 'more' professionalization, since it enables us to disassemble the elements of professionalization for purposes of analysis and identify alternative routes and critical stages of professional development. It may be that we should anticipate a two-tier set of characteristics, a short, economical list of basic, constant characteristics and a secondary list of optional variables.[5]

In sum, a satisfactory working definition of the professions will therefore be both institutional and 'political', in the sense that it will refer to claims made by the professions. It will also provide or suggest operational indicators so that we may disaggregate the phenomenon of professionalization and trace its development over time. Of necessity, therefore, it will also be provisional. For purposes of comparative analysis it might also help if it was seen as competitive, that is to say, as one possible way in which certain occupations have been distinguished from others. Its merits or demerits might then be compared with the terms used in other cultures for a similar purpose. Clearly the intent and usage of the French term *profession libérale* and the German *freie Berufe* are different. The terms *cadres* and *akademische Berufsstände* are closer equivalents, though they have quite different connotations and imply different collective aspirations, as well as different modes of analysis.

A comparative social history of these terms to identify the self-conceptions and the theories of social order they imply would substantially assist the analysis of the professions. It might also prompt us to ask why we are analysing French and German professions rather than English cadres or American *akademische Berufsstände*. Is it merely a consequence of the hegemony of the English language? Or is it a response to a significant social change in France and Germany? Such an analysis, however, presupposes that we have a firmer grip on the place of the professions in the social order of English-speaking societies and a sharper picture of what it is that has distinguished them over time. It will therefore be expected to accompany or follow further comparative investigation of the professions rather than precede it.

Four actors and their resources

Any satisfactory analysis of the professions requires a clear identification of the groups and organizations whose actions determine the form and the success or failure of professionalization. Most sociologists now employ an interactive triangle with professionals, clients and the state, but there can be little doubt that for comparative analysis it would be better to distinguish practising members of the profession from the specialists in the production and reproduction of professional knowledge, whom we may collectively describe as professors or academics. This addition is crucial if we wish to extend our analysis across the channel and identify the key differences between the continental and English profession. It might also enable us to deal rather better with the literature on professionalization in the history of science and discuss occupations which by many criteria look like professions, such as physicists, biologists and chemists, but emerged almost exclusively within the universities.

Abbott's work suggests we might add a fifth actor – namely, other professions – but for the moment we think that the four actors identified are sufficient.[6] While every profession involves a relationship of some kind between these four actors, it is by no means certain that it also entails a relationship of comparable significance and continuity with neighbouring and competing professions, even though conflicts with other professions, or more commonly with non-professionals, may at times be of some concern to its members.

Practising professionals themselves are obviously the key actors in their own development. Their basic aim may be described as self-government, that is, to control entry to their profession and practice of it and to protect and enhance the corporate interests. However, in order to pursue these goals and to realize them, they require the cooperation of the other actors, of the state, of universities and of their users, and we may reasonably assume that they endeavour to obtain this cooperation at minimum cost to their autonomy. Their major resources in these endeavours are organization, ideology and what we might call proximity and persistence. We will explain and illustrate each of them in turn.

Practising members of professions have organized for a variety of purposes, in an immense variety of ways. Unfortunately, historians and sociologists do not work with any agreed typology of organization; indeed, they have an unsettling tendency to see any form of organization as more or less equivalent to any other. One may nevertheless begin by distinguishing four major, ideal types of organization. First are those that give primary emphasis to the knowledge base of the profession, the discussion circle, learned society or academy. Second, there are those which primarily seek to represent and lobby on behalf of the profession and to obtain some legislative relief or support. Third are those which negotiate on behalf of their members and are often therefore barely distinguishable from trade unions. Finally, there are those that seek to regulate the members of the profession, the examining, certifying or as Millerson called them, the 'qualifying' associations.[7] These may be either state-sponsored, like the American 'integrated' bar associations, or voluntary, like the English Inns of Court.

In reality, these types of organization may be combined in a variety of ways, and the goals of associations may shift from one priority to another, or fail to shift, as associations formed to deal with one set of circumstances are compelled to deal with another. This may provoke conflicts within the profession on various grounds, between 'generalists' and 'specialists', between the elite and ordinary practitioners, between those in the capital and provinces and between those in different work settings, and any of these conflicts may lead to the emergence of factions within their associations or of rival, competing forms of association.

The goals and forms of organizations are not, however, solely a matter of the practitioners' volition, since they seem to be determined to some degree by the demands and pressures of the other three actors. These have rarely been investigated in detail, but it does not appear to be coincidental that the four types distinguished roughly correspond to the main concerns of the four actors. The learned society, for instance, gives primacy to developing the knowledge base of the profession and hence shares the same goal as the universities. The representative association is primarily oriented towards the state. The trade-union type of organization is primarily concerned to protect members having to deal with organized users of professional services, whether public or private. The regulatory association is of course concerned with practitioners themselves. This correspondence corroborates the suggestion that the dominant form of professional association is the product of historically specific constraints and opportunities presented to practitioners.

Ideology might well have preceded organization as a practitioner resource, since a profession might be said to begin to exist when those who perform the same kind of work recognize their kinship. A profession is an abstraction before it develops institutions. It largely exists in the aspirations and loyalties of practitioners or in the eye of the beholder, more, in other words, in perception than in reality. That circumstance suggests that ideology is of crucial importance for professionalization, both in terms of internal cohesion and of outside recognition or acceptance. Although practitioners may work successfully without a particular, professional consciousness, it takes an elevated and codified self-image to distinguish 'professional' from other kinds of behaviour. A professional ideology not only inspires practice and constrains practitioners, but also justifies privilege via public service to central social values. In order to distinguish professionalization from related phenomena, it is essential to identify a specifically 'professional' component in these actions, based upon a separate ideology that dictates strategies that are distinguishable from the activities of other groups.

Organization and ideology are resources that professions share with many other kinds of interest or pressure group, but professions have another resource which distinguishes them from every other such organized group. We have sought to capture this by the terms 'persistence' and 'proximity'. By 'persistence', we refer to the remarkable uniformity and consistency in the goals of professions. Whereas state institutions and state policies have changed out of all recognition, the goals of the professions have remained virtually constant, even though the strategies for reaching them may have changed. The mechanism of this continuity is of course the formal or informal socialization of new members, which leads one to suggest that the continuity will be greatest whenever practitioners remain in complete control of professional training.

Proximity, like persistence, is an inherent resource of any profession. States and pressure groups may intermittently be interested in the provision of one or other professional service, but practitioners themselves are of necessity always interested and always involved. Hence, though there may be room for disagreement, as we shall see, about the role of the knowledge base of professions, the knowledge *of* the profession as we might call it, there can be no doubt that the profession's knowledge *about* the intricacies of professional practice, the official and unofficial procedures, and the opportunities for manoeuvre and circumvention that these provide, is rarely rivalled. This is an immense source of power since it means that any attempt to change or control professional behaviour by instituting new rules and procedures has to be negotiated with resident procedural experts, the practitioners who will actually implement the change.

The second actors, *states*, are both regulators of professional life and instruments of professional advancement. They are directly or indirectly involved in every facet of professional existence, their organization, their education and licensing, their relationships with other professions as well as the market for their services. The power, wealth and prestige of any profession therefore depends largely on the policies of the state to which they are subject.

The crucial importance of states is demonstrated by the fact that the typology used immediately, and almost instinctively, in any comparative discussion of the professions is based on forms of political domination. Thus the discussion of professions in the English-speaking world rests implicitly on the boundaries of British imperialism. Further differentiation within this category refers to the divergent development from the original English model made possible by the end of British domination and the creation of new, independent states. The Napoleonic empire was similarly the means by which French professional institutions were diffused throughout Europe. Even instances of cultural diffusion, such as French and English influence on the bar of imperial Russia, or German influence on the development of Japanese attorneys, in fact depended on state action rather than the spontaneous, voluntary adoption of foreign models by members of the professions themselves.

In early discussions of the professions, the state was nevertheless treated as a silent, supportive partner to professional endeavours, partly, one suspects, because the emergence of the professions was seen as a consequence of the development of capitalism and partly because of the peculiar conditions under which many professions emerged in late-nineteenth-century Britain, when the state did in fact little more than facilitate the establishment of professional self-government. In recent times, prompted by the study of continental professions, far more attention has been paid to the role of the state, though much still remains to be discovered about the relationship between the state and professions.

To begin with, the interests of the state in the professions are rarely explicitly identified or documented. The analysis of their relationship is therefore frequently unbalanced, for while the interests of the profession are declared or self-evident, the state frequently appears to have no particular purpose of its own when dealing with the professions. The absence of concrete and specific accounts of state interests and actions has hindered the development of an adequate typology or periodization of state–profession relationships. Some students of the professions tend therefore to work with a basic variable of high and low stateness and then utilize a number of other familiar, available labels devised for some other purpose such as those used to describe states' political institutions, like absolutist, authoritarian, fascist or communist. Alternatively, they use terms that describe state relationships with manufacturing industry, such as '*laissez-faire*', 'liberal', 'interventionist' or 'corporatist'. It is by no means certain, however, that these terms can capture the relationship between states and professions satisfactorily.

Thus, the term '*laissez-faire*' is used to describe the relationship between the state and manufacturing industry and to draw a contrast with an interventionist state that regulates or nationalizes private industry. Such a distinction only tends to confuse the analysis of the state–profession relationship. To begin with, one might observe that during the heyday of '*laissez-faire*' in the middle of the nineteenth century, the British and American states adopted fundamentally different policies towards the professions. Moreover, the English legal and medical professions extended their powers still further under an 'interventionist' Labour government which nationalized many industries and, in a sense, sought to 'nationalize' health care by creating a National Health Service and legal advice by financing legal aid. Any analogy at this point with the dispossession of the owners of the railway, steel or ship-building industries is obviously misleading, since the medical profession extended its powers with the introduction of national health insurance and still more with the creation of the National Health Service. The legal profession similarly extended its powers with the creation of publicly funded legal aid.

The analysis of the professions therefore awaits some typology of state policies that is more appropriate and helpful for its purposes. In its absence, we will identify some of the different kinds of state interests in the professions. First, the aim shared by all new states is to establish their authority. This prompts a particular interest in legal institutions and the legal profession, and also in public health and therefore in the medical profession. Second, states have strategic interests in the professions. This was perhaps first shown by the interest of French monarchs of the sixteenth and seventeenth centuries in siege warfare and military engineering, but it has subsequently been demonstrated by most modern states, especially when at war. Third, states have had a political interest in the forms of government and collective action of the professions. The most outstanding example is the interest of French revolutionary assemblies in the forms of professional self-government. Finding these inconsistent with their ideals of equality and the sovereignty of the people, they were all abolished. Authoritarian regimes, such as the French through the first three-quarters of the nineteenth century, the Soviet and the Nazi have had a more or less continuous interest in the political potential of professional organizations and activities of whatever kind. Finally, one may distinguish a fiscal, and therefore electoral, interest in the professions. This is a relatively modern concern, stemming from state involvement in professional services as third-party payers, and it accounts for the interest of contemporary states in the legal, medical, teaching and social-work professions.

Somehow or other we need to relate these state interests to state policies towards the professions. Unfortunately, with a few notable exceptions,[8] research into state policy towards the professions has, for obvious reasons, tended to concentrate on those moments when the relationship 'surfaces' as public politics, usually when one or other of the actors has proposed a significant change in the relationship. And it may be that this intermittent, episodic state interest is one of the most significant characteristics of state–profession relationships. However, we obviously cannot draw conclusions about this until we know more about the continuous, covert relationships and the links between the executive agencies of the state and professions that precede or follow public legislative and judicial decisions. To what degree are professionals dealing with fellow members of their profession in the public service? Have professions been able to exploit state indifference or ignorance? Or, as Cleaves has asked, to what extent do states rely on professionals to provide a degree of insulation and autonomy from powerful interests in civil society?[9]

The *users* of professional services are the third significant actors in the professional domain. There are several different types. They have different resources at their disposal and accordingly present different kinds of threat and establish different relationships with the professions whose services they use. There can be little doubt that the user determines to a considerable extent the organization and strategy adopted by professional practitioners. An analysis of the variations in the resources of users, and how they have changed over time, must therefore figure largely in any satisfactory historical or comparative analysis of the professions. To illustrate the point, we may distinguish some major types of user, indicate their resources and suggest their effects on practitioner organization and strategy.

First, there is the individual fee-for-service client or patient. In the very first instance, these were usually drawn from a restricted royal or elite circle, but they progressively came to include the landowning classes and the urban middle class. The desire of practitioners to emancipate themselves from the arbitrary patronage of individual clients appears to have been associated with the initial emergence of professional institutions, indeed to have been the foundation of a golden age of professional organization. The legal and medical professions of many societies initially organized when the main demand for their services came from this kind of user. And this is perhaps not surprising, since the individual client has few resources that can be deployed against organized professional practitioners. Their only resources are their fees, their gossip perhaps, since word-of-mouth publicity may be an additional sanction or reward for professional behaviour and they may, of course, have sought redress in the courts. In the United States in the mid-nineteenth century, to cite one outstanding example, individual patients started to use the courts and malpractice suits against doctors, and these grew into an extremely potent form of client redress. However, all these resources could be used only to reward or sanction or control individual members of the profession, not to control an organized profession as a whole.

From the practitioner point of view, therefore, the individual fee-for-service client is the ideal user of their services. And their pre-eminence is associated with the golden age of professional organization because practitioners were able to develop their corporate institutions without significant, organized response from the users of their services. It may also have been a golden age in a normative sense since the kind of institutions which the legal and medical professions developed when serving an expanding, but unorganized, middle-class clientele seems to have had a decisive, formative impact on their institutions and ideology, indeed to have had a lasting influence on the actions and ideologies of professions that emerged later and with quite different clienteles.

Although individual users have not always remained powerless, user power generally depends on organization. One notable form of user organization emerged in the late nineteenth century when the mass demand for medical care was organized by private third-party payers, such as friendly societies and trade unions. Few other professions have had to face this kind of organized private user.

The nearest comparable cases, apart from medically related professions, are American lawyers and accountants since in recent decades they have begun to create mass markets for their services.

Judging by the experience of the French, German and British medical professions, this kind of organized user imposed one of the harshest, most punitive regimes that medical practitioners have ever had to endure.[10] All three professions therefore welcomed the emergence of the third type of user, the state, when it took over as the dominant third-party payer, and, in all three countries, state intervention seems to have augmented the autonomy of the profession.

A fourth kind of user is the private employer. In most countries, private employers have been the most numerous users of the services of engineers. The resources at the disposal of employers are considerable, since they determine the entire income of the employed professional and may also offer other inducements and rewards, including, as is commonly the case for engineers, advancement up a managerial career ladder. To counter employer demands and to try to defend their autonomy and status, professionals may rely on collective organization, or on their ideology, which an employer may or may not respect.

In the case of engineers, neither strategy seems to have been effective. It appears, in fact, that the upward, managerial 'exit' route is the Achilles' heel of the profession, undermining both their solidarity and their ideology.[11] To put the point another way around, and in more general terms, it may be that the power of professions has depended on the fact that their members commonly anticipate that their work as a member of a particular profession is life-long, terminal. Strong professions, we may suggest, have no alternative career outside the profession, no exit.

A fifth type of user is the public employer. If the state is the ultimate user of professional services, it has at its disposal the resources of private employers, plus those normally monopolized by the state – namely, legal and penal sanctions. In the case of the military and public service professions, states invariably use all these resources. In other cases, professionals may have alternative, political means of retaliating against public employers. This politicization of the employer–professional relationship is even more likely when the state employs professionals not as the ultimate user but to provide services for its citizens. Teaching was the first profession of this kind but since the emergence of the welfare state it has been joined by many more, including in some societies both the medical and legal professions.

These publicly employed professionals are distinctive because they have both clients and employers. The resources that might, potentially, be used to contain professional autonomy are therefore overwhelming since, in addition to those normally at the disposal of the state and of an employer, they may also face organized clients who might use protest or votes to force state action against the professions. However, it is by no means inevitable that employers and clients will combine their resources to control the professions. Professionals may be able to use one to resist the other and hence establish a high degree of autonomy. The outcomes of this kind of state–profession–user confrontation have varied greatly, by profession, by time and by country.

There is, it need hardly be added, no uniform or necessary pattern of development from one type of user to another. Contemporary professions face all types, as did some of the early professions. The twentieth century is nevertheless distinctive in the relative importance of the organized user, and the task of comparative analysis will be to try to identify the impact of the shift from one kind of user to another. The English bar has been able to convert every user, even the state, into an individual fee-for-service client and therefore long resisted any organizational response to the presence of organized users. Others, like French doctors, responded to the organized patients by adopting trade-union forms of organization. Accountants and lawyers in the United States appear to have been especially ready to develop forms of organization similar to those of their organized private users and thereby to have pioneered a sixth type of user, namely, the professional employer.

Universities, or other forms of advanced training institutions, are the fourth actor in the professional domain. Their major resources are the knowledge on which professions may depend and the status which their degrees may provide. In some countries the formation of professional training institutions has been part of the emergence of the professions and for that reason universities and practitioners are frequently not identified as distinct actors in the professional domain. In others, most notably England and the early United States, the organization of practitioners and professional training institutions has been quite separate and the distinct, and even conflicting, interests of practitioners and academics were explicit and self-evident.[12] Thus the universities had little interest in restricting entry to the profession and wished to convey knowledge which they judged to be interesting or important, without regard to the day-to-day requirements of professional practice.

The role of knowledge in the development of the professions remains a conspicuous area of disagreement. Talcott Parsons' claim that professions are mainly based on expertise seems to accept uncritically their own rhetoric. However, in criticizing this argument, Collins seems to deny the importance of professional knowledge altogether and equate it with rhetoric or ideology.[13] Even if some professionalization can take place before the establishment of a scientific knowledge base (as in nineteenth-century medicine), professionals' demands for autonomy and material rewards rest on some evaluation of their claimed expertise. The decline of theologians demonstrates the limits of the self-creation of problems and of claimed skill versus testable performance. A third position in this debate (derived from Foucault) treats the professions as 'a field of discourse', as though they were dominated by disciplinary concerns and never had to practise their profession. This approach seems more suitable for analysing the professionalization of academic disciplines than for the study of practising professionals.

The framework directs attention to other issues, to the balance of power between professor and practitioners. Who controls and transmits the knowledge required for admission to the profession? In some cases, the English bar is again the extreme case, the practitioners' knowledge was until recently the sole requirement for professional practice. In others, academic knowledge alone is mandatory, while in yet others, perhaps the majority of cases, some combination of formal, school-based and practice-based training is required. However, over the long run there has been an unmistakable trend toward university-based professional training. Practitioners who originally insisted that practice-based training was sufficient, such as English and American lawyers and engineers, now accept the major role of universities. In the United States, the transfer was made possible by state action against bar admission rules in the first half of the nineteenth century, and the English professions have slowly moved in the same direction in the second half of the twentieth.[14]

Although practitioners now accept the role of universities in training entrants to the profession and share academic interest in developing the knowledge base of their profession, we cannot assume that the interests of practitioners and academics invariably coincide. Their different career paths and their different roles and expectations with respect to the development of the knowledge of the profession are potential sources of disagreement and conflict. Practitioners seem to want a stable body of knowledge, each cohort of graduates acting as though the knowledge acquired during their training will constitute a secure base for practice during their entire careers. Practitioner solidarity is built on a relatively stable corpus of knowledge. In some professions, notably the law, this expectation is not altogether unrealistic, since legal knowledge changes in a predictable and cumulative manner. In others, most notably medicine since the late nineteenth century, such an expectation has been hopelessly inaccurate and the universities have developed entirely new specialities, which have substantial impact on intra-professional status relationships.

Practitioners and professors therefore have different kinds of investment in the knowledge base of the profession. Their interests in knowledge *about* the profession, as distinct from knowledge *of* the profession, may diverge sharply. If, for instance, practitioners have complaints about their fellow practitioners or about the activities of their corporate institutions, they usually avoid airing them in public. Academics, by contrast, who conduct research on the activities of the profession may have an interest in disseminating their findings and complaints to the widest possible audience and if they can provoke some kind of response from the state or from public opinion, so much the better.

Practitioners and professors also differ in their attitude towards the ideology and ethics of the profession. For the practitioner, the ideology of the profession is often converted into 'maxims of everyday life' that need not be examined, reassessed or criticized too frequently or too closely. For professors they are intellectual constructs, and may be accorded the same kind of scrutiny and review as the knowledge of the profession. Professors similarly have little direct interest in the rules of ethics that govern practitioners' behaviour. They have often therefore contributed to the rational examination and discrediting of practitioner ideologies and codes of ethics. Professors similarly have little direct interest in the jurisdictional concerns of practitioners. From the practitioners' point of view, they are therefore somewhat unreliable allies, often providing ammunition to their enemies and sowing the seeds of doubt in the minds of those who are shortly to enter the profession.

The relationship between practitioners and professors, like those between the other three actors, is therefore a variable one, and any historical or comparative analysis must be sensitive to these variations over time, between professions or between countries. There appears to be, for instance, a recurring difference between the law and medicine in this respect, with the practising lawyers often distinguishing themselves sharply from their academic 'colleagues' and seeking to resist or delimit academic control of legal training. Medicine, by contrast, is one of the few professions whose practice can be conducted within universities. Medical professors may be near full-time practitioners in a way that law professors seldom are. For this reason the distance between academic medicine and 'the real world' is not so great and there is less potential for antagonism in the relationship between practitioners and professors.

This, however, is merely to scratch at the surface of a neglected aspect of professionalization, since the relationship between practical and academic professional knowledge has only begun to be studied in recent years. One suspects that, wherever the state has empowered the universities to train and license future members of the profession or wherever practitioners have sought to locate their professional training in universities, professors have higher status, and perhaps higher incomes, than practitioners. Moreover, in these circumstances academic knowledge seems to be treated more deferentially and professors are more likely to be chosen as representatives, even leaders, of their professions.

Patterns of interaction

This framework is not a substitute for historical and sociological analyses of the professions. It does not explain how or why practitioners, civil servants, users and professors interacted to shape the modern professions. It may, however, help us to explore the interrelationships between these actors, first, by providing an initial checklist of the resources at their disposal. It may therefore facilitate the specification of the peculiarities of both particular professions and of professionalization in particular countries. It may also assist the identification of sequences or phases in the relationships between these actors and the attempt to identify typical patterns of development. It clearly avoids the structural reductionism that sees the professions as products of macro-processes such as 'modernization'[15] and, since all the actors may obviously be affected by events external to the professional domain, leaves open the question of how war, revolution, economic depression and other social changes may have affected a given social structure and political system and thereby the interaction of these four actors.

If one could identify the interests, resources and strategies of each of these four actors in a number of professions, in a number of countries, and how their interaction has changed over time, we would be able to advance general propositions about professionalization and be on our way to a general theory of the professions. However, the materials for such an inductive approach are not currently available, nor likely to be for some considerable time. A few preliminary speculations may, however, illustrate the uses to which this framework might be put.

To begin with, the framework provides a means of classifying and comparing different kinds of profession on the basis of the relative importance of the actors in their organization. Thus, as we have argued above, medicine seems always to have been more dependent on universities than law for the generation and transmission of their professional knowledge, and as a result medical practitioners have ceded more control over admission to professional practice to the universities than lawyers. Moreover, since the users of medical and legal services have organized at different times and in different ways, states have taken a different interest in the two professions. Engineering is distinctive in that it has never had a large proportion of individual fee-for-service clients and has therefore always had to deal with public or private employers, either of whom can overwhelm practitioner claims to autonomy. One might, in the same way, consider the other relationships of the framework, between practitioners and professors, between states and universities, and identify distinctive characteristics of specific professions.

In studying empirical cases, however, it soon becomes clear that the inter-professional differences are combined with inter-societal ones. One may therefore also use the framework to distinguish national patterns according to the actor that initiated professionalization. In England, professionalization has, almost invariably, been practitioner-led. Their associations have sought and usually obtained state authority to maintain control of entry and training, to extend their power over members of their own profession and to protect their jurisdiction against the claims of rival occupations. The British state has therefore played a rather passive role in the development of the professions, and the universities have hesitated to assert their interest in professional knowledge or in training of future members of the professions.

Initially, the legal and medical professions in the American colonies and in the new republic followed a similar pattern, but in the early nineteenth century the new state legislatures began to defend the interests of other actors; of clients, of practitioners dispossessed by the privileges granted to these professions, and of universities and other training institutions. Over the first four decades of the nineteenth century, state legislation undermined the existing bar associations and pre-empted the role of practitioner organizations. Professionalization was thereafter university-led, since the universities, together with private, commercial institutions, were the only remaining organized actors with an interest in the development of the professions.[16]

In France and other continental societies the state has played a much more important role in the training, licensing and regulation of both lawyers and doctors, and it has both empowered the universities and other institutions of professional training and circumscribed the freedom of practitioner organizations. The professionalization of French engineers seems to be the best-documented example of a set of relationships which is also found among professions in Germany, Italy and the Hapsburg empire where the state trained, employed and organized the profession. It therefore controlled and coordinated the strategies of three actors, leaving virtually no role at all for practitioner organizations.

The German case suggests a mixed model of state initiation followed by corporate self-assertion. While cameralist states reformed the older occupations into modern professions, practitioners in the mid-nineteenth century restructured their callings as 'free professions'. Under pressure from over-crowding, practitioners eventually turned back on the state to achieve a kind of neo-corporate compromise of self-government through professional chambers coupled with state protection against excessive competition. The role of universities and other institutions of higher learning tended to be stronger than the influence of clients except in the more controversial field of medical insurance funds where, with state assistance, doctors eventually succeeded in restoring their authority.[17]

With a broad characterization of national patterns, one may also identify the more significant discontinuities and changes in the relationships between the actors. In the case of France, the Revolution is obviously of primary importance, since the state and professional schools emerged from it with significantly greater powers and the practitioners with virtually none. Revolution is also of some importance in the United States, though the changes in the legal and medical professions followed it over some decades. The next significant change in the United States was the revival of a state interest in the delivery of professional services at the end of the nineteenth century and the accompanying resurgence and diffusion of practitioner organization.

In Britain there has been a continuous and progressive change in the relationship between practitioners and universities since World War II, as the older professions have come to rely on the universities and polytechnics to play a greater role in professional training and the rise of the so-called 'all-graduate' profession. The distinctive British professional configuration has therefore begun to resemble those of other societies, though the reasons for this belated change have still to be explained. Presumably, it reflects the progressive discrediting of practitioner-controlled methods of training and the wider acceptance of university degrees as status credentials.

These speculations lead one in turn to wonder whether one can distinguish phases of professional development. Many studies adopt or imply a 'traditional' versus 'modern' dichotomy similar to and probably derived from that once used in discussions of industrialization. By assigning greater weight to political factors, as this framework does, one is led to expect more complex sequences. In many European societies one can identify a succession from self-regulated guilds, to mercantilist state regulation, followed in some instances by a revolutionary or liberal disestablishment and then by a neo-corporatist re-establishment in the twentieth century. The inter-war period was one of crisis for the professions in many countries and their growth and general prosperity after World War II led some observers to speak of an era of neo-professionalism. More recently, in several professions, in several countries, one can detect a convergence with trade-union strategies, sometimes described as 'de-professionalization'.[18] This may perhaps be identified as another distinct phase.

Obviously, the timing and length of these phases differ from country to country. And the direction of change is not irreversible, since new socio-economic conditions and political struggles can arrest or reverse outcomes. Such a loose sequence cannot therefore be presented as a unilinear development. It might, in fact, be more fruitful to compare several typical sequences according to the relative power and initiative of the four actors. In any event, some conceptualization of the process of change, some sense of sequence and phases, is the prerequisite to crucial questions about the timing and sources of change in particular cases, and to the recognition of cases where continuity is itself worthy of intensive investigation.

Implications: politics and policy

In the past much of the discussion of the professions has been concerned with internal, domestic affairs and has paid little attention to the place of professionalization within the wider structural, political and moral transformations of modern society. The framework described above does not specify which transformations are critical, but it does at least break out of the narrow confines of much previous discussion and offer some means of relating the professions to other elements of the social structure to the state, to the educational system, to the markets for labour and services.

By presenting the development of the professions as the interplay of four actors, each with their own distinctive resources, interests and strategies, it gives primary place to politics. Since all the actors involved depend on the state, and their actions are mediated by the state, the decisions and policies of the state towards professional knowledge and professional services are therefore a subject of particular importance. Indeed, as we have already had reason to note, the advance of the comparative study of the professions depends, in large measure, on a concomitant advance in the comparative analysis of states. Are some states more responsive to their desires than others? How do professionals achieve their aims within the political process? In what ways has professional self-government changed the state? What was the nature of the link between the emergence of the modern professions in the last decades of the nineteenth century? Did their reiterated social service rhetoric contribute to the emergence of the liberal state?

Economic changes enter the analysis via the interests or resources of one or other of the four actors, and no special priority is given to industrial revolutions or the development of capitalist, industrial economies. Industrial revolutions do not, in fact, appear to have a decisive impact on the relationships between these four professional actors. Industrialization led to the expansion of the older professions and to the emergence of many new professions, and had a significant impact on the organization and resources of the four actors, especially the users of professional services. However, capitalist societies at similar stages of development still show remarkably different professional configurations which suggest that the economic interests of practitioners and of the users of professional services have been constrained, directed and shaped by the outcome of the political struggles and political relationships among the four actors.

In a similar manner the framework does not attempt to prejudge the question of the relationship between the professions and the class structure, since it is a matter for investigation to determine how far the strategies of the four actors have coincided with class action and class interests. In protecting their own interests, organized practitioners have, of necessity, helped to create and maintain structured social inequality. In cooperation with the state and universities, they have helped to stabilize and legitimize a highly differentiated and competitive occupational stratification. However, the extent to which their strategies have involved other actors, or have promoted society-wide, class organization and action is another question. It may be that the configuration of the four actors will help to explain apparent variations in the extent to which professions combine in pursuit of class interests.

In nineteenth-century Germany, for instance, graduates of higher educational institutions, far from being 'free-floating' intellectuals outside the class struggle, frequently had very concrete interests which led them time and again to ally themselves with other bourgeois groups in political campaigns.[19] In twentieth-century France, professional solidarity seems to have been commonly submerged, or transcended, by that of cadres.[20] In Britain, by contrast, histories of the professions seldom refer, or apparently need to refer, to class loyalties or associations.[21] One is therefore led to ask whether the greater degree of state control and state employment in the first two cases, as well as the common educational experience might help to explain their greater willingness to embrace wider, class loyalties.

Similar questions might also be also raised about gender inequalities. It is of course known that the professions have until very recently restricted access by women and that their access to the professions has followed certain common paths, starting with certain professions or semi-professions thought to be closer to female tastes and talents, such as nursing, social work and primary school teaching, and even when they finally entered the ancient professions they have tended to be found in particular female specialities. These patterns of access, however, need to be specified more exactly so that the kind of professional configuration that favours gender equality can also be identified. At first glance, it would appear that professions where entry is practitioner-controlled are least accessible to women, and correspondingly those where entry is controlled by universities or by the state are more open to them. Moreover, the impact of 'feminization' on the ideologies and strategies of the professions also merits further investigation.[22]

While this framework can claim to have something to offer to the study of the professions, it cannot claim to resolve many of the most heated disputes, since these are frequently ethical rather than empirical. There is a highly critical tone in much of the current literature on the professions, which often seeks to debunk the moral claims of the professions, and to show that their behaviour falls short of their proclaimed ideals, while the critics themselves, by implication at least, assert the superiority of their own moral position, in pointing out the excessive power and privileges that the professions enjoy, that their ethical codes are bogus and a cover for the pursuit of their material interests and so on. There is a certain irony in this literature inasmuch as professional power is nothing but the successful realization of a widely cherished goal, a form of workers' control or *auto-gestion*. A case might therefore be made not for less professionalism but for more, indeed for the professionalization of everyone, but no critic of the professions has followed this logic.

Since the framework is intended for analytical purposes, its neutrality with respect to this critical literature is scarcely surprising. It might none the less be of some relevance to the reform of the professions since, at the end of the day, the critics are obliged to suggest alternative forms for the delivery of professional services. In practice, there appears to be only one alternative to the complete abolition of the professions, namely, bureaucracy. One might, it is true, propose or desire some other alternative, such as independent, individual self-employed, fee-for-service practitioners, operating entirely independently of one another. It would, however, be inordinately difficult to maintain anything of this kind, since these independent practitioners would probably collude, which means some form of covert re-professionalization, or be taken over by larger enterprises, which means bureaucracy.

Few critics have been ready to face this stark, bureaucratic alternative, let alone suggest it was desirable. Most therefore seem to hope for the reform of professional organizations, the amendment of their rules, the curtailing of their privileges, making them more accountable. Historical and comparative research can play a part in this kind of discussion, since history has provided many diverse forms for the delivery of professional services and many different types and levels of professional development. Gathering and utilizing knowledge of these alternatives, however, depends on understanding the patterns of interaction which we have sought to clarify in this chapter.

Notes

1 This was the common goal of conferences organized by Rolf Torstendahl in Uppsala, Arnold Heidenheimer in Florence and Jürgen Kocka and Hannes Siegrist in Bielefeld. These comments are indebted to the discussions at these meetings. Most of the papers of the Bielefeld conferences are published in Siegrist, 1988a and in Kocka, 1988a.
2 Heidenheimer, 1986.
3 Collins, 1987.
4 Conze and Kocka, 1985.
5 McClelland, 1985.
6 Abbot, 1988.
7 Millerson, 1964.
8 Honigsbaum, 1979; Wortman, 1976.
9 Cleaves, 1987.
10 Leonard, 1978; Green, 1985; Huerkamp, 1985b.
11 Zussman, 1985.
12 Calvert, 1967; Jarausch, 1983.

13 Parsons, 1968; Collins, 1979.
14 Lundgreen, 1988.
15 Wehler, 1975.
16 Burrage, 1989.
17 Siegrist, 1988a; Cocks and Jarausch, 1990.
18 Jarausch, 1988.
19 Kocka, 1988b.
20 Boltanski, 1987.
21 Abel-Smith and Stevens, 1967.
22 Menkel-Meadow, 1989.

References

Abbott, Andrew (1988) *The System of Professions: An Essay on the Division of Expert Labor*. Chicago: University of Chicago Press.

Abel, Richard (1988a) 'United States: The Contradictions of Professionalism', in Richard Abel and Philip S. C. Lewis (eds), *Lawyers in Society*. vol. 1, *The Common Law World*. Berkeley, Los Angeles, London: University of California Press.

Abel, Richard (1988b) *The Legal Profession in England and Wales*. Oxford: Blackwell.

Abel-Smith, Brian and Stevens, Robert (1967) *Lawyers and the Courts: A Sociological Study of the English Legal System 1750–1965*. London: Heinemann.

Abelshauser, W. (ed.) (1987) *Die Weimarer Republik als Wohlfahrtsstaat*, Stuttgart.

Abercrombie, Nicholas and Urry, John (1983) *Capitalism, Labour and the Middle Classes*. London: Allen & Unwin.

Ackernecht, Erwin H. (1967) *Medicine at the Paris Hospital 1794–1848*. Baltimore, MD.

Adlercreutz, A. (1954) *Kollektivavtalet*. Lund.

Ahlstrom, G. (1982) *Engineers and Industrial Growth*. London: Croom Helm.

Åmark, C. (1948) 'Aktuella frågeställningar i det fackliga arbetet inom svensk psykiatri', *Nordiskt Psykiatriskt medlemsblad*, II.

Åmark, C. (1976) 'Klinik 4 – återblick och framtidsvyer', *Psykisk hälsa*, 1.

Åmark, Klas (1986) *Facklig makt och fackligt medlemsskap. De svenska fackförbundens medlemsutveckling 1890–1940*. Lund: Arkiv.

Åmark, Klas (1987) *Konkurrensbegränsning och arbetsmarknadsorganisering*.

Åmark, Klas (1989) *Maktkamp i byggbransch*. Lund.

Åmark, Klas (1990) 'Open Cartels and Social Closures: Professional Strategies in Sweden, 1860–1950', in this volume.

Anderson, Perry (1974) *Passages from Antiquity to Feudalism*. London: New Left Books.

Arnö, I. (1964) *Publicistklubben 90 år 1874–1964*. Stockholm.

Arthurs, Harry, Weisman, Richard, and Zemens, Frederick (1988) 'Canadian Lawyers: A Peculiar Profession', in Richard Abel and Philip S. C. Lewis (eds), *Lawyers in Society*, vol. 1, *The Common Law World*. Berkeley, Los Angeles, London: University of California Press.

Atiyah, P. S. (1979) *The Rise and Fall of Freedom of Contract*. Oxford.

Austin, J. L. (1961) *Philosophical Papers*. Oxford: Clarendon Press.

Bailes, Kendall (1978) *Technology and Society under Lenin and Stalin: Origins of the Soviet Technical Intelligentsia, 1917–1941*. Princeton: Princeton University Press.

Barbaret, J. (1886) *Le Travail en France: Monographies Professionelles*, 3 vols. Paris: Berger-Levrault.

Baumgarten, S. von and Corneliusson, E. (1986) *Vi behöver varandra. En historiebok om SKTF.* Stockholm.

Becher, Tony (1990) 'Professional Education in a Comparative Context', in R. Torstendahl and M. Burrage (eds), *The Formation of Professions: Knowledge, State and Strategy.* London: Sage.

Beckman, Svante (1981) *Kärlek på tjänstetid.* Stockholm.

Bell, Daniel (1973) *The Coming of Post-Industrial Society: A Venture in Social Forecasting.* New York: Basic Books.

Berg, O. (1980) 'The Modernization of Medical Care in Sweden and Norway', in Arnold Heidenheimer and Nils Elvander, *The Shaping of the Swedish Health System.* London.

Bergstrand, H. (1958) *Läkaresällskapet 150 år.* Stockholm.

Bergstrand, H. (1962) 'Läkarekåren och provinsialväsendet', in W. Kock (ed.), *Medicinalväsendet i Sverige 1913–1962.* Stockholm.

Berlanstein, Lenard R. (1975) *The Barristers of Toulouse in the Eighteenth Century, 1740–1793.* Baltimore, MD: Johns Hopkins University Press.

Berlant, Jeffrey L. (1985) *Professions and Monopoly: A Study of Medicine in the United States and Great Britain.* Berkeley, CA: University of California Press.

Bernstein, Basil (1971/1973) *Class, Codes, and Control.* London: Routledge & Kegan Paul.

Bertilsson, Margaretha (1990) 'The Welfare State, the Professions and Citizens', in Rolf Torstendahl and Michael Burrage (eds), *The Formation of Professions: Knowledge, State and Strategy.* London: Sage.

Best, H. (1989) 'Soziale Morphologie und politische Orientierungen bildungsbürgerlicher Abgeordneter in der Frankfurter Nationalversammlung und in der Pariser Assemblée nationale constituante 1848/49', in Jürgen Kocka (ed.), *Das Bildungsbürgertum in Gesellschaft und Politik.* Stuttgart.

Björnhaug, I. (1986) 'Profesjonalisert arbid og faglig radikalisme – naert forhold eller tilfeldige forbindelser?', *Tidskrift for Arbeiderbevaegelsens historie,* 2.

Blanc, Louis (n.d.) *Historical Pages from the French Revolution of February 1848.* Trans. J. E. Smith. London: Vickers.

Blau, Peter M. (1964) *Exchange and Power in Social Life.* New York: Wiley.

Blau, Peter (1974) 'Parameters of Social Structure', *American Sociological Review,* 39.

Bloomfield, Maxwell (1976) *American Lawyers in a Changing Society, 1776–1876.* Cambridge, MA: Harvard University Press.

Boalt, G. and Bergryd, U. (1974) *Centralförbundet för socialt arbete. Ett kapitel svensk socialpolitik.*

Bok, Derek and Dunlop, John (1970) *Labour and the American Community.* New York: Simon & Schuster.

Boltanski, Luc (1987) *The Making of a Class: Cadres in French Society.* Cambridge: Cambridge University Press.

Bourdieu, Pierre (1979/1984) *Distinction. A Social Critique of the Judgement of Taste.* Cambridge, MA: Harvard University Press.

Bourdieu, Pierre (1979) *La Distinction: Critique social du jugement.* Paris.

Bourdieu, Pierre and Passeron, Jean-Claude (1970/1977) *Reproduction: in Education, Society, and Culture.* Beverly Hills, CA: Sage.

Boyer Chammard, G. (1976) *Les Avocats.* Paris.

Brambilla, E. (1982) 'Il sistema letterario di Milano. Professioni nobili e professioni borghesi dall'età spagnola alle riforme teresiane', in A. de Maddalena et al. (eds),

Economia, istituzioni, cultura in Lombardia nell'età di Maria Teresa, vol. 3. Bologna.

Brante, Thomas (1988) 'Sociological Perspectives on the Professions', *Acta Sociologica*, 31(2).

Braudel, Fernand (1969) 'La longue durée', in F. Braudel, *Écrits sur l'histoire*. Paris.

Braun, R. (1985) 'Zur Professionalisierung des Ärztestandes in der Schweiz', in Werner Conze and Jürgen Kocka (eds), *Bildungsbürgertum im 19. Jahrhundert. Teil I: Bildungssystem und Professionalisierung in internationalen Vergleichen*, Stuttgart: Klett-Cotta.

Brentano, Lujo von (1870) *On the History and Development of Gilds and the Origin of Trade Unions*. London: Trubner.

Brooks, C. W. (1986) *Pettyfoggers and Vipers of the Commonwealth: The 'Lower Branch' of the Legal Profession in Early Modern England*. Cambridge: Cambridge University Press.

Brundage, James A. (1987) 'The Professionalization of Canon Lawyers in the Thirteenth Century'. Unpublished paper given to Law and Society Seminar. Institute of Historical Research, University of London.

Burchhardt, Lothar (1980) 'Professionalisierung oder Berufskonstruktion? Das Beispiel des Chemikers im Wilhelminischen Deutschland', *Geschichte und Gesellschaft*, 6.

Burns, Tom and Flam, Helena (1987) *The Shaping of Social Organization: Social Rule System Theory with Applications*. London: Sage.

Burrage, Michael (1988a) 'Revolution and the Collective Action of the French, American and English Legal Professions', in *Law and Social Inquiry, Journal of the American Bar Foundation*, 13(2).

Burrage, Michael (1988b) 'Unternehmer, Beamte und freie Berufe. Schlüsselgruppen der bürgerlichen Mittelschichten in England, Frankreich und den Vereinigten Staaten', in Hannes, Siegrist, *Bürgerliche Berufe. Zur Sozialgeschichte der freien und akademischen Berufe im internationalen Vergleich*. Göttingen.

Burrage, Michael (1989) 'Revolution as a Starting Point for the Comparative Analysis of the French, American and English Legal Professions', in Richard L. Abel and Philip S. C. Lewis (eds), *Lawyers in Society*. vol. 3, *Comparative Theories*. Berkeley, CA: University of California, pp. 322–374.

Calhoun, Daniel H. (1965) *Professional Lives in America, Structure and Aspiration 1750–1850*. Cambridge, MA: Harvard University Press.

Calvert, Monte (1967) *The Mechanical Engineer in America, 1830–1910. Professional Cultures in Conflict*. Baltimore, MD.

Carlsson, Sten (1968) *Yrken och samhällsgrupper. Den sociala omgrupperingen efter 1866*. Stockholm.

Carr-Saunders, A. M. and Wilson, P. A. (1933) *The Professionals*. London: Frank Cass.

Carr-Saunders, A. M. et al (1958), *A Survey of Social Conditions in England and Wales as Illustrated by Statistics*. Oxford: Clarendon Press, 1st edn 1937.

Chaigneau, V-L. (1945) *Histoire de L'Organization Professionelle en France: La Loi du 4 Octobre 1941*. Paris.

Clark, George (1964, 1966) *A History of the Royal College of Physicians of London*, 2 vols. Oxford: Clarendon Press.

Cleaves, Peter S. (1987) *Professions and the State: The Mexican Case*. Tucson, AZ: University of Arizona Press.

Clegg, Hugh, et al. (1964) *A History of British Trade Unions since 1889*, vol. 1, *1889–1910*. Oxford: Oxford University Press.

Cocks, G. and Jarausch K. H. (eds) (1990) *The German Professions 1800–1950*. New York: Oxford University Press.

Cocks, Raymond (1983) *Foundations of the Modern Bar*. London: Sweet & Maxwell.

Cole, G. D. H. (1953) *Attempts at General Union: A Study in British Trade Union History 1818–1834*. London: Macmillan.

Collins, Harry (1981) 'Son of Seven Sexes', *Social Studies of Science*, 11.

Collins, Randall (1975) *Conflict Sociology*. New York: Academic Press.

Collins, Randall (1979) *The Credential Society: An Historical Sociology of Education and Stratification*. New York: Academic Press.

Collins, Randall (1981) 'Crises and Declines in Credential Systems', in *Sociology since Midcentury: Essays in Theory Cumulation*. New York: Academic Press.

Collins, Randall (1986) *Weberian Sociological Theory*. New York: Cambridge University Press.

Collins, Randall (1987) 'Comments on "A framework for the history of the professions" ', MS, Riverside.

Collins, Randall (1988) *Theoretical Sociology*. San Diego: Harcourt, Brace, Jovanovich.

Commons, J. R. (ed.) (1921) *History of Labour in the United States*, vol. 1, New York: Macmillan.

Conze, Werner and Kocka, Jürgen (eds) (1985) *Bildungsbürgertum im 19. Jahrhundert. Teil I: Bildungssystem und Professionalisierung in internationalen Vergleichen*. Stuttgart: Klett-Cotta.

Cope, Zachary (1959) *The Royal College of Surgeons of England: A History*. London: Anthony Blond.

Daheim, H. (1969) 'Berufssoziologie', in R. König (ed.), *Handbuch der empirischen Sozialforschung*, vol. 8(2), rev. ed. Stuttgart.

Dawson, John P. (1960) *A History of Lay Judges*. Cambridge, MA: Harvard University Press.

Dawson, John P. (1968) *The Oracles of the Law*. Ann Arbor, MI: University of Michigan Law School.

De Geer, Hans (1986) *SAF i förhandlingar. Svenska Arbetsgivareföreningen och dess förhandlingsrelationer till LO och tjänstemannaorganisationerna 1930–1970*. Stockholm.

Desroisières, A. (1977) 'Eléments pour l'histoire des nomenclatures socioprofessionnelles', in *Pour une histoire de la statistique*. Paris.

Desroisières, A. (1988) 'How to Make "Things": The Contribution of Statistics to the Construction of the Social Sciences. A Problem-oriented Historical Perspective'. Unpublished paper, Berlin: Wissenschaftskolleg.

Dezelay, Yves (1989) 'Le Droit des faillites: du notable à l'expert. La réstructuration du champ des professionnels de la réstructuration des entreprises', in *Actes de la Recherche en sciences sociales*, 76–77 (March).

Dilcher, G. (1986) 'Die preussischen Juristen und die Staatsprüfungen. Zur Entwicklung der juristischen Professionalisierung im 18. Jahrhundert', in *Festschrift für Hans Thieme*. Sigmaringen.

Dingwall, R. and Lewis, P. (eds) (1983) *The Sociology of the Professions*. London: Macmillan.

Dobson, C. R. (1980) *Masters and Journeymen: A Prehistory of Industrial Relations 1717–1800*. London: Croom Helm.

Douglas, Mary (ed.) (1982) *Essays in the Sociology of Perception*. London: Routledge & Kegan Paul.

Dubofsky, M. (1968) *We Shall All Be All: a History of the International Workers of the World*. Chicago: Quadrangle.

Duman, Daniel (1983) *The English and Colonial Bars in the Nineteenth Century*. London: Croom Helm.

Durkheim, Emile (1912/1954) *The Elementary Forms of the Religious Life*. New York: Free Press.

Dyson, Roger and Spary, K. (1979) 'Professional Associations', in Nick Bosanquet (ed.), *Industrial Relations in the National Health Service – the Search for a System*, King Edward's Hospital Fund.

Elbow, M. H. (1953) *French Corporative Theory, 1789–1948*. Columbia University Studies in History, Economics and Public Law, 577. New York.

Ellis, Richard, E. (1971) *The Jeffersonian Crisis: Courts and Politics in the Young Republic*. New York.

Engelhardt, U. (1986) 'Bildungsbürgertum', *Begriffs- und Dogmengeschichte eines Etiketts*. Stuttgart.

Engels, Friedrich (1972) *Die Lage der arbeitenden Klasse in England*. 1844, published in Karl Marx and Friedrich Engels, *Werke*, vol. 2. Berlin.

Evans, Peter, Rueschemeyer, Dietrich, and Skocpol, Theda (eds) (1985) *Bringing the State Back In*. Cambridge: Cambridge University Press.

Festy, O. (1891) *Le Mouvement ouvrier au début de Monarchie de Juillet 1830–1834*. Paris.

Feuchtwanger, S. (1922) *Die freien Berufe. Im besonderen: Die Anwaltschaft. Versuch einer Kulturwirtschaftslehre*. Leipzig.

Feyerabend, Paul (1975) *Against Method*. London: New Left Books.

Field, Mark (1967) *Soviet Socialized Medicine*. New York.

Fitzsimmons, M. P. (1987) *The Parisian Order of Barristers and the French Revolution*. Cambridge, MA: Harvard University Press.

Flanders, A. (1964) *The Fawley Productivity Agreements*. London: Faber.

Flexner, Abraham (1910) *Medical Education in the United States and Canada, A Report to the Carnegie Foundation for the Advancement of Teaching*. Bulletin no. 4.

Flexner, Abraham (1912) *Medical Education in Europe: A Report to the Carnegie Foundation for the Advancement of Teaching*. Bulletin no. 6.

Flexner, Abraham (1930) *Universities: American, English, German*. Oxford: Oxford University Press.

Florin, Christina (1987) *Kampen om katedern. Feminiserings- och professionaliseringsprocesser inom den svenska folkskolans lärarkår 1860–1906*. Acta Universitatis Umensis, Umeå Studies in the Humanities, 82. Almqvist & Wiksell International.

'Formerna för auktorisation av revisorer mm. Betänkande avgivet av Auktorisationsutredningen'. H 1971:3, Stockholm 1971.

Franzen, Gunnar (1977) *Byggnormer* (Standards of Construction). Lund: Studentliteratur.

Freidson, E. (1970) *Professional Dominance: The Social Structure of Medical Care*. New York: Atherton Press.

Freidson, Eliot (1970a) *Profession of Medicine: A Study of the Sociology of Applied Knowledge*. New York: Dodd and Mead.

Freidson, Eliot (1983) 'The Theory of Professions: State of the Art', in R. Dingwall and P. Lewis (eds), *The Sociology of the Professions*. London: The Macmillan Press.

Freidson, Eliot (1986) *Professional Powers: a Study of the Institutionalization of Formal Knowledge*. Chicago: University of Chicago Press.

Frevert, U. (ed.). (1988) *Bürgerinnen und Bürger. Geschlechterverhältnisse im 19. Jahrhundert* Göttingen: Vandenhoeck & Ruprecht.

Frieden, Nancy Mandelker (1981) *Russian Physicians in an Era of Reform and Revolution, 1865–1905*. Princeton, NJ: Princeton University Press.

Furåker, Bengt (1987) *Stat och offentlig sektor*. Stockholm: Rabén och Sjögren.

Gaudry, J. A. J. (1864) *Histoire du barreau de Paris. Depuis son originale jusqu'à 1830*. Paris: reprint, Geneva, 1977.

Gawalt, Gerard W. (1979) *The Promise of Power. The Emergence of the Legal Profession in Massachusetts, 1760–1840*. Westport, CT.

Geiger, T. (1949) *Aufgaben und Stellung der Intelligenz in der Gesellschaft*. Stuttgart.

Geison, Gerald (ed.) (1984) *Professions and the French State, 1700–1900*. Philadelphia: Pennsylvania University Press.

Gelfand, Toby (1987) 'The Annales and Medical Historiography: Bilan et Perspectives', in Roy Porter and Andrew Wear (eds), *Problems and Methods in the History of Medicine*. London: Croom Helm.

Gesser, Bengt (1985) *Utbildning, jämlikhet, arbetsdelning*. Lund: Arkiv.

Gilb, Catherine (1966) *Hidden Hierarchies, The Professions and Government*. New York: Harper & Row.

Glaser, William A. (1963) 'American and Foreign Hospitals: Some Sociological Comparisons', in E. Freidson (ed.), *The Hospital in Modern Society*. New York.

Glover, Ian A. and Kelly, Michael P. (1987) *Engineers in Britain: A Sociological Study of the Engineering Dimension*. London: Allen & Unwin.

Goldstone, Jack (1989) *State Breakdown. Revolution and Rebellion in the Early Modern World, 1640–1848*. In press.

Goodrich, C. L. (1920) *The Frontier of Control: A Study in British Workshop Politics*. London.

Gottfried, Robert S. (1986) *Doctors and Medicine in Medieval England, 1340–1520*. Princeton, NJ: Princeton University Press.

Green, David G. (1985) *Working Class Patients and the Medical Establishment: Self-help in Britain from the Mid-nineteenth Century to 1948*. London: Gower.

Grimm, Dieter (1987) *Recht und Staat der bürgerlichen Gesellschaft*. Frankfurt.

Hall, Kermit L. (ed.) (1987) *The Legal Profession: Major Historical Interpretations*. New York: Garland.

Hall, R. H. (1968) 'Professionalism and Bureaucratization', in *American Sociological Review*, 33.

Hall, R. H. (1983) 'Theoretical Trends in the Sociology of Occupations', *Sociological Quarterly*, 24 (Winter).

Haller, John S., Jr (1981) *American Medicine in Transition, 1840–1910*. Urbana, IL, University of Illinois Press.

Handlin, O. and Handlin, M. (1969) *Commonwealth: a Study of the Role of Government in the American Economy, Massachusetts 1774–1861*. Cambridge, MA: Harvard University Press, rev. ed.

Hansson, S. (1981) *Svenska Teknologföreningen – de andra femtio åren*.

Harré, Rom (1979) *Social Being*. Oxford: Blackwell.

Hattenhauer, H. (1980) *Geschichte des Beamtentums*. Cologne.

Havland, A. (1958) 'Tandläkarsammanslutningar i Sverige före 1908. Krisår och tillväxtår', in *Sveriges Tandläkareförbund 1908–1958*.

Hazard, John N. (1964) *The Soviet System of Government*. 3rd ed. Chicago: University of Chicago Press.

Heidenheimer, Arnold (1980) 'Conflict and Compromises Between Professional and Bureaucratic Health Interests 1947–1972', in Arnold Heidenheimer and Nils Elvander, *The Shaping of the Swedish Health System*. London.

Heidenheimer, Arnold (1986) 'Guardians Transformed: Exploring the Evolution of State–Professional Relationships', MS, St Louis, MO.

Heidenheimer, Arnold (1989) 'Professional Knowledge and State Policy Variations: Law and Medicine in Britain, Germany and the United States'. Mimeographed paper, University of Bielefeld, Centre for Interdisciplinary Research (March).

Hellberg, Inga (1978) 'Studier i professionell organisation. En professionsteori med tillämpning på veterinäryrket? Dissertation, Göteborg.

Hellkvist, O. and Wingqvist, T. (1926) *Svenska Journalistföreningen. De första tjugofem åren i ord och bild*.

Henning, H. (1972) *Das westdeutsche Bürgertum in der Epoche der Hochindustrialisierung 1860–1914. Soziales Verhalten und soziale Strukturen I: Das Bildungsbürgertum in den Preussischen Westprovinzen*. Wiesbaden.

Henning, H. (1978) 'Soziale Verflechtungen der Unternehmer in Westfalen 1860–1914', in *Zeitschrift für Unternehmensgeschichte*, 23.

Hetzler, Antoinette et al. (1985) *Ramlagstiftning*. Nordiska Institutet för Samhällsplanering 10, Stockholm.

Hobsbawm, E. J. (1988) 'Die englische "middle-class" 1780–1920', in Jürgen Kocka (ed.), *Bürgertum im 19. Jahrhundert. Deutschland im europäischen Vergleich*, Vol. 1. Munich: Deutscher Taschenbuch Verlag.

Holmes, Geoffrey (1982) *Augustan England: Professions, State and Society, 1680–1730*. London: Allen & Unwin.

Honigsbaum, Frank (1979) *The Division in British Medicine: A History of the Separation of General Practice from Hospital Care 1911–1968*. London: Kogan Page.

Hubert, Henri and Maus, Marcel (1902–3, 1975) *A General Theory of Magic*. New York: Norton.

Hubert-Valleroux, Paul (1885) *Les Corporations d'Arts et Métiers et les Syndicats Professionnels en France et à l'étranger*. Paris: Guillaumin.

Huerkamp, Claudia (1985a) 'Die preussisch-deutsche Ärzteschaft als Teil des Bildungsbürgertums: Wandel in Lage und Selbstverständnis vom ausgehenden 18. Jahrhundert bis zum Kaiserreich', in Werner Conze and Jürgen Kocka (eds), *Bildungsbürgertum im 19. Jahrhundert. Vol. I: Bildungssystem und Professionalisierung in internationalen Vergleichen*. Stuttgart: Klett-Cotta.

Huerkamp, Claudia (1985b) *Der Aufstieg der Ärzte im 19. Jahrhundert. Vom gelehrten Stand zum professionellen Experten: Das Beispiel Preussens*. Göttingen.

Huerkamp, Claudia (1987) 'The Professionalization of Medical Men in the Nineteenth Century: A Comparison between England and Prussia', paper given at the Council of European Studies Seminar on the State and Professions, Bielefeld.

Huerkamp, Claudia (1988) 'Frauen, Universitäten und Bildungsbürgertum. Zur Lage studierender Frauen 1900–1930', in Hannes Siegrist (ed.), *Bürgerliche Berufe: Zur Sozialgeschichte der freien und akademischen Berufe im internationalen Vergleich*. Göttingen: Vandenhoeck & Ruprecht.

Huskey, Eugene (1986) *Russian Lawyers and the Soviet State: The Origins and Development of the Soviet Bar 1917–1939*. Princeton, NJ: Princeton University Press.

Illich, Ivan (1972) *De-Schooling Society*. New York: Harper & Row.

Illich, Ivan (1975) *Medical Nemesis: the Expropriation of Health*. London: Calder and Boyars.

Illich, Ivan et al. (1977) *Disabling Professions*. London: Boyars.

Indebetou, G. and Hylander, E. (1936) *Svenska Teknologföreningen 1861–1936*. Stockholm.

Ives, Eric W. (1983) *The Common Lawyers of Pre-Reformation England: Thomas Kebell, A Case Study*. Cambridge: Cambridge University Press.

Jamous, H. and Peloille, B. (1970) 'Changes in the French University-Hospital System', in J. A. Jackson (ed.), *Professions and Professionalization*. Cambridge: Cambridge University Press.

Jarausch, Konrad (ed.) (1983) *The Transformation of Higher Learning, 1860–1930*. Chicago, IL: Chicago University Press.

Jarausch, Konrad H. (1985) 'The Crisis of the German Professions 1918–1933', *Journal of Contemporary History*, 20.

Jarausch, Konrad H. (1986a) 'The Perils of Professionalism. Lawyers, Teachers and Engineers in Nazi Germany', *German Studies Review*, 9.

Jarausch, Konrad (1986b) 'Professionalization German Style', The Swedish Collegium for Advanced Study in the Social Sciences (SCASSS), Uppsala (MS).

Jarausch, Konrad H. (1987) 'Die Not der geistigen Arbeiter. Akademiker in der Berufskrise 1918–1933', in W. Abelshauser (ed.), *Die Weimarer Republik als Wohlfahrtsstaat*. Wiesbaden: Franz Steiner Verlag.

Jarausch, Konrad H. (1988) 'Die unfreien Professionen. Überlegungen zu den Wandlungsprozessen in deutschen Bürgertum', in Jürgen Kocka (ed.), *Bürgertum im 19. Jahrhundert. Deutschland im europäischen Vergleich*, vol. 2. Munich: Deutscher Taschenbuch Verlag.

Jarausch, Konrad (1990) *The Unfree Professions: German Lawyers, Teachers and Engineers between Democracy and National Socialism, 1900–1950*. New York: OUP.

Jeffreys, J. B. (1945) *The Story of the Engineers 1800–1945*. London: Lawrence & Wishart.

Jensen, Merrill, (1974) *The American Revolution within America*. New York.

Johansson, O. (1971) 'SYLF 50 en tillbakablick med glimtar från de gångna årens verksamhet', *Läkartidningen*, 51.

Johnson, Dale L. and O'Donnell, Christine (1982) 'The Dequalification of Technical, Administrative and Professional Labor', in D. L. Johnson (ed.), *Class and Social Development. A New Theory of the Middle Class*. Beverly Hills, CA: Sage.

Johnson, Terrence (1972) *Professions and Power*. London: Macmillan.

Kagan, Richard L. (1981) *Lawsuits and Litigants in Castile, 1500–1700*. Chapel Hill, NC: University of North Carolina.

Karady, V. (1985) 'Teachers and Academics in Nineteenth-Century France', in Werner Conze and Jürgen Kocka (eds), *Bildungsbürgertum im 19. Jahrhundert. Vol. I: Bildungssystem und Professionalisierung in internationalen Vergleichen*. Stuttgart: Klett-Cotta.

Karpik, Lucien (1985) 'Avocat: une nouvelle profession?', *Revue Française de Sociologie*, XXVI.

Karpik, Lucien (1988) 'The State, the Market and the Public: Lawyers and Politics in France 1814–1950', *Law and Social Inquiry*, 13(4) (Fall).

Kaupen, W. (1974) 'Über die Bedeutung des Rechts und der Juristen in der modernen Gesellschaft. Ein strukturell-funktionaler Ansatz', in W. Kaupen and R. Wehrle (eds), *Soziologische Probleme juristischer Berufe*. Göttingen.

Kett, Joseph F. (1968) *The Formation of the American Medical Profession: The Role of Institutions*. New Haven, CT: Yale University Press.

Kindleberger, C. P. (1967) *Europe's Postwar Growth: The Role of Labour Supply*. Cambridge MA.

King, Desmond (1987) 'The State and the Social Structures of Welfare in Advanced Industrial Democracies', *Theory and Society*, 16.

Kock, W. (1963) 'Lasaretten och den slutna kroppssjukvården', in W. Kock (ed.), *Medicinalväsendet i Sverige 1913–1962*. Stockholm.

Kocka, Jürgen (1969) *Unternehmensverwaltung und Angestelltenschaft am Beispiel Siemens 1847–1914. Zum Verhältnis von Kapitalismus und Bürokratie in der deutschen Industrialisierung*. Stuttgart.

Kocka, Jürgen (1980a) 'The Rise of the Modern Industrial Enterprise in Germany', in A. D. Chandler, Jr. and H. Daims (eds), *Managerial Hierarchies. Comparative Perspectives on the Rise of the Modern Industrial Enterprise*. Cambridge, MA.

Kocka, Jürgen (1980b) *White-collar Workers in America 1890–1940. A Social-political History in International Perspective*. London.

Kocka, Jürgen (1981) 'Capitalism and Bureaucracy in Germany Industrialization before 1914', *The Economic History Review*, Sec. Ser. 33.

Kocka, Jürgen (1987a) 'Eisenbahnverwaltung in der industriellen Revolution. Deutsch-amerikanische Vergleiche', in H. Kellenbenz and H. Pohl (eds), *Historica socialis et oeconomica. Festschrift für Wolfgang Zorn*. Stuttgart: Steiner, Franz.

Kocka, Jürgen (ed.) (1987b) *Bürger und Bürgerlichkeit im 19 Jahrhundert*. Göttingen: Vandenhoeck & Ruprecht.

Kocka, Jürgen (1987c) 'Einleitung', in J. Kocka (ed.), *Bürger und Bürgerlichkeit im 19. Jahrhundert*. Göttingen: Vandenhoeck & Ruprecht.

Kocka, Jürgen (1987d) 'Bürgertum und Bürgerlichkeit als Probleme der deutschen Geschichte vom späten 18. zum frühen 20. Jahrhundert', in Jürgen Kocka (ed.), *Bürger und Bürgerlichkeit im 19. Jahrhundert*. Göttingen: Vandenhoeck & Ruprecht.

Kocka, Jürgen (ed.) (1988a) *Bürgertum im 19. Jahrhundert. Deutschland im europäischen Vergleich*. Vols I–III. Munich: Deutscher Taschenbuch Verlag.

Kocka, Jürgen (1988b) 'Bürgertum und bürgerliche Gesellschaft im 19. Jahrhundert. Europäische Entwicklungen und deutsche Eigenarten', in J. Kocka (ed.), *Bürgertum im 19. Jahrhundert. Deutschland im europäischen Vergleich*. Vol. I. Münich: Deutscher Taschenbuch Verlag.

Kocka, Jürgen (1988c) 'German History before Hitler. The debate about the German "Sonderweg" ', *Journal of Contemporary History*, 23.

Kocka, Jürgen (ed.) (1989a) *Das Bildungsbürgertum in Gesellschaft und Politik*. Stuttgart.

Kocka, Jürgen (1989b) *Les employés en Allemagne 1850–1980. Histoire d'un groupe social*. Paris.

König, M. (1988) 'Angestellte am Rande des Bürgertums. Kaufleute und Techniker in Deutschland und in der Schweiz 1860–1930', in Jürgen Kocka (ed.), *Bürgertum im 19. Jahrhundert. Deutschland im europäischen Vergleich*. Vol. II. Munich: Deutscher Taschenbuch Verlag.

Kornhauser, William, Jr (1965) *Scientists in Industry: Conflict and Accommodation*. Berkeley, CA: University of California Press.

Kucherov, Samuel (1953) *Courts, Lawyers and Trials under the Last Three Tsars*. New York: Praeger.

Kuhn, Thomas (1962/1974) *The Structure of Scientific Revolutions*. Chicago: University of Chicago Press.

Lagardelle, Hubert (1901) *L'Evolution des syndicats ouvriers en France de l'interdiction à l'obligation*. Paris.

Lane, David (1976) *The Socialist Industrial State: Towards a Political Sociology of State Socialism*. London: George Allen & Unwin.

Larson, Magali Sarfatti (1977/1979) *The Rise of Professionalism: A Sociological Analysis*. Berkeley, CA: University of California Press.

Latreille, Genevieve (1980) *La Naissance des métiers en France, 1950–1975: Etude psycho-sociale*. Lyon: Presses Universitaires de Lyon.

Layton, Edwin (1971) *The Revolt of the Engineers, Social Responsibility and the American Engineering Profession*. Cleveland, Ohio: Case Western Reserve Press.

Leeson, R. A. (1979) *Travelling Brothers: The Six Centuries from Craft Fellowship to Trade Unionism*. London: Allen & Unwin.

Lemercier, M. Le Vicomte Anatole (1857) *Etudes sur les Associations Ouvrières*. Paris.

Lennmalm, F. (1908) *Svenska Läkaresällskapets historia 1808–1908*.

Leonard, Jacques (1978) *Les Médecins de l'ouest au XIXe siècle*. Thesis of the University of Paris, 3 vols, University of Lille.

Lepsius, M. R. (1987) 'Zur Soziologie des Bürgertums und der Bürgerlichkeit', in Jürgen Kocka (ed.), *Bürger und Bürgerlichkeit im 19. Jahrhundert*. Göttingen: Vandenhoeck & Ruprecht.

Lévi-Strauss, Claude (1949/1969) *The Elementary Structures of Kinship*. Boston: Beacon.

Lévi-Strauss, Claude (1984) 'The Origin of Historical Societies', Public lecture, University of California, Los Angeles.

Lindenberg, Siegwart (1985) 'An Assessment of the New Political Economy', *Sociological Theory*.

Lindh, G. (ed.) (1988) *Vägledningsboken*. Lund (Studentlitteratur).

Lipset, Seymour Martin and Schneider, William (1983) *The Confidence Gap*. New York: Free Press.

Loft, Anne (1988) *Understanding Accounting in its Social and Historical Context: The Case of Cost Accounting, 1914–1975*. New York: Garland.

Lundgreen, Peter (1980) 'The Organization of Science and Technology in France: a German Perspective', in Robert Fox and George Weisz (eds), *The Organization of Science and Technology in France 1808–1914*. Cambridge: Cambridge University Press.

Lundgreen, P. (1988) 'Wissen und Bürgertum. Skizze eines historischen Vergleichs zwischen Preussen/Deutschland, Frankreich, England und den USA, 18.–20. Jahrhundert', in Hannes Siegrist (ed.), *Bürgerliche Berufe. Zur Sozialgeschichte der freien und akademischen Berufe im internationalen Vergleich*. Göttingen: Vandenhoeck & Ruprecht.

Lundgreen, Peter (1989) 'Engineering Education in Europe and the U.S.A., 1750–1930: The Rise to Dominance of School Culture and the Engineering Professions', Unpublished mimeograph, Bielefeld.

McClelland, Charles (1985) 'Zur Professionalisierung der akademischen Berufe in Deutschland', in Werner Conze and Jürgen Kocka (eds), *Bildungsbürgertum im 19. Jahrhundert. Vol. I: Bildungssystem und Professionalisierung in internationalen Vergleichen*. Stuttgart.

McDaniel, W. B. (1959) 'A Brief Sketch of the Rise of American Medical Societies', in Marti-Ibanez, Felix (ed.), *A History of American Medicine: A Symposium*, M.D. International Symposium Series, no. 5. New York: M.D. Publications.

Macdonald, K. M. and Ritzer, G. (1988) 'Sociology of the Professions: Dead or Alive?' in *Work and Occupations* (Aug.).

McKean, D. D. (1963) *The Integrated Bar*. Boston: Houghton Mifflin.

McKinlay, John B. (1982) 'Toward the Proletarianization of Physicians', in Charles Derber (ed.), *Professionals as Workers*. Boston: G. K. Hall & Co.

Marcson, Simon (1960) *The Scientist in American Industry: Some Organizational Determinants in Manpower Utilization*. Princeton University Dept of Economics and Sociology, Industrial Relations Section, Research Report Series, No. 99, Princeton, NJ.

Marland, Hilary (1987) *Medicine and Society in Wakefield and Huddersfield 1780–1870*. Cambridge: Cambridge University Press.

Marshall, T. H. (1939) 'The Recent History of Professionalism in Relation to Social Structure and Social Policy', *Canadian Journal of Economics and Political Science*, 5 (Aug.).

Martin, George (1970) *Causes and Conflicts: The Centennial History of the Association of the Bar of the City of New York, 1870–1970*. Boston: Houghton Mifflin.

Marx, Karl and Engels, Friedrich (1972) 'Manifest der kommunistischen Partei', in Karl Marx and Friedrich Engels, *Werke*, vol. 4. Berlin.

Marx, Karl (1972a) 'Das Elend des Philosophie', in Karl Marx and Friedrich Engels, *Werke*, vol. 4. Berlin.

Marx, Karl (1972b) 'Das Kapital', in Karl Marx and Friedrich Engels, *Werke*, vol. 23. Berlin.

Marx, Karl (1982) Wage Labour and Capital, (1849) published in Karl Marx and Friedrich Engels, *Selected Works*. Moscow.

Mauss, Marcel (1925/1967) *The Gift*. New York: Norton.

Mayntz, Renate (1982) 'Problemverarbeitung durch das politisch-administrative System: Zum Stand der Forschung', in S. J. Hesse (ed.), *Politikwissenschaft und Verwaltungswissenschaft*. Opladen: Westdeutscher Verlag.

Menkel-Meadow, Carrie (1989) 'Feminization of the Legal Profession: The Comparative Sociology of Women Lawyers', in Richard L. Abel and Philip S. C. Lewis (eds), *Lawyers in Society*, vol. 3, *Comparative Theories*. Berkeley, CA: California University Press. pp. 196–255.

Meriggi, M. (1987) *Il Regno Lombardo-Veneto*. Turin.

Meriggi, M. (1988) 'Italienisches und deutsches Bürgertum im Vergleich', in Jürgen Kocka (ed.), *Bürgertum im 19. Jahrhundert. Deutschland im europäischen Vergleich*. Vol. II. Munich: Deutscher Taschenbuch Verlag.

Millerson, Geoffrey (1964) *The Qualifying Associations*. London: Routledge.

Minville, G. (1954) *Ordres et syndicats professionnels*. Paris: Dalloz.

Mok, A. L. (1969) 'Alte und neue Professionen', *Kölner Zeitschrift für Soziologie und Sozialpsychologie*, 21.

More, C. (1980) *Skill and the English Working Class 1870–1914*. London: Croom Helm.

Mosher, Frederick C. (1968) *Democracy and the Public Service*. New York: Oxford University Press.

Moss, Bernard (1976) *The Origins of the French Labour Movement, 1830–1914: The Socialism of Skilled Workers*. Berkeley, CA: University of California Press.

Motpol, 4–5 (1986).

Mousnier, Roland (1979) *The Institutions of France under the Absolute Monarchy 1598–1798, Society and State*, Volume I. University of Chicago.

Murphy, Raymond (1983) 'The Struggle for Scholarly Recognition: The Development of the Closure Problematic', *Theory and Society*, 12.

Murphy, Raymond (1984) 'The Structure of Closure: A Critique and Development of Weber, Collins, and Parkin', *British Journal of Sociology*, 35.

Murphy, Raymond (1985) 'Exploitation or Exclusion?', *Sociology*, 19.

Murphy, Raymond (1986) 'Weberian Closure Theory: A Contribution to the Ongoing Assessment', *British Journal of Sociology*, 37.

Murphy, Raymond (1988) *Social Closure. The Theory of Monopolization and Exclusion*. Oxford: Clarendon Press.

Murphy, Raymond (1990) 'Proletarianization or Bureaucratization: The Fall of the Professional?' in R. Torstendahl and M. Burrage (eds), *The Formation of Professions: Knowledge, State and Strategy*. London: Sage.

Musson, A. E. (1972) *British Trade Unions 1800–1875*. London: Macmillan.

Nader, R. and Green M. (1976) *Verdicts on Lawyers*. New York.

Nilsson, T. (1985) *Från kamratföreningar till facklig rörelse. De svenska tjänstemännens organisationsutveckling 1900–1980*. Lund: Arkiv.

Nipperdey, T. (1983) *Deutsche Geschichte 1800–1866. Bürgerwelt und starker Staat*. Munich: Beck.

Noble, David F. (1977) *America by Design: Science, Technology, and the Rise of Corporate Capitalism*. Oxford: Oxford University Press.

Osborne, T. R. (1983) *A Grande Ecole for the Grand Corps. The Recruitment and Training of the French Administrative Elite in the Nineteenth Century*. New York.

Ostler, F. (1971) *Die deutschen Rechtsanwälte 1871–1971*. Essen.

Parkin, Frank (1974) *The Social Analysis of Class Structure*. London: Tavistock Publications.

Parkin, Frank (1979) *Marxism and Class Theory: A Bourgeois Critique*. London: Routledge.

Parry, Noel and Parry, Jose (1976) *The Rise of the Medical Profession: A Study of Collective Social Mobility*. London: Croom Helm.

Parsons, Talcott (1939) 'The Professions and Social Structure', *Social Forces*, 17.

Parsons, Talcott (1951) *The Social System*. Glencoe, IL: Free Press.

Parsons, Talcott (1963) 'The Professions and Social Structure', in T. Parsons, *Essays in Sociological Theory*. Glencoe IL: Free Press.

Parsons, Talcott (1968) 'Profession', in *International Encyclopedia of the Social Sciences*, vol. 12.

Pascal, O. and Sirinelli, J-F. (1986) *Les Intellectuels en France, de l'Affaire Dreyfus à nos jours*. Paris: A. Colin.

Perkin, Harold (1969) *The Origins of Modern English Society, 1780–1880*. London: Routledge & Kegan Paul.

Perkin, Harold (1989) *The Rise of Professional Society*. London: Routledge.

Perrucci, Robert and Gerstl, Joel (eds) (1969) *The Engineers and the Social System*. New York: Wiley.

Person, S., Lindblom, B. and Odmark, I. (1980) *Vägledning*. Stockholm: Liber.

Personalutbildning – En kartläggning (1988) LO, Stockholm.

Peterson, Jeanne M. (1978) *The Medical Profession in Mid-Victorian London*. Berkeley, CA: University of California Press.

Prandy, K., Stewart, A., and Blackburn, R. (1983) *White Collar Unionism*. London: Macmillan.

238   *Professions in theory and history*

Prest, Wilfred R. (1972) *The Inns of Court under Elizabeth and the Early Stuarts, 1590–1640*. London: Longman.

Prest, Wilfred (1981) *Lawyers in Early Modern Europe and America*. New York: Croom Helm.

Prest, Wilfred (1984) 'Why the History of Professions is not Written', in G. R. Rubin and D. Sugarman, *Law, Economy and Society 1750–1914*. Abingdon, Oxon: Professional Books.

Prest, Wilfred R. (1986) *The Rise of the Barristers: A Social History of the English Bar 1590–1640*. Oxford: Clarendon Press.

Price, Roger (1972) *The French Second Republic: A Social History*. London: Cornell University Press.

Price, R. (1980) *Masters, Unions and Men*. Cambridge: Cambridge University Press.

Raelin, Joseph A. (1986) *The Clash of Cultures: Managers and Professionals*. Boston: Harvard Business School Press.

Ramsey, Matthew (1983) 'History of a Profession, Annales Style: The Work of Jacques Leonard', *Journal of Social History*, 17 (Fall).

Ramsey, Matthew (1984) 'The Politics of Professional Monopoly in Nineteenth-Century Medicine: The French Model and Its Rivals', in Gerald L. Geison (ed.), *Professions and the French State 1700–1900*. Philadelphia: University of Pennsylvania Press.

Ramsey, Matthew (1988) *Professional and Popular Medicine in France 1770–1830: The Social World of Medical Practice*. Cambridge: Cambridge University Press.

Rayack, Elton (1967) *Professional Power and American Medicine: The Economics of the American Medical Association*. Cleveland, OH: World Publishing.

Reader, W. J. (1966) *Professional Men: The Rise of Professional Classes in Nineteenth Century England*. London: Weidenfeld & Nicolson.

Reed, Alfred Z. (1921) 'Training for the Public Profession of Law', Carnegie Foundation for the Advancement of Teaching, Bulletin No. 15, New York.

Reedy, B. L. (1978) *The New Health Practioners in America: a Comparative Study*. London: King Edward's Hospital Fund for London.

Rekryteringen till och avhoppen från domarbanan. Domstolsverket' (1987) 1, Rapport.

Riper, P. van (1958) *History of the United States Civil Service*. Evanston, IL: Row, Peterson.

Roberts, J. M. (1972) *The Mythology of the Secret Societies*. London: Secker & Warburg.

Rothblatt, Sheldon (1968) *The Revolution of the Dons: Cambridge and Society in Victorian England*. London: Faber.

Rothstein, William G. (1972) *American Physicians in the Nineteenth Century: From Sects to Science*. Baltimore, MD: Johns Hopkins.

Rottleuthner, H. (1988) 'Die gebrochene Bürgerlichkeit einer Scheinprofession. Zur Situation der deutschen Richterschaft zu Beginn des 20. Jahrhunderts', in Hannes Siegrist (ed.), *Bürgerliche Berufe. Zur Sozialgeschichte der freien und akademischen Berufe im internationalen Vergleich*. Göttingen: Vandenhoeck & Ruprecht.

Roux, Xavier (1867) *La Corporation des Gantiers de Grenoble avant et après la Révolution*. Paris.

Rubin, G. R. and Sugarman, David (eds) (1984) *Law, Economy and Society*. Abingdon, Oxon: Professional Books.

Rueschemeyer, Dietrich (1973) *Lawyers and their Society: A Comparative Analysis of the Legal Professions in Germany and in the United States.* Cambridge: Harvard University Press.

Rueschemeyer, Dietrich (1980) 'Professionalisierung. Theoretische Probleme für die vergleichende Geschichtsforschung', *Geschichte und Gesellschaft, 6.*

Rueschemeyer, Dietrich (1986) 'Comparing Legal Professions Cross-Nationally: From a Professions-centered to a State-centered Approach', *American Bar Foundation Research Journal, 3.*

Rueschemeyer, Dietrich (1987) 'Bourgeoisie, Staat und Bildungsbürgertum. Idealtypische Modelle für die vergleichende Erforschung von Bürgertum und Bürgerlichkeit', in Jurgen Kocka (ed.), *Bürger und Bürgerlichkeit im 19. Jahrhundert.* Göttingen: Vandenhoeck & Ruprecht.

Runeby, Nils (1976) *Teknikerna, vetenskapen och kulturen. Ingenjörsundervisning och ingenjörsorganisationer i 1870-talets Sverige.* Uppsala: Studia Historica Upsaliensia, vol. 83.

Saks, M. (1983) 'Removing the Blinkers? A Critique of Recent Contributions to the Sociology of Professions', *The Sociological Review.*

Sandberg, P. (1969) *Tjänstemannarörelsen.* Stockholm: TCO.

Schluchter, W. (1980) *Rationalismus der Weltbeherrschung. Studien zu Max Weber.* Frankfurt: Suhrkamp.

Schumpeter, Joseph A. (1911/1961) *The Theory of Economic Development.* New York: Oxford University Press.

Schumpeter, Joseph A. (1942) *Capitalism, Socialism, and Democracy.* New York: Harper.

Sewell, W. H. (1980) *Work and Revolution in France: The Language of Labour from the Old Regime to 1848.* Cambridge: Cambridge University Press.

Shafer, Henry B. (1936) *The American Medical Profession 1783–1850.* New York: Columbia University Press.

Sheldrake, John and Vickerstaff, Sarah (1987) *The History of Industrial Training in Britain.* Avebury.

Shinn, Terry (1980) *L'Ecole Polytechnique, 1794–1914.* Paris: Presses de la Fondation Nationale des Sciences Politiques.

Sialleli, Jean-Baptiste (1987) *Les Avocats de 1920 à 1987, L'Association Nationale des Avocats, La Confédération Syndicale des Avocats.* Paris: Litec.

Siegrist, Hannes (1985) 'Gebremste Professionalisierung – Das Beispiel der schweizer Rechtsanwaltschaft im Vergleich zu Frankreich und Deutschland im 19. und 20. Jahrhundert', in Werner Conze und Jürgen Kocka (eds), Bildungsbürgertum im 19. Jahrhundert. Stuttgart: Klett-Cotta.

Siegrist, Hannes (1986) 'Professionalisation with the Brakes On: The Legal Professions in Switzerland, France and Germany in the Nineteenth and Early Twentieth Centuries', in R. F. Tomasson (ed.), *Comparative Social Research. An Annual Publication, 9.*

Siegrist, Hannes (ed.) (1988a) *Bürgerliche Berufe. Zur Sozialgeschichte der freien und akademischen Berufe im internationalen Vergleich.* Göttingen: Vandenhoeck & Ruprecht.

Siegrist, Hannes (1988b) 'Bürgerliche Berufe. Die Professionen und das Bürgertum', in Hannes Siegrist (ed.), *Bürgerliche Berufe. Zur Sozialgeschichte der freien und akademischen Berufe im internationalen Vergleich.* Göttingen: Vandenhoeck & Ruprecht.

Siegrist, Hannes (1988c) 'Die Rechtsanwälte und das Bürgertum. Deutschland, die Schweiz und Italien im 19. Jahrhundert', in Jürgen Kocka (ed.), *Bürgertum im 19.*

Jahrhundert. Deutschland im europäischen Vergleich, vol. II. Munich: Deutscher Taschenbuch Verlag.

Siegrist, Hannes (1989) 'Public Office or Free Profession. German Attorneys in the Nineteenth and Early Twentieth Centuries', in G. Cocks and Konrad H. Jarausch (eds), *German Professions 1800–1950*. New York.

Siegrist, Hannes (1990) *Advokaten und Bürger* (forthcoming).

Smelser, Neil J. (ed.) (1988) *Handbook of Sociology*. London: Sage.

Smith, W. Rand (1987) *Crisis in the French Labour Movement: A Grassroots Perspective*. London: Macmillan.

Soboul, Albert (1962) *Précis d'histoire de la Révolution Française*. Paris: Editions Sociales.

Sombart, N. (1986) *Jugend in Berlin 1933–1943. Ein Bericht* (1984). Frankfurt.

Soreau, E. (1931) 'La Loi Le Chapelier', *Annales Historiques de la Révolution Française*, vol. 8.

SOU, 1935:52, *Betänkanden med undersökningar och förslag i anledning av tillströmningen till de intellektuella yrkena.*

SOU, 1944:29, *Socialutbildningssakkunniga i den högre socialpolitiska och kommande utbildningen.*

SOU, 1947:23, *Betänkande med förslag till statens allmänna avlöningsreglemente mm.*

SOU, 1954:15, *Om kompetenskrav.*

SOU, 1958:15, *Hälsovård och öppen sjukvård i landstingsområdena.*

SOU, 1962:43, *Socionomutbildningen.*

SOU, 1987:50, *Högskolans journalistutbildning.*

Späth, M. (1988) 'Der Ingenieur als Bürger. Frankreich, Deutschland und Russland im Vergleich', in Hannes Siegrist (ed.), *Bürgerliche Berufe. Zur Sozialgeschichte der freien und akademischen Berufe im internationalen Vergleich*. Göttingen: Vandenhoeck & Ruprecht.

Starr, Paul (1982) *The Social Transformation of American Medicine: The Rise of a Sovereign Profession and the Making of a Vast Industry*. New York: Basic Books.

Statistics Canada, Education in Canada: A Statistical Review for 1982–83 (1984) Cat 81–229. Ottawa: Ministry of Supply and Services.

Stevens, Rosemary (1966) *Medical Practice in Modern England: The Impact of Specialization and State Medicine*. New Haven, CT: Yale University Press.

Stevens, Rosemary (1971) *American Medicine and the Public Interest*. New Haven, CT: Yale University Press.

Strong, H. A. R. (1909) 'The Machinations of the American Medical Association: an Exposure and a Warning', *National Druggist*, St Louis.

Svenska Läkaresällskapet 175 år: dess sektioners tillkomst och utveckling, 1983.

Svensson, L. (1988) *Arkitekternas och psykologernas yrkesutveckling.*

Sveriges Tandläkareförbund 1908–1958, 1958.

Süle, T. (1988) *Preussische Bürokratietradition. Zur Entwicklung von Verwaltung und Beamtenschaft in Deutschland 1871–1918*. Göttingen: Vandenhoeck & Ruprecht.

Swedish Statistical Yearbook 1988.

Tawney, R. H. (1921) *The Acquisitive Society*. London.

Thapar, Romila (1966) *A History of India*. Baltimore, MD: Penguin Books.

Thompson, Edward P. (1963/1972) *The Making of the English Working Class*. Harmondsworth: Penguin.

Thuillier G. (1980) *Bureaucratie et bureaucrats en France XIXe siècle*. Geneva.

Tierney, Kevin (1979) *Darrow*. New York: Crowell.

Torstendahl, Rolf (1975) *Dispersion of Engineers in a Transitional Society. Swedish Technicians 1860–1940*. Uppsala: Studia Historica Upsaliensia, vol. 73.

Torstendahl, Rolf (1982) 'Byråkratisering, yrkesstolthet och klassmedvetande 1870–1940', in Bo Öhngren (ed.), *Organisationerna och samhällsutvecklingen*. Stockholm: TCO.

Torstendahl, Rolf (1984a) 'Technology in the Development of Society 1850–1980. Four Phases of Industrial Capitalism in Western Europe', *History and Technology*.

Torstendahl, Rolf (1984b) 'Vom Berufsstolz zum Angestelltenbewusstsein in Schweden 1900–1940', in Jürgen Kocka (ed.), *Angestellte im europäischen Vergleich. Die Herausbildung angestellter Mittelschichten seit dem 19. Jahrhundert*. Göttingen: Vandenhoeck & Ruprecht.

Torstendahl, Rolf (1985a) 'Das Konzept des organisierten Kapitalismus und seine Anwendung auf Schweden', *Geschichte und Gesellschaft*, 11.

Torstendahl, Rolf (1985b) 'Engineers in Sweden and Britain 1820–1914, Professionalisation and Bureaucratisation in a Comparative Perspective', in W. Conze and J. Kocka (eds), *Bildungsbürgertum im 19. Jahrhundert*. Stuttgart: Klett-Cotta.

Turner, H. A. (1962) *Trade Union Growth, Structure and Policy: A Comparative Study of the Cotton Unions*. London: Allen & Unwin.

Turner, R. S. (1980) 'Das Bildungsbürgertum and the Learned Professions in Prussia, 1770–1830: The Origins of a Class', *Histoire sociale – Social History*, 13.

Vasseur, Edmond (1900) *L'Ordre et le tableau des avocats*. Paris: Thorin.

Vess, David M. (1975) *Medical Revolution in France, 1789–1796*. Gainesville, FL: University of Florida.

Vial, Jean (1895) *La Coutume Chapelière*. Paris.

Vierhaus, R. (1980) 'Umrisse einer Socialgeschichte der Gebildeten in Deutschland', in *Quellen und Forschungen aus italienischen Archiven und Bibliotheken*, 60.

Vondung, Klaus (ed.) (1976) *Das Wilhelminische Bildungsbürgertum. Zur Socialgeschichte seiner Ideen*. Göttingen: Vandenhoeck & Ruprecht.

Waddington, I. (1985) 'Medicine, the Market and Professional Autonomy: Some Aspects of the Professionalisation of Medicine', in Werner Conze and Jürgen Kocka (eds), *Bildungsbürgertum im 19. Jahrhundert. Vol. I: Bildungssystem und Professionalisierung in internationalen Vergleichen*. Stuttgart: Klett-Cotta.

Waddington, Ivan (1984) *The Medical Profession in the Industrial Revolution*. London: Humanities Press.

Walker, M. (1971) *German Hometowns. Community, State and General Estate 1648–1871*. Ithaca, NY.

Waller, Willard (1937) 'The Rating and Dating Complex', *American Sociological Review*, 2.

Wallerstein, Immanuel (1974, 1980, 1988) *The Modern World System*, Vols 1–3. New York: Academic Press.

Walster, Elaine and Walster, G. William (1978) *A New Look at Love*. Reading MA: Addison-Wesley.

Ware, Norman J. (1929) *The Labor Movement in the United States 1860–1895: A Study in Democracy*. New York.

Warren, Charles (1911) *A History of the American Bar*. Boston.

Webb, S. and Webb, B. (1920) *The History of Trade Unionism*. London, rev. ed.

Weber, Max (1922/1968) *Economy and Society*, Guenter Roth and Klaus Wittich (eds). New York: Bedminster Press.

Weber, Max (1963) *A General Economic History*. New York.

Weber, Max (1964) *Wirtschaft und Gesellschaft. Grundriss der verstehenden Sozio-logie.* Tübingen, 1956: Cologne, 1964: Studienausgabe.

Weber, Max (1972) *Wirtschaft und Gesellschaft.* Studienausgabe, 5. rev. ed. Tübingen.

Weber, Max (1983) *Ekonomi och samhälle.* Lund: Argos.

Wehler, Hans-Ulrich (1975) *Modernisierungstheorie und Geschichte.* Göttingen.

Wehler, Hans-Ulrich (1987) *Deutsche Gesellschaftsgeschichte,* vols I-II. Munich: Beck.

Weiss, John Hubbel (1982) *The Making of Technological Man: The Social Origins of French Engineering Education.* Boston: MIT Press.

Weiss, John Hubbel (1984) 'Bridges and Barriers: Narrowing Access and Changing Structure in the French Engineering Profession, 1800–1850', in Gerald L. Geison (ed.), *Professions and the French State, 1700–1900.* Philadelphia, University of Pennsylvania Press.

Weissler, A. (1905) *Geschichte der Rechtsanwaltschaft.* Leipzig.

Weisz, George (1978) 'The Politics of Medical Professionalization in France 1845–1848', *Journal of Social History,* 12(1).

Weisz, George (1983) *The Emergence of Modern Universities in France, 1863–1914.* Princeton, NJ: Princeton University Press.

Whalley, Peter (1986) *The Social Production of Technical Work: The Case of British Engineers.* Albany, NY: State University of New York.

Whitley, Richard (1984) *The Intellectual and Social Organization of the Sciences.* Oxford: Clarendon Press.

Wickenden, William E. (1930) 'A Comparative Study of the Engineering Education in the US and Europe', *Report of the Investigation of Engineering Education,* Society for the Promotion of Engineering Education. Pittsburgh, PA.

Wikland, H. (1962) 'Sveriges Advokatsamfund 75 år', *Tidskrift för Sveriges Advo-katsamfund.*

Wilder, Alexander (1901) *History of Medicine and Especially a History of American Eclectic Practice of Medicine.* New Sharon, ME.

Wilensky, Harold L. (1964) 'The Professionalization of Everyone?' *American Jour-nal' of Sociology,* 70.

Wilensky, Harold L. (1972) 'Jeder Beruf eine Profession', in T. Luckman and W. Sprondel (eds), *Berufssoziologie.* Cologne.

Williamson, Oliver E. (1975) *Markets and Hierarchies. A Study of the Economics of Internal Organization.* New York: Free Press.

Winch, Peter (1958) *The Idea of Social Science and its Relation to Philosophy.* London: Routledge & Paul.

Wirén, Agnes (1980) *G. H. von Koch Banbrytare i svensk socialvård.* Rabén and Sjögren.

Woodworth, Richard (1973) 'Some Influences on the Reform of Schools of Law and Medicine, 1890–1930', *Sociological Quarterly,* 14.

Wortman, Richard S. (1976) *The Development of a Russian Legal Consciousness.* Chicago: University of Chicago Press.

Wunder, B. (1986) *Geschichte der Bürokratie in Deutschland.* Frankfurt.

Zunkel, F. (1986) 'Das Verhältnis des Unternehmertums zum Bildungsbürgertum im Vormärz und Ersten Weltkrieg'. Unpublished paper.

Zussman, Robert (1985) *Mechanics of the Middle Class: Work and Politics Among American Engineers.* Berkeley, CA: University of California Press.

Index

Index compiled by Peva Keane